Station Master
on the
Underground Railroad

Station Master *on the* Underground Railroad

The Life and Letters of Thomas Garrett

REVISED EDITION

James A. McGowan

with a foreword by William C. Kashatus

McFarland & Company, Inc., Publishers
Jefferson, North Carolina, and London

In memory of Dorothy Biddle James,
great-great-granddaughter of Thomas Garrett

Frontispiece: Thomas Garrett, 1789–1871
(courtesy Historical Society of Delaware).

The present work is a reprint of the illustrated case bound edition first published in 2005 by McFarland.

LIBRARY OF CONGRESS CATALOGUING-IN-PUBLICATION DATA

McGowan, James A.
    Station master on the Underground Railroad : the life and letters of Thomas Garrett / James A. McGowan ; with a foreword by William C. Kashatus.— Rev. ed.
       p.   cm.
    Includes bibliographical references and index.

    ISBN 978-0-7864-4240-9

    softcover : 50# alkaline paper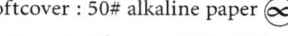

    1. Garrett, Thomas, 1789–1871. 2. Garrett, Thomas, 1789–1871—Correspondence. 3. Abolitionists—Delaware—Wilmington—Biography. 4. Quakers—Delaware—Wilmington—Biography. 5. Underground railroad—Delaware—Wilmington. 6. Wilmington (Del.)—History. 7. Wilmington (Del.)—Race relations. 8. Wilmington (Del.)—Biography. I. Title.
    E450.G23M32   2009   973.7'115 — dc22   2004020170

British Library cataloguing data are available

©2005 James A. McGowan. All rights reserved

No part of this book may be reproduced or transmitted in any form or by any means, electronic or mechanical, including photocopying or recording, or by any information storage and retrieval system, without permission in writing from the publisher.

On the cover: Background ©2009 Clipart; Thomas Garrett's handwriting; Thomas Garrett 1789–1871 (courtesy Historical Society of Delaware)

Manufactured in the United States of America

McFarland & Company, Inc., Publishers
  Box 611, Jefferson, North Carolina 28640
    www.mcfarlandpub.com

Contents

Foreword by William C. Kashatus	1
Preface	5
1. The Underground Railroad	11
2. Early Accounts of Garrett's Life	17
3. Upper Darby Ancestry	24
4. Quakers and Quakerism	28
5. The Road to Damascus	31
6. The Move to Wilmington	37
7. Wilmington	40
8. Rachel (Mendinhall) Garrett	46
9. The Trial of 1848	52
10. Thomas Garrett, the Man	82
11. How Important Was Thomas Garrett?	93
12. Thomas Garrett and Harriet Tubman	98
13. How Many Runaways Did Garrett Assist?	115
14. The End of the Line	129
15. Letters to William Still & J. Miller McKim	134
16. Letters to William Lloyd Garrison	154
17. Letters to Eliza Wigham & Mary Edmundson	162
18. Miscellaneous Letters	184

Appendix A: Thomas Garrett Genealogy	197
Appendix B: Letters from John Hunn to The Blue Hen's Chicken	201
Appendix C: Letter from Thomas Garrett to The Blue Hen's Chicken	207
Chapter Notes	211
Bibliography	217
Index	221

Foreword

FOR THOSE WHO ARE UNFAMILIAR with the Religious Society of Friends, the most dangerous phrase to come from the mouth of a Quaker is: "I have a concern." In lay terms a "concern" is a grievance that is so distressing to the individual that redressing it is pursued with an almost fanatical compulsion. Thomas Garrett, a Wilmington, Delaware, Quaker who favored broad-brimmed hats and long dark waistcoats, struggled with a lifelong concern over the peculiar institution of slavery.

Garrett projected a genial disposition unless provoked to defend his anti-slavery beliefs. When challenged he could become outspoken, if not abrasive. Found guilty of harboring a family of fugitive slaves in 1848, Garrett was heavily fined and warned by the court "not to meddle with slaves again." He grew defiant. "I have assisted over fourteen hundred runaways in twenty-five years on their way to the North," he told the federal marshal, "and I now consider the penalty imposed upon me as a license for the remainder of my life."

To make matters worse, Garrett turned to the spectators who attended the trial and added, "If any of you know of any slave who needs assistance, send him to me, as I now publicly pledge myself to double my diligence and never neglect an opportunity to assist a slave in obtaining his freedom."

To be sure, Thomas Garrett was not a typical Quaker. While most Friends may have considered African Americans their "spiritual equals," they did not welcome them into their religious body as brethren. Abolitionism had been a movement of individuals within the Society of Friends until 1776, when Philadelphia Yearly Meeting made slaveholding a cause for disownment of members. Even then, Friends tended to limit their abolitionist activities to boycotting goods produced by slave labor and calling on non–Quaker neighbors to free their black field hands. They were more concerned about their own salvation and the spiritual integrity of the Yearly Meeting than with welcoming blacks into the fold. Nor were Quaker abolitionists unified in how they opposed slavery.

Civil war, for example, was not an alternative for the overwhelming majority, who saw pacifism as fundamental to the Quaker faith. Many Friends also feared that the illegal nature of the Underground Railroad compromised the integrity and legal status of all Quaker religious practice. Some of these Quakers belonged to Kennett Monthly Meeting in southeastern Pennsylvania, which in 1853 disowned members who felt otherwise. Not only did Garrett circulate among these dissident Quakers, many of whom were later involved in establishing the Pennsylvania Yearly Meeting of Progressive Friends, but he also mobilized them as the nucleus of an Underground Railroad network that began at his home in Wilmington, Delaware, wove its way north through Chester County, Pennsylvania, and ended in Philadelphia at the station of William Still, the secretary of the Pennsylvania Anti-Slavery Society's General Vigilance Committee and the coordinator of the entire Eastern Line.

Unlike most other white abolitionists who saw slavery in more abstract or constitutional terms, Garrett, like free black abolitionists and the slaves themselves, saw the peculiar institution in very personal terms. He, too, felt as if his own family had been violated by slavery when, in 1813, a slave catcher kidnapped a free black woman who worked on his parents' farm in Upper Darby, Pennsylvania. Garrett sped off to rescue her and on the way experienced a spiritual revelation about the utter sinfulness of slavery. Vowing to assist any fugitive slave, he joined the Pennsylvania Anti-Slavery Society and dedicated himself to the Underground Railroad. So zealous was he that he chafed under the Quaker principle of nonviolence when acts of force seemed the only way to win freedom for the slaves. Although he never physically took up arms, he supported the Union's war effort. He also joined freely with the black community whose Underground Railroad activities sometimes resulted in riots, and he counted many of the zealots among his intimates.

No wonder that when Garrett died in 1871, Wilmington's black community saluted him as "their Moses" and carried his coffin through the streets of the city to his final resting place near the Friends Meeting House where he had worshiped.

Station Master on the Underground Railroad: The Life and Letters of Thomas Garrett was a seminal work in the field of antebellum reform when it was first published in 1977. James McGowan challenged earlier accounts that argued that white abolitionists were unified in their opposition to slavery and credited them with the success of the Underground Railroad, while the fugitives were depicted as helpless, frightened passengers who took advantage of a well-organized national network. Instead, McGowan offered an important corrective to what had become a rich but fanciful mix of historical fact and legend by documenting Garrett's activities with the free black community and the runaways themselves and placing them in the broader context of the Underground Railroad's Eastern Line.

In this expanded edition, McGowan offers new information of Garrett's relationship with Harriet Tubman, the most noted conductor on the Eastern Line, and the abolitionist newspaper editor, William Lloyd Garrison. He also gives us a more human perspective of Thomas Garrett, recognizing his shortcomings as well as the uncompromising nature of his Quaker faith.

More than a quarter century after its initial publication, *Station Master on the Underground Railroad* continues to be one of the most critical works in a growing body of literature on this important chapter of American history.

William C. Kashatus
West Chester County Historical Society
West Chester, Pennsylvania

Preface

WHEN I WAS A LITTLE BOY growing up in Brooklyn during the 1930s there was very little of what we know today as Black History. All we learned was that we people, then called "Negroes"— sometimes "colored"— were the descendants of slaves in the South. We learned that one day the white people in the North thought slavery was wrong and so they told the president, Abraham Lincoln, to put an end to it. So President Lincoln started a Civil War, the North won the war and slavery was ended, and we were free. That was the alpha and omega of Black History as I knew it.

What heroes did we have? Well, we were taught that there were two famous Negroes, George Washington Carver and Booker T. Washington, and both of them, I was told, were named after a white man, George Washington. And that was it.

I *accepted* what I was taught. I looked around and saw no black policemen, or firemen, or sanitation workers, or trolley car drivers. I saw no black lawyers, or judges, or doctors. So to my young mind I concluded that we Negroes ... well ... we were just hanging around. We had no history. All we had were our modern day popular figures— athletes Joe Louis and Jessie Owens and music people, Ella Fitzgerald and Louis Armstrong. We had no historical figures to point to other than Booker T. Washington and George Washington Carver.

Then came the Civil Rights Movement of the 1960s. And out of the riots and the lynchings, the sit-ins, the police dogs and the billy clubs, the fire hoses and the bombing of churches, there began to emerge in my consciousness a new reality: that black men and women had indeed made significant contributions to history, not only in America, but all over the world. I began to hear about such people as Harriet Tubman, Frederick Douglass, Sojourner Truth, Toussaint L'Ouverture, and Alexander Pushkin. I began to hear about the black soldiers and sailors who also fought in the Civil War. And I began to hear about a mysterious institution called the Underground Railroad. Not till then did I learn that we Negroes ... well ... we were *not* just hanging around!

Still, it was not until the next decade, the '70s, that this history would finally take root in my mind. By then we were no longer called "Negroes" or "Colored." We were "Black Americans." The year was 1973. As I was leaving a friend's house, my eye caught a small yellow pocket book on a bookshelf near her door. It was *Harriet Tubman, Conductor on the Underground Railroad*, by Ann Petry. Although I would one day discover that Harriet Tubman's life contained far more than was in that book, it was really my introduction to *serious* Black History. As I read the book, I came across a single paragraph in which the author stated that on her way to freedom, Harriet Tubman stopped at the home of a white Quaker, Thomas Garrett. He gave her money and shoes to help her on her way.

I had to find out who this man was. So I called the local library and asked if they had books about Thomas Garrett. The librarian said, "No," and asked for more information. I said he was a Quaker. She said, "Why don't you call the Quaker Libraries, Swarthmore and Haverford?" I did, and the librarian at Swarthmore said, "We have no books about Thomas Garrett. All we have are a few letters written by him to two ladies in Scotland. Would you like to have copies of these?" I said "yes." She asked, "Are you going to write a book about Thomas Garrett?" I said, "yes." I hung up the phone and said to myself, "Why did you say that?" You know absolutely nothing about this man other than what you've read in that single paragraph in Ann Petry's book. Not only that, you've never even written a book! But something inside me said, "You may not have written a book before but you're going to write one now." And so I did.

I spent the next three years totally absorbed in the life of this man. To my dismay most of the information about him at that time was scattered throughout various early books about the Underground Railroad, as well as brief notices in articles and books about Harriet Tubman. Most of the information was inconsistent. There was exaggeration and a bit of sensationalism. The most consistent and valuable source of information about him was William Still's historic book, *The Underground Railroad*. As there was close collaboration and communication between them, Still saw fit to print 25 letters from Garrett. I decided at that time that the greatest contribution I could make to his life was to bring together in one place — in one book — all the available information about Thomas Garrett; to dissect it, analyze it, and try to present a consistent account of his life. I collected every available letter he'd written about his activities as an UGRR agent. I read every article about him and every book in which he was mentioned. Early on I recognized that the single significant event in his life — that which I call "the defining moment" — was in the trial of 1848, when he was tried and convicted for helping a family of slaves to escape. However, it was in that area where the most inconsistency and shortage of information existed. My biggest hurdle then was not only procuring, but actually transcribing the court records. I spent weekends and parts of my vacations and stayed awake sometimes far into the night with a magnifying glass trying to transcribe the court records, as well as letters he had written more than a hundred years before I was born. Three years later, I met Thomas Garrett's great-great-granddaughter, Dorothy Biddle James. She had heard about my manuscript through UGRR historian Charles Blockson. Mrs. James introduced me to publisher Walter Kahoe, and in 1977 the first and only full-length biography of Thomas Garrett was published.

With the exception of an unpublished manuscript entitled *The Land of Boasted Freedom*, by James F. Conlin, OSFS, and Cornelius Desmond, OSFS, there has been no major scholarship *exclusively* about Thomas Garrett since that first biography. The above thesis, however, largely comprises articles and chapters about Thomas Garrett that appeared in newspapers and books, as well as information taken from a scrapbook left with the Historical Society of Delaware by Garrett's granddaughter, Helen Sellers Garrett. In 1985 Priscilla Thompson, with a grant from the Delaware Humanities Forum, published a 45-page dual biography, *Harriet Tubman, Thomas Garrett and the Underground Railroad in Delaware*. Although this work is not exclusively about Thomas Garrett, Ms. Thompson does include some valuable additional information about other UGRR workers in Wilmington who assisted Garrett, as well as Garrett's participation in the Longwood Progressive Friends Meeting, as well as his relationship with the Wilmington Friends Meeting.

In 1997 writer and community college teacher Judith Bentley published a very readable dual biography, *Dear Friend: Thomas Garrett & William Still, Collaborators on the Underground Railroad* (New York, Cobblehill Books/Dutton, 1997), and in 2002, Teleduction, a Wilmington, Delaware-based, television documentary company, produced "Whispers of Angels: A Story about the Underground Railroad," starring television/movie stars Ed Asner and Blair Underwood. This again is a dual biography about the collaboration between Thomas Garrett and William Still.

There have been numerous short articles about Thomas Garrett in local papers and magazines, and excerpts of his life and Underground Railroad activities will be found in every major book about the UGRR, Harriet Tubman, and abolitionists in general. However, few if any of these works include the vital statistics of his life that are necessary to present a full and complete picture of the man that are in my original work; one example is Garrett's genealogy, in which I traced his family back to 1682, when they were among the first Quaker immigrants to this country under the influence of William Penn. I give a synopsis of his faith (The Religious Society of Friends—"Quakers"), the cornerstone of his unshakable belief that his mission in life was to help free the runaway slave. I include a biographical sketch of his second wife, Rachel Mendinhall, who, though she remained largely in the background, shared his goal of liberating the runaway slave. Also included in the first edition is a brief history of Thomas Garrett's adopted city, Wilmington, Delaware, the city that was his base of operation wherein he gave succor to hundreds of runaway slaves. There is, as well, a detailed discussion of the trial of 1848, in which he was tried and convicted for following the command he believed he received from God.

Since 1973, when I began research for the original biography, library science was in the earliest stages of upgrading its system with computers. So, much of the information available then was acquired through dogged determination on my part, as well as the patience, persistence and helpfulness of librarians, archivists, historians and friends. Today, there exists a host of new Underground Railroad literature based on a large body of information made available mainly by computers and the diligence of a new breed of UGRR and Quaker historians and writers. These works, though not all directly related to Thomas Garrett, nevertheless add additional light on his contributions as an UGRR agent. Chief among these is William C. Kashatus's *Just Over the Line*, a major work about the Underground Railroad in Chester County, only five miles from Garrett's home in Wilmington, Delaware, and a hotbed of individual abolitionists and anti-slavery communities, black and white. It was the county where Thomas Garrett sent most of the runaways he assisted on their way to Philadelphia, to the home of the outstanding African American UGRR worker, William Still.

In Chester County also lived Thomas Garrett's in-laws, Isaac and Dinah Mendinhall, to whom he also sent fugitives. Thus, *Just Over the Line* is one of the works that enables us to offer a critical evaluation of the number of slaves Thomas Garrett is said to have helped escape, as well as why he was so successful.

Two related works are Frances Cloud Taylor's *The Trackless Trail* and *The Trackless Trail Leads On*, about the Underground Railroad in Kennett Square, the city known as the "hub" of Underground Railroad activity in the important Chester County. Among these recent works is historian James Newton's article "Diamonds of Delaware and Maryland's Eastern Shore: Seven Black Men of Distinction." This article sheds light on the contributions of the African American churches in Wilmington, particularly the African Methodist Union (AMU) Church under the outstanding leadership of an ex-slave, the Reverend Peter Spencer.[1] Peter J. Delleo's article, "The Growth of Delaware's Antebellum Free African American Community," is of the contributions of individual African American UGRR workers in Wilmington, many of whom were Thomas Garrett's helpers. These works were very helpful.

Someone once said, "Discoveries are made by people who look at the same things as every one else but see something different." That seems quite true of Vincent Leggett, a writer and historian specializing in African American Maritime History and Culture. In my research I came across an extremely interesting internet website, "Blacks on the Chesapeake Foundation, Inc." In it was an article by Leggett, entitled "Chesapeake Underground, Charting a Course Toward Freedom" (which is also the title of his book). Mr. Leggett's thesis, simply put, is that thousands of slaves—including Harriet Tubman and Frederick Douglass—also escaped by boat, using the Chesapeake, with the help of numerous black UGRR maritime workers. That is a simple observation, but its significance may very well have been overlooked by UGRR historians and writers—myself included. Yet that simple observation explains to me why Thomas Garrett, in his letters, frequently referred to runaways escaping by boat.

Meanwhile, one can hardly write about the Underground Railroad without referring to historian Charles Blockson's pioneering books about the Underground Railroad, as well as his article about the Underground Railroad that appeared in *National Geographic* magazine. They have been helpful in bringing to light the contributions of UGRR workers in Delaware, Maryland, Virginia, and various counties in Pennsylvania, which sheds further light on why Thomas Garrett was so successful in assisting large numbers of runaways to escape.

All of the above has made this new edition necessary. Although it includes all the essential original material—as well as additional letters and photographs—this volume contains new material. In the chapter, "Thomas Garrett, the Man," I offer an in-depth look at the major source of Garrett's motivation, that which drove him to make his lasting commitment to freeing the runaway slave. With this has also come consideration of the question, "How important was Thomas Garrett as an UGRR agent?" Also included is an in-depth discussion of Thomas Garrett's close relationship with the most outstanding conductor on the Underground Railroad, Harriet Tubman. And finally, I offer a critique of the number of runaway slaves Thomas Garrett is said to have helped escape. In short, along with the important genealogical, oral and factual history, and primary source material (Garrett's letters), in this edition, I put a human face on Thomas Garrett.

The poet Kahlil Gibran once wrote, "Your friend is your needs answered." How true I found that to be. Hence, I wish to extend my heartfelt thanks to my friend and colleague, William C. Kashatus, PhD, who suggested, *insisted*, that this new edition be written. Another friend and colleague I wish to thank is Kate Larson, PhD, who unselfishly shared with me her own research and findings about the Eastern Shore where Thomas Garrett received large numbers of runaways. I am also grateful to both Kate Larson and Bill Kashatus for reviewing parts of the manuscript and making suggestions for accuracy. If there are any inaccuracies, they must be attributed to myself for following my own judgment.

I am deeply indebted to my friends, Paul Ressler and Margaret Swantko, who generously donated material that made it possible for this book to be written, and to my brother-in-law, Alwin Woodall, and his wife—my sister—Cheryll Woodall, who contributed their computer know-how, time and energy to assist me with the scanning that made it possible to include the essential material from the original edition. Thanks also to Elizabeth Williams, for her continuous interest in this work. I am especially grateful to Caron Williams, for his computer expertise and generous donation of time to keep my computer operative. Without the works of all of those writers, and the assistance of all of these friends, it would have been extremely difficult for me to complete this edition. They answered my needs.

James A. McGowan
Newtown, Pennsylvania
Fall 2004

1

The Underground Railroad

EVER SINCE HUMAN BEINGS became "civilized," they have practiced what is known as "slavery;" they have held each other as personal property to be used in any way fitting to the owners' purposes. The Romans enslaved the Greeks, the Spanish, Africans, and everyone else they conquered, while the Greeks and Spanish themselves held slaves—and so did the Egyptians. The Muslims raided parts of Black Africa for slaves, and during the Crusades, Christians enslaved the Saracen and other Muslim people they captured. Between the eighth and tenth centuries, the Germans enslaved the Slavonic people. In South America, the Mayans, the Aztecs, and the Incas also practiced slavery and were in turn enslaved by the Spanish. The English not only enslaved the Irish; the Irish, French, Dutch, Spanish, Portuguese, all enslaved the African Negro to be used as cheap labor in South America, the Caribbean, and North America, and some African Negro tribes enslaved other African Negro tribes.

Slavery began officially in America in 1619, when a Dutch ship landed 20 African Negro slaves at Jamestown, Virginia. The slaves were put to work on the tobacco plantations, and the rest is history. By 1681 there were only 2,000 Negro slaves as against 6,000 indentured laborers of European origin. After the intensive cultivation of tobacco developed, and a little later, rice, slavery took root. By 1714 there were 59,000 slaves. From then on they increased steadily, mainly through new arrivals, reaching 263,000 by 1754.[1]

Most opponents of slavery believe that the desire to be free is something inherent in all human beings. Frederick Douglass, an ex-slave, once said, "If a slave has a cruel master, he longs for a kind master. And if he has a kind master, then he longs to be his own master."

In the United States those slaves who longed to be free ran away. In the beginning that is all they did; they ran away from slavery. For the most part they had no idea where they were running. Hence, they inevitably became in need of direction and assistance from other human beings. As it has been a practice of human beings to enslave one another, it has always been a practice of human beings to help one another. Hence, those slaves that ran away and needed help did receive it from other human beings. And from this simple act of one human being helping another, there grew up in the United States a "mysterious institution" known as "The Underground Railroad," herein referred to as the "UGRR."

History books are replete with the names of heroic men and women who made outstanding contributions by helping the runaway slaves along the UGRR, but for the most part the work was done by plain and simple people from many walks of life. To be sure, these "ordinary" people were probably afraid for their own lives and property, but nevertheless they helped the runaway slaves. As one writer put it: "They took up the issue in their hard and capable hands, weighed it thus against their own strength, and decided what was to be done. Then they did that, backed by nothing but the bidding of their own consciences, and because it made them feel good to behave as they did."[2] They hid the slaves in their attics, woodsheds, churches, outhouses, cellars, corn-cribs, woodpiles, smokehouses, hay-mows, and every place conceivable. They smuggled them on board ships, hid them in the bottoms of wagons, and disguised them in their own clothes.

The heroism of the runaway slaves themselves can scarcely be exaggerated. In spite of the help that sometimes could be provided along the way, they were the ones who took the greatest risks and endured the worst hardships. They were physically conspicuous and were under the special handicap of almost total ignorance of where they were going. With only a few exceptions, most of the slaves who attempted to escape were striking out into something completely unknown.[3] Help was dangerous for fugitive slaves to seek and dangerous for their well-wishers to give. Both were at hazard.

To be sure, not all of those human beings who helped the runaway slaves were motivated by sympathy for their condition. To some it was profitable; money was paid by friends of the runaways, as well as by the runaways themselves, to buy their own freedom. A few steamship captains did "good business" running slaves to freedom, and slaves and free Negroes also earned money piloting fugitives across rivers, especially the Ohio.[4]

Again, to others, it was not so much the money as it was the thrill of adventure, or even the idea of breaking the law! These people were always able to supply their consciences with the "good excuse" that they had to do what they did because slavery was morally wrong and "against the will of God"—even as there were those who argued that slavery was morally right and that God sanctioned it.

Whatever their reasons, many otherwise ordinary people risked their lives and their belongings to assist the runaway slave. Thomas Garrett of Wilmington, Delaware, was one such person.

The formation of the UGRR began slowly at first, with one slave running away here, and another there, and so on. In time, of course, the flights increased. More and more slaves fled to, or at least toward, freedom. Literature on the UGRR gives a variety of reasons for this; reasons which cover perhaps the entire range of human reactions against adverse conditions. They ran away because they were mistreated, because they were afraid of being sold, and so separated from those they loved and the place that was familiar to them; they ran away because they would rather be free than slave, because they were enticed to run away, and for many more reasons. What ever the cause of slaves running away, the UGRR became such an important means of assistance to them that one writer thought it was "…one of the greatest forces which brought on the Civil War, and thus destroyed slavery."[5] Others believed that the UGRR was a "natural safety valve" for the South. They saw it as a means by which the natural leaders, malcontents, and more militant among the slaves fled, individuals who, had they no means of escape, would have surely contributed to a vast insurrection.

How did the UGRR get its name?

There is no reliable or exact answer to this question. R.C. Smedley, an early researcher on the UGRR, and one who considered it to be a highly organized system, tells the following story:

> In the early part of this concerted management slaves were hunted and tracked as far as Columbia. There the pursuers lost all trace of them. The most scrutinizing inquiries, the most vigorous search, failed to educe any knowledge of them. Their pursuers seemed to have reached an abyss, beyond which they could not see, the depth of which they could not fathom, and in their bewilderment and discomfiture they declared there must be an underground railroad somewhere. This gave origin to the term by which this secret passage from bondage to freedom was designated ever after.[6]

However, Wilbur H. Siebert, another researcher on the UGRR, points out that, as Smedley, in the above account, was referring to the early part of the 19th century, his account of the origin of the term seems to contain an anachronism. "Railroads were not known either in England or the United States until about 1830," says Siebert, "so that the word 'railroad' could scarcely have received its figurative application as early as Mr. Smedley implies."[7]

Siebert then quotes from The *Firelands Pioneer* (July 1888) an account by the Honorable Rush Sloan of Sandusky, Ohio:

> In the year 1831, a fugitive named Tice Davids came over the line and lived just back of Sandusky. He had come direct from Ripley, Ohio, where he crossed the Ohio River.... When he was running away, his master, a Kentuckian, was in close pursuit and pressing him so hard that when the Ohio River was reached he had no alternative but to jump in and swim across. It took his master some time to secure a skiff, in which he and his aid followed the swimming fugitive, keeping him in sight until he had landed. Once on shore, however, the master could not find him; and after a long ... search the disappointed slave-master went into Ripley, and when inquired of as to what had become of his slave, said ... he thought "the nigger must have gone off on an underground road." The story was repeated with a good deal of amusement, and this incident gave the name to the line: First the "Underground Road," afterwards "Underground Railroad."[8]

Some people believed that the UGRR was a real railroad. Thomas Drake, in *Quakers and Slavery in America*, tells the following story:

> An Indiana school teacher gravely told a friend of mine that she had actually seen the entrance of the tunnel through which the fugitives were shipped to Canada. Apparently her imagination had been so stimulated by the sight of the caves on the Indiana shore of the Ohio River, caves in which slaves were hidden after they had escaped across the river from Kentucky, that she pictured to herself a real tunnel extending all the way from southern Indiana to the Lake Erie shore.[9]

Once the name and concept "Underground Railroad" became popular, those human beings who felt called to work upon it began to use appropriate terms and names in connection with their self-appointed duties. They referred to themselves as "Conductors," "Station Masters," "Signal Men," and so on. Railroad terms caught on.

What were their duties? Briefly, the Conductors were the men and women who often went right into the heart of the slave territory and enticed the slaves to escape, after which they led them along secret routes to freedom. Along these routes were houses of friends and sympathizers who hid and gave succor to the fugitives, and passed them on to other friendly houses. These houses, or places of friendship, were known as "Stations," or "Depots," and the men and women who ran them were known as "Station Masters." There were other contributors to the UGRR; people who played a less active and less dangerous (but equally important) role. These contributed money (which was often needed for bribes, transportation, etc.), food and clothing. These contributors were known as "Stockholders." There were also synonyms. Conductors were also referred to as "Pilots," and "Station Masters" (especially in towns and cities, where a higher degree of organization existed) were referred to as "Managers." The term "Agent" was used to designate anyone who worked on the UGRR.

How well was the UGRR organized?

As mentioned, R.C. Smedley believed that the UGRR was a highly organized system, but most others disagree with this. The general consensus of opinion, particularly among recent authorities, is that the UGRR was essentially a loosely connected system, relying for the most part on the concern of those who participated. It was a means through which one human being could help another, and this help arose mostly spontaneously, for it is generally accepted that most of the Negroes who ran away from slavery did so of their own accord and were inclined to be distrustful, even of other slaves.

In some areas, of course, there was organization. According to Siebert, "The first reference to an organization devoted to the business of aiding fugitive slaves occurred in 1786."[10] He writes, "Two letters of George Washington, written in 1786, give the first reports, as yet known, of systematic efforts for the aid and protection of fugitive slaves. One of these letters bears the date May 12, and the other, November 20. In the former Washington speaks of the slave of a certain Mr. Dalby, residing at Alexandria, who has escaped to Philadelphia, and 'whom a society of Quakers in the city, formed for such purposes, have attempted to liberate.'"[11]

Between some parts of Maryland, Delaware and Pennsylvania (where Thomas Garrett operated), some degree of organization did exist. Harriet Tubman, a runaway slave from lower Maryland who later became one of the most outstanding conductors on the UGRR and one of Thomas Garrett's closest friends, "...made use of stations at Camden, Dover, Blackbird, Middletown and New Castle in the state of Delaware." Siebert describes the Maryland-Delaware routes as follows:

> Along the western shore of the Chesapeake runaways passed northward to Havre de Grace, where they usually crossed the Susquehannah, and with others from the Eastern Shore found their way to established stations in the southern part of Lancaster and Chester counties in Pennsylvania. From the territory adjacent to the Delaware the movement was to Wilmington, and thence north through Chester and Delaware counties. The routes developed in the three regions just indicated formed three systems of the underground travel, the first of which may, be called the western, the second, the middle, and the third, the eastern system. These systems comprised, besides the main roads ... numerous side-tracks and branches.... Their common goal was Phoenixville, the home of Elijah F. Penneypacker, and from here fugitives were sent to Philadelphia, Norristown, Quakertown, Reading and other stations as occasion required. While Phoenixville may be regarded as the central station for the three systems mentioned, it did not receive all the Negroes escaping through this section, and Smedley says that "Hundreds were sent to the many branch stations along interlacing routes, and hundreds of others were sent from Wilmington, Columbia, and stations westward direct to the New England States and Canada. Many of these passed through the Vigilance Committee connected with the anti-slavery office in Philadelphia."[12]

Siebert lists six other people from Wilmington in addition to Thomas Garrett who were agents on the UGRR: Isaac Flint, John Hunn, Joseph G. Walker, Benjamin Webb, Thomas Webb, and William Webb. Strictly speaking, John Hunn was from Middletown; Smedley also lists Evan Lewis and states that he "was a zealous and active abolitionist. His house was a much frequented station on the UGRR. The fugitives who came his way were generally forwarded in the direction of Philadelphia."[13] Meanwhile, Joseph G. Walker, Benjamin, Thomas and William Webb were all African American UGRR workers in Wilmington. We will have occasion to speak of their contributions to the UGRR in Wilmington in a later chapter.

Chester County, in the free State of Pennsylvania, lying just north of the State of Delaware, was arguably the most important location for runaway slaves. According to Smedley:

> After leaving Wilmington, the main route came by way of Allen and Maria Agnew, Isaac and Dinah Mendinhall, Dr. Bartholomew Fussell, and John and Hannah Cox, near Kennett; Simeon and Sarah D. Barnard, East Marlborough; Eusebius and Sarah Marsh Barnard and William Barnard, Pocopsin; Isaac and Thamazine P. Meredith, Mordecai and Esther Hayes, Newlin; James Fulton, Jr., and Gideon Pierce, Ercildoun; Dr. Eshelman, Zebulon Thomas and daughters, Downington; Micajah and William Speakman, Uwehlan; John Vickers and Charles Moore, Lionville; Esther Lewis and daughters Mary Elizabeth, and Graceanna, William Fussell, Dr. Edwin Fussel and

Narris Maris, Vincent West; Emmor Kimbor, Kimberton; and Elijah F. Penneypacker, near Phoenixville.

This route was relatively successful in transporting fugitives, and this was probably due to its fairly high degree of organization. However, for a more recent study of the Chester County contribution to the UGRR, see William C. Kashatus's *Just over the Line*.[14] Kashatus includes the vital contributions made by individual African American UGRR workers, communities and churches in Chester County, which Smedley leaves out. Kashatus's study also includes the contributions of other individuals and denominations besides the Quakers.

Larry Gara declares, "It was the interest and perseverance of Garrett that provided essential leadership for the cause. He spared neither time nor expense, and threw himself into underground work with enthusiasm."[15]

2

Early Accounts of Garrett's Life

AFTER THE CIVIL WAR, several accounts of the UGRR were published. One of the very first of these was by William Still, a black man, who made his home in Philadelphia.[1] Still was the Chairman of a four-man "Acting Committee" (which was part of the "Vigilance Committee") of The Pennsylvania Anti-slavery Society, and had the assignment of personally interviewing the slaves that the Society had helped pass on to freedom. In the execution of his duties, Still recorded his personal observations; he told what the slaves looked like, what their personal attitudes were, and, in his own opinion, their individual level of intelligence. From them he heard and recorded their personal histories: where they came from, who their masters were, how they escaped, what motivated them to escape, and the dangers they encountered during their flight. In his foreword to the 1970 edition of Still's book, Benjamin Quarles refers to Still as being "resourceful, energetic and courageous," and that he "proved to be an admirable choice for this work. [Still's] mother and father had been slaves, thus deepening his dedication to his work."[2]

Those who worked on the UGRR were wary of keeping records of their activities and of their passengers. Such evidence, if found, made them not only liable for court suits, which could result in their losing large sums of money and property, but could also lead to the recapture of runaways and to the incrimination of others. Except when writing to fellow UGRR workers, they used code terms. They referred to the slaves as "bales of wool," or "dark cargo," and others. Garrett often referred to the slaves he helped as "God's poor."

"But William Still kept his records," says Quarles. "He guarded them carefully, and during one stretch he concealed them in a cemetery building. In 1872, with slavery buried in the ashes of the Civil War, Still decided that the time had come 'to show what efforts were made and what success was gained for freedom under difficulties.' Bringing together a goodly portion of his collected material, Still published *The Underground Railroad*...."[3]

William Still, an early record-keeper, author and participant on the Underground Railroad who worked closely with Thomas Garrett.

Most of the people who forwarded the runaway slaves to the office of the Vigilance Committee in Philadelphia were people William Still knew personally, and he presented biographical sketches of them in his book. Among these is a sketch of the life of Thomas Garrett. In his lifetime Thomas Garrett is reported to have helped more than 2,700 slaves find their way to freedom. Most — or at least a large portion — of them he sent to William Still. So great was the slave traffic (and communication) that resulted between these two men that Still saw fit to publish more than 25 letters from Thomas Garrett in his book. We may assume there must have been many more letters that Still received from Garrett but did not publish.

The biographical sketch of Garrett appearing in Still's book is the earliest. It is a reprint of a series of articles originally printed in January, 1871, by the local newspaper, *The Wilmington Daily Commercial*. All later accounts of Garrett's life apparently took most of their information from this original source. As copies of this newspaper are no longer in existence, we owe much thanks to William Still for reprinting these articles.

The first article, printed soon after Garrett's death (January 25, 1871), gives a brief outline of his life, covering his birth in Upper Darby, Pennsylvania, his business career as an iron merchant in the city of Wilmington, his two marriages, and his trial in 1848. The focus of the article is on Garrett's labors in behalf of the abolition of slavery and his assistance to runaway slaves.

The second article (which appeared on January 30) is an extract of the funeral service. This is followed by a letter to the editor of the *Commercial*, in which the writer commends the editors for their "admirable" sketch of Garrett's life, but wishes to correct inaccurate statements made by the editors regarding certain particulars of the trial of 1848. After this, Mr. Still presents letters from a few of Garrett's friends. The first of these is from William Lloyd Garrison to Garrett's second son, Henry. The next letter is also to Henry. It is from Elizabeth J. Williams, a friend. There follows a testimony from Wendell Phillips, which was printed in the *National Standard* (an anti-slavery newspaper) and a tribute from Aaron M. Powell, taken from the same newspaper.[4] The last is a letter from T. Israel to George Stone, in which Israel speaks warmly of his friendship with Garrett and of "Garrett's greatness of soul." This whole account of Garrett's life comprises approximately 15 pages.

A second account of Garrett's life was written by Dr. Robert C. Smedley, an early researcher on the UGRR. Smedley was the first non-participant to write about the UGRR. His book began "simply with the view of writing a newspaper article on the main lines and general management of the UGRR in Chester county." However, as he inquired further, he writes, "the character of the persons engaged in the work, revealed such well-established and well-conducted plans, such nobleness of purpose, such an amount of secret charity and unrecompensed labors freely given, that the idea suggested itself that the true Christian principles and commendable works of those noble philanthropists, should not be allowed to die with the times in which they lived." Hence he wrote his *History of the Underground Railroad In Chester and the Neighboring Counties of Pennsylvania*, a full-length book of almost 400 pages.

Smedley's book, first published after his death in 1883, was considered one of the most widely read books about the UGRR, besides William Still's. It has been the object of some criticism, the chief one being that the author concentrates mostly on the contributions made by white abolitionists — mostly Quakers. Even William Loren Katz, who wrote the introduction to the 1969 edition of Smedley's book, and who defended Smedley against one of his critics, was himself inclined to say that Dr. Smedley was "less conscious of the part both black fugitives and the local black population played in the events that he described. He is more concerned and aware of the selfless devotion of local whites," says Katz, "particularly those motivated by deep religious conviction," and ends by saying, "If Dr. Smedley erred, he did so on the side of the angels, but unfortunately only the white ones."

In reviewing the book I find, it is true that the main characters are the white abolitionists and the local white population, but the reader should not be misled to believe that Dr. Smedley totally ignores the contributions made by either the black fugitives or the local black population. For example, Smedley gives a sketch of the life of William Parker, the Negro leader of the famous "Christiana Riot," in which he speaks of Parker in as favorable a light as I believe anyone totally sympathetic to the Negro cause would have done. "Neither unequal numbers, nor pistols pointed at him could impress him with a thought of fear," says Smedley, then adds, "It was a remark of Lindley Coats that 'he [Parker] was as bold as a lion, the kindest of men, and the warmest and most steadfast of friends.'" In another passage, Smedley says, "How many more [free Negroes] might have been swept away from their homes without legal warrants, by those mercenary negro-stealers who infested that part of Lancaster county, had they not been afraid of, and measurably held at bay by the powerful and dauntless Parker, it would be impossible to tell."[5] The following are two of numerous references that Smedley makes to the contributions of the local Negro population:

> Abraham Johnson, a young slave, belonging to a Mr. Wheeler, of Cecil County, Md., hearing that he was to be sold next day, told his mother. Early in the night they, with his sister and her child, fled to that well known colored man, on the Susquehannah, Robert Loney, who ferried fugitives across the river in the night at various places

below Columbia, and gave them into the care of William White (a white conductor), who distributed them to other agents.[6]

In the second incident, slave hunters had actually captured a slave, bound his hands and carried him off. The local abolitionists ascertained where the party was going to put up for the night:

> Then riding in advance they notified the colored people of that vicinity, who assembled with arms after dark, and surrounded the house in ambush. While the party was at supper, Hannah Quiggs, the landlady, secretly loosened the slave's handcuffs, when with the bound of a liberated hare, he opened the door and fled. The slave holders and their guide rushed out to pursue him, but a dusky phalanx of resolute men arose before their eyes, and presented a solid front, which they knew it was death to encounter.[7]

Smedley's sketch of the life of Thomas Garrett covers approximately the same information that is in William Still's book — Garrett's birthdate and death, where he was born, the incident that led him to take up the cause of helping runaway slaves, his move to Wilmington, and the events that led to the trial of 1848. There are eight and a half pages in all. Smedley also included several incidents involving Garrett in the sketches of the lives of some of the other characters in the book, and in the appendix he includes six letters from Garrett to William Still, which he copied from Still's book. These letters are included in the present book.

In 1898, Wilbur H. Siebert, a professor of history at Ohio State University, published his "carefully documented" history of the underground railroad, *The Underground Railroad: From Slavery to Freedom.*

Through correspondence and travel, Siebert gathered reminiscences from many surviving abolitionists or their families. He collected recollections of fugitive slave days from books, newspapers, letters and diaries. He took up residence in Ohio, where he was able to investigate and collect information on the UGRR in that state, southern Michigan, and from the surviving fugitives along the Detroit River, in the province of Ontario. He also lived in Massachusetts, where he secured information regarding the UGRR in New England. In all, the material Siebert collected related to "Iowa, Wisconsin, Illinois, Indiana, Ohio, Michigan, Pennsylvania, New York, New Jersey, Connecticut, New Hampshire, Rhode Island, Massachusetts and Vermont."[8] Quarles says, "Siebert's book immediately stamped him as the foremost authority in the field, a position that has gone unchallenged."[9] However, contemporary UGRR historian, Charles Blockson, finds that Siebert, like Smedley, accords only a minor role to the efforts of blacks on the UGRR. He writes:

> The most often cited early study of the network is Wilbur H. Siebert's *The Underground Railroad, From Slavery to Freedom*, published in 1898. The bulk of his field work over forty years was conducted in Ohio and Massachusetts, where he resided. Thus the celebrated Underground Railroad chronicler accorded a minor role to the efforts of blacks on the Freedom Train.[10]

Siebert mentions Garrett several times throughout his book in connection with Harriet Tubman and various UGRR activities, and gives a brief account of Garrett's life (one paragraph), including a photograph of Garrett.

A fourth account of Thomas Garrett's life is a "Memorial Address" commemorating the 100th anniversary of his birth. This address was given on January 28, 1889, by the Reverend William P. Tilden (who was also a practicing physician) in the First Unitarian Church in Wilmington.

Tilden gathered the material for this address from the local newspapers, *The Wilmington Daily Commercial, The Delaware Gazette* and *The Blue Hen's Chicken,* as well as from incidents told to him by people who knew Garrett personally. Tilden's address is 19 and a half pages long, and repeats most of the same facts of Garrett's life that Still and Smedley report in their books. However, Tilden's address is sprinkled with a few more personal anecdotes that bear on the human side of Garrett.

Doctor Robert C. Smedley, 1832–1883, an early researcher on the Underground Railroad.

In 1935, Tilden's "Memorial Address" was printed privately by one of Thomas Garrett's great-grandsons, and copies can probably be acquired from the Quaker colleges, Swarthmore and Haverford, in Pennsylvania, as well as from the Historical Society of Delaware.

Friends in Wilmington is a compilation of addresses and papers, most of which were presented at the Bicentennial Celebration of the Wilmington Monthly Meeting of Friends. It was compiled by a committee of Friends (Quakers) of the Meeting under the editorship of Edward P. Bartlett. The purpose of this book, as stated by Bartlett, is "to present historical material of the factual type and to tell the story of Friends in northern Delaware as it has been written into ancient and in most cases unpublished records."[11]

This book is significant because Wilmington was Thomas Garrett's adopted city—he lived there for 49 years—and the Friends Meeting House is where he and his second wife, Rachel Mendinhall, were married. They were both buried on the Meeting House grounds, along with his first wife, Mary Sharpless, and his youngest son, Eli, by Rachel Mendinhall.

Among the various addresses and papers that appear in this book is a biographical sketch of Thomas Garrett. This was one of the addresses originally presented at the Bicentennial Celebration by Thomas E. Drake, a professor of American History and Curator of The Quaker Collection of Haverford College — also the author of *Quakers And Slavery in America* (New Haven, Yale University Press, 1950), in which he mentions Thomas Garrett very briefly several times.

Drake, like Tilden, gathered his material for this address from many of the people in Wilmington and from newspaper files. He also gathered material from the public library, Historical Society Archives and Federal Records, as well as consulting a scrapbook of material concerning Thomas Garrett from Miss Helen Garrett, Thomas' granddaughter by his son, Eli. As to the content of the address, Drake himself says it "adds only a little that is new about the life of Thomas Garrett."

A Dictionary of American Biography contains only a brief outline of some of the highlights of Garrett's life, and there is even less in *Dictionary of Quaker Biography*. *History of Upper Darby* mentions Thomas Garrett only briefly, but it is an excellent source of information on the Garrett family, from the first settlers (1684) to Arthur Sellers Garrett (early 1900s).

A recent study of the UGRR was conducted by Larry Gara, a history professor from Pennsylvania. In his book, *Liberty Line: The Legend of the Underground Railroad*, Professor Gara is critical of the earlier writing on the UGRR, believing that the "Reminiscent accounts" [particularly as reported by Smedley and Siebert] were taken uncritically from the "faulty memories" of aging abolitionists who, for the most part romanticized and exaggerated their deeds. "Reminiscent accounts are bound to be full of inaccuracies," says Professor Gara. "Facts are elusive even to the diligent scholar, but even more so to rambling old folk who are recalling the heroic deeds of their more active days."[12] In commenting on Siebert's book, he says:

> He [Siebert] accepted the elderly abolitionists statements at face value and defended the use of such material on the ground that the memories of the aged were more accurate than those of young people.[13]

Professor Gara cites pages 11–12 of Siebert's book as evidence. Turning to those pages we find that it is Gara, himself, who is guilty of an inaccuracy! Let us read what Siebert really said:

> If it be argued that the surviving abolitionists are now old persons, it should not be forgotten that it is a fact of common observation that *old persons ordinarily remember occurrences of their youth and prime better than events of recent date* [italics added].

It is probably important to also point out that Siebert was aware of the nature of the material comprising his book; he was aware that reminiscent accounts were not a substitution for facts, and he dealt with this in his book (see pages 11 to 13). Professor Gara does not mention this.

In other words, Professor Gara has shown himself to be as fallible in recording facts as those "aged abolitionists" he criticizes—diligent scholar though he may be. However, his book is a valuable source of information for anyone interested in another perspective of the popular stories of the UGRR. Professor Gara's implication that the runaway slave did far more for himself than he is generally given credit for is more than likely a correct one and is a point of view that future researchers of the UGRR would do well to bear in mind. I have also found his assertion that "reminiscent accounts are bound to be full of inaccuracies" to be painfully true in many instances, though I would not say that they are "bound" to be so. However, in his attempt to correct the offences of past historians and writers of memoirs, I think Professor Gara unfairly minimizes their contributions. He accuses those abolitionists who wrote their memoirs of being "no more capable of objectivity in the post war years than they had been in the days before the war."[14] He adds:

> Although the Underground Railroad was a reality, much of the material relating to it belongs in the realm of folklore rather than history.... Fantastic exaggerations of the exploits of such persons as Harriet Tubman, Thomas Garrett and Levi Coffin make them as much a part of our folklore as of our national history.[15]

What Professor Gara seems to overlook is that slavery was an extreme condition and thus required men and women of an extreme nature to oppose it. William Lloyd Garrison was considered a fanatic. The New Jersey-born Quaker, Isaac T. Hopper, was considered a fanatic, and even the gentle Lucretia Mott was considered a fanatic. In fact, abolitionists, in general, were considered a fanatical breed. They went to extremes to oppose the condition of slavery. We, today, are far removed from that condition, and therefore can view it with detachment and criticism, but the men and women who dedicated their lives to oppose it knew well the extremely oppressive conditions under which the slave lived and toiled and were kept in ignorance. It can only be a total lack of ability to empathize with that other point in time which will lead us to believe that their deeds were "fantastic exaggerations." In the case of Harriet Tubman, I believe that most investigators of black history would strongly disagree with Professor Gara. However, in the case of Thomas Garrett, I have found instances which I believe were exaggerated, and I have pointed them out.

3

Upper Darby Ancestry

From 1822 until his death in 1871, Thomas Garrett lived in Wilmington, Delaware. However, he was born and raised in what is now Upper Darby, Pennsylvania. His birthdate was August 21, 1789.

The Garrett family were members of The Religious Society of Friends (popularly known as "the Quakers"), and were among the first Quaker immigrants to leave England and come to the New World under the influence of William Penn.

William Penn, the son of an English naval officer and a convert to Quakerism, was made proprietor of an ill-defined tract of land in America by King Charles II. The land lay between New York and Maryland, and extended from the Delaware River indefinitely westward.[1]

As a young man, Penn became deeply influenced by the preaching of the Quaker preacher, Thomas Loe, and almost at once began a long career of crusading for religious toleration. Hence, when he received the grant of land from Charles II, his first concern was to establish political and religious toleration in the new colony. Penn was eventually to become one of the outstanding voices of the Quaker doctrine that all men are equal in the eyes of God, and also to settle that land which today bears his name — "Pennsylvania."

William Penn first arrived in the new world in 1682. The following year Darby was settled and recognized as a definite locality.[2] Its name is reminiscent of the old world, "Derbyshire," England. Today, Upper Darby includes much of suburban Philadelphia.[3] Darby Creek and Cobbs Creek form the east and west boundaries, respectively.[4]

In 1687 the first Quaker Meeting House was established. John Blunston, a mill owner, acknowledged a deed for one acre of land in the township of Darby to build the meeting house.[5] Prior to this time the meetings were held in Blunston's home.

In 1747 Darby was divided into two townships, Upper Darby and Lower Darby, but it was not until 1786, however, that this division was legally carried out.[6]

3. Upper Darby Ancestry

Thomas Garrett's great-grandfather, William Garat — as the name was then spelled — arrived in Darby from Leicestershire County, England, in 1684. With him was a friend, Samuel Levis. He and Levis acquired 1,000 acres of land from a Joshua Fearn. According to *A History of Upper Darby*, the property was originally deeded to Fearn by William Penn. The indenture, or deed, upon which the transaction of the property took place contains the signature of William Penn and is today considered the most prized possession of the Garrett family.

> The deeds of long ago were called indentures because of the manner in which they were protected against counterfeit. When a deed was written before the time of recorders, it was the custom to write two copies of the document on a single piece of parchment. The purchaser would receive one copy and the court clerk the other. When the two were cut apart with scissors, no set design was followed. But they were never cut in a straight line. If a dispute arose, and more than one copy appeared, a trip was made to the court house. The holder of the deed whose indenture fitted that of the copy on record was judged the rightful owner of the disputed property.[7]

The 1,000 acres of land was divided between William Garat and Samuel Levis, and on the 500 acres that he farmed, William Garat built his homestead. William Garat's son, Samuel, first changed the spelling of the name to Garratt, and later it was Samuel's son, Nathan, who made the second change in the spelling of the name, to Garrett.

"Riverview Farm" was the name of the Garrett farm, and the house was located at 463 Shadeland Avenue.[8] *A History of Upper Darby* contains a photo of the old Garrett House (p. 118) with a caption noting that the house was torn down to make way for the School of the Holy Child Jesus. This is apparently an error. The author visited the spot, in April of 1975, and took the photograph of the house. There have been some changes in the house, to be sure, but it is the same house. In 1975 the house was owned by a family named Isard.

The house stands on the corner of Shadeland Avenue and Garrett Road; the latter was so named because it ran through the Garrett land to the Garrett mills, which were located on Cobbs Creek.[9]

When William Garat moved to the New World in 1684, with him were his wife, Ann, and eight children — Ann, Mary, Samuel, Hannah, Sarah, Alice, William, and Thomas. After their arrival, a son, John, was born.

The oldest boy, Samuel, married Jane Pennel, of Middletown, Pennsylvania. They had nine children — Mary, Joseph, Hannah, Samuel (who died in infancy), Samuel, Nathan, James (who died in youth), Thomas, and Jane.

Of the boys, it was Nathan who inherited the farm and homestead when the father died. Nathan married Ann Knowles of Oxford Township. They had five children — Hannah (who died in childhood), Jane, Nathan, Thomas, and Ann.

Nathan's son, Thomas, fell heir to the Garrett homestead. Thomas was married twice. His first wife was Margaret Levis, who died three years later. He then married Sarah Price of Kingsessing, Pennsylvania. By his first marriage, he had two children —

The Garrett family home in Upper Darby, Pennsylvania, birthplace of Thomas Garrett. (Photograph taken by the author, James McGowan, in April 1975.)

Mary (who died in infancy) and Samuel. By his second marriage, he had 11 children. The eldest were Phillip and Sarah, a set of twins. Following the twins was a boy, Thomas, who died in youth. Then followed Charles, Margaret, and another boy named Thomas, and it is *this* Thomas Garrett, the second son of this name, who is the subject of this biography. The remaining five children were Benjamin, John Knowles, Isaac, Ann, and Edward.

So Thomas Garrett, who eventually moved to Wilmington, Delaware, to become that state's most outstanding station master on the UGRR, was one of 13 children.

The Garrett family owned and operated a number of mills in the Darby area. In *History of Delaware County, Pennsylvania*, Henry Graham Ashmead reports that the name Garrett appears on the assessment roll in connection with mills in Upper Darby a number of times. In 1766, William Garat was assessed on a leather mill and a blade mill, and in 1774 on a fulling mill and a blade mill. In 1782, William Garat and Oborn Levis were assessed on a fulling mill, and in 1788 on a skin mill and a plaster mill.

In 1805, Thomas Garrett's father built a tilt mill at the site of the Union Mills—

at that time owned by a Thomas Kent. Samuel, his son by his first marriage, owned and operated an oil mill at the same locality, and in 1822, the father erected a stone cotton factory.

Other branches of the Garrett family also owned and operated mills in the area. Casper S. Garrett, a cousin, purchased the unexpired lease from a mill owned by a Samuel Hartranft, and converted it from oil to manufacturing paper. This was known as The Keystone Mills. Casper's grandson, Edwin T. Garrett, bought a grist mill from Robert Palmer in 1872, and converted it to a paper mill.[10]

In 1692, the Quakers established the first school in Delaware County. This was recorded in the minutes of Darby Friends Meeting. During the following century other Quaker schools were established. These were at Haverford, Concord, Radnor, Marple, Springfield, Middletown and Upper Chichester.[11]

When William Penn first came to the colony in 1682, a large company of English and Welsh Quakers came with him. They were "followed later by Scotch-Irish Presbyterians, by Moravians and members of other German groups, all seeking religious liberty, all firmly resolved to make new homes in a land free from the persecutions which had beset them in the old."[12] They set up their own schools to preserve their religious beliefs, language and customs. Thomas Garrett's education undoubtedly included this ancestral resolution. His religious teaching embodied the fundamental tenet of Quakerism, that all men are equal in the eyes of God. His boyhood years were spent working on the farm and in the mills. Both Ashmead and William Still mention that Garrett's father was a scythe and edged toolmaker, and that, besides working on the farm, Thomas learned the blacksmith trade.

4

Quakers and Quakerism

Thomas Garrett was a Quaker. His family were members of that faith probably from its very beginning. He was married twice under the Quaker faith to two women who were also Quakers. He was buried in the burial grounds of a Quaker Meeting House. It is therefore necessary to say a brief word about the Quakers in order to tell his life story. Although the subject of Quakers and Quakerism is vast, all that is here necessary is a general statement, and for this I have borrowed quite liberally from those whose knowledge of the subject is greater than my own.

The Religious Society of Friends is the official name for that body of people popularly called, "Quakers," and the terms are used interchangeably or, as one writer put it, "indifferently," even among Quakers themselves.[1] Capital "F" Friends, are called "Quakers," and vice versa.

"Quakerism" started in the 17th century in England, from the spiritual experience of one man, George Fox. A fundamental belief of Quakerism is that "…God has endowed every human being with some measure of 'Inward Light,' by which everyone can have some direct experience of communion with God, some reliable knowledge of God's purpose. Holding this belief, early Quakers were convinced of the essential equality of all men in the sight of God…."[2] Although Thomas Garrett's great-niece, Margaret H. Garrett, writing in *Garrett Family Recollections*, was to say that although he was "not very settled or clear" in his religious views, Thomas Garrett's life, nevertheless, was an example of his deep belief in this fundamental idea.

A Quaker Meeting can be held anywhere and at any time. It does not require a special place consecrated for the purpose of worship. "To the Quaker no day, no place is more sacred than any other. All places, all days, all actions are equal opportunities to find and follow the will of God."[3] What is most important to a Quaker meeting is the religious attitude; the sense of communion with the Inward Light, that each individual brings to the group, when and wherever they meet.

"In the early days of the Quaker movement, Quaker meetings were held in barns, farmhouses, kitchens, or in the open air. Today most meetings take place in properties owned by the Society of Friends. Some of these are buildings erected in the seventeenth, eighteenth, and nineteenth centuries, and represent the modes of architecture typical of those periods."[4] Although a Meeting House is primarily used for worship, it may be used for a variety of purposes, including non–Quaker meetings.

The procedure of a Quaker meeting for worship is simple:

> ...there is no liturgy or programmed order of service with hymns, set prayers and readings; so no prayer or hymn books are required. There is no priest or minister to conduct or lead the worship, for these are responsibilities shared by all who are present. No outward sign marks the beginning of the meetings; it starts when the first person arrives, enters the room and sits down in silence.[5]

Silence is historically an important part of Quaker worship; it is this which gives it its distinctive character. The silent worship is based on the Quaker tenet that a portion of God (the *Inward Light*) is in every human being. This inward light is accessible to each individual, and can be made known to him by his *own* inward seeking, and "waiting." Each individual then is his own minister, and when a member rises to speak in meeting it is assumed that he has been moved by that "light within" to do so, to share his ministry with those who are present. Until then the meeting is silent — although, during the course of an hour's meeting, three or four people may rise and speak for a few minutes each. However, most meetings for worship generally have more silence than speaking.

The Society is structured in the following way: There is, first, a Monthly Meeting, which consists of a local group of Quakers worshipping in the same Meeting House and gathering at least once a month for business. The Quarterly Meeting is a larger unit of several Monthly Meetings, coming together every three months for both worship and business. A Yearly Meeting is an associated group of Quarterly Meetings, meeting annually.[6]

There are a few Quaker customs that bear mentioning, also; the first is the Quaker manner of speech. Throughout Thomas Garrett's letters we find him using the second-person singular pronouns, "thee," and "thy." The origin of this "plain language," as the Quakers call it, has its roots in the Quaker belief in the essential equality of all men. Tradition has it that kings and royalty of the 17th century "began to refer to themselves in the plural — 'we shall proceed to Coventry' or 'your majesty.' Gradually you and your became general for all the elect, and the second person singular pronouns were used only for intimates or social inferiors. With early Quakers, therefore, using the 'plain language' was a mark of democracy, a denial of caste in human relationships."[7]

This denial of caste was also true of the Quaker manner of dress — the familiar broad-brimmed hat and Quaker waistcoat. Wearing this "plain dress" did not come from a desire to be different. It was the same apparel worn by most during the period of Quakerism's beginning. The Quakers simply took the ornamentation off. Convinced of the essential equality of all men, they also refused to remove their hats to those who, by worldly standards, were above them in rank. Today, however, "The Quaker garb has become largely a Quaker costume, to be used for pageants or to be placed in museums, and thee and thy (thou has never been common among Friends in America) are now used by Quakers mostly among themselves ... A practice that was clung to in order to further inclusiveness with all God's children has become a harmless peculiarity, a rather charming anachronism...."[8]

5

The Road to Damascus

As a birthright Quaker, Thomas Garrett inherited a strong antipathy to slavery. George Fox, the founder of Quakerism, "early perceived the spiritual danger inherited in the master-slave relationship," writes Thomas E. Drake in *Quakers and Slavery in America*.

> In 1657, before either Puritan or Anglican had published a word about slave-holding, and only two years after the first Quaker missionaries reached the New World, Fox wrote from England a letter of caution "To Friends Beyond Sea, That Have Blacks and Indian Slaves." In this, his first discussion of slavery, [Fox] made only a beginning: he did not condemn slave holding as such. But he did expound the idea of equality of men in the eyes of God; and this idea — the touchstone to the Truth — finally, more than a century later, freed the Quakers' slaves. Fox urged Quaker converts in the New World "to have the mind of Christ, and to be merciful, as your heavenly Father is merciful"; he reminded them that God had made all nations of one blood; and that His gospel should be preached to all, because it is "the power that giveth liberty and freedom, and is glad tidings to every captivated creature under the whole heaven."[1]

In 1688, a group of Quakers in Germantown, Pennsylvania (not far from Upper Darby), were the first Quakers in America to urge that there was an inconsistency between Quakerism and slavery. "They hated the sight of slavery in a land where they had come to find freedom," says Drake.

> They ... drew up a formal remonstrance against slavery and the slave trade and submitted it to the monthly meeting of Friends in nearby Dublin. ...They remembered ... the fear which had gripped them on their voyage across the sea when they thought they might be captured by Turkish pirates and sold into slavery. Was it not worse, they asked, for Christians to act like the Turks, and steal Negroes from their native Africa to keep them in lifelong bondage?

The Germantown Quakers could see no more reason for enslaving black men than white. They had come to Pennsylvania themselves to find liberty of conscience: "liberty of the body should also prevail."[2]

Several years later, in 1693, George Keith's "Christian Quakers" printed the first American anti-slavery tract, *An Exhortation to Friends Concerning Buying or Keeping of Negroes*. Keith's followers "maintained that Christians ought to assist runaway slaves to escape, for God had commanded his people not to restore an escaped servant to bondage. Christians could not possibly hold slaves," argued Keith's followers, "for the Bible said that servants should not be oppressed, and what oppression could possibly equal slavery!"[3]

These ideas about slavery, particularly the latter, undoubtedly were impressed upon Thomas Garrett's mind during his formative years in Upper Darby. During those years there were certainly many occasions when he heard Friends rise and speak on the evils of slavery at the meetings for worship. Indeed, the Garrett homestead in Upper Darby was itself a station on the UGRR where runaway slaves were hidden and given succor.[4]

Yet, those who have written about Thomas Garrett say that his lifelong commitment to helping the runaway slave began with a single incident.

The incident occurred in approximately 1813. The place was the Garrett farm house in Upper Darby. Present were Thomas' mother, a Negro servant named Mary and her two children, and two white children. Here is the version told by Tilden in his "Memorial Address":

> Living in a free state [Pennsylvania] the household servants of the [Garrett] family were free. One day as he came home, he found the family in sorrow and indignation at the kidnapping of a free colored woman in their employ. Thomas immediately started in hot pursuit of the kidnapper, hoping, if possible to rescue the poor woman before she was sold in hopeless bondage. It was during this pursuit, that a light above the brightness of the sun shone in upon his soul revealing to his awakened conscience, the utter enormity of slavery as he had never before seen it .... It was borne in upon his mind so vividly as to appall him, and he seemed to feel a voice within telling him that his work in life must be to help and defend this persecuted race.[5]

He tracked the kidnapper and his victim by some peculiarity of wheelmarks in the road to a place near the Navy Yard in Philadelphia, "and thence, by a keen scent, sharpened by his mental agony, to Kensington, where he found them and returned rejoicing."

Drake, in *Quakers and Slavery in America*, referred to this experience as "a kind of road to Damascus vision of the sinfulness of slavery..."[6] meaning, of course, that Thomas Garrett, like the Biblical Paul of Tarsus, had a spiritual or mystical revelation which profoundly influenced the course of his life. This comparison by Drake seems at first to be an exaggeration, an attempt — mildly perhaps— to dramatize Garrett's life. But, as we shall see, from that moment on, assisting the runaway slave became an activity which dominated Thomas Garrett's life until slavery was ended.

The best example of Garrett's sense of "divine purpose" comes after his trial in 1848, when he and John Hunn, a fellow Quaker from Middletown, Delaware, were tried and found guilty of harboring fugitive slaves. Both were fined a considerable sum of money, and unsubstantiated reports claim that Garrett also lost much of his property and household goods. At the time Garrett was almost 60 years old, and the year just prior to the trial had also taken a "great" financial loss in business. After the sentence was passed, the Marshal of the court said to Garrett, "I hope you will now mind your own business and not meddle with slaves again." Our first impression on hearing this remark is that the Marshal was taunting Garrett, or attempting to humiliate him. But it may also be that the Marshal had weighed the awful consequences which could befall a man (particularly at Garrett's age) whom he thought was foolhardy in engaging in such a dangerous activity, and was therefore, benevolently perhaps, warning Garrett to cease. Garrett's response was not only with the defiance which came to characterize him as one of the most fearless station masters on the UGRR, but firmly reassures us that the experience he had on the road to Philadelphia had definitely influenced the course of his life. He told the Marshal publicly in the courthouse that he had assisted over 1,400 slaves to freedom in 25 years. Then he added, "and I now consider the penalty imposed might be a license for the rest of my life: but be that as it may, if any of you know of any poor slave who needs assistance, send him to me, as I now publicly pledge myself to double my diligence, and never neglect an opportunity to assist a slave to obtain freedom" (letter to Eliza Wigham, No. 1).

What was the state of the country during this period?

The first year of the 19th century gave birth to a number of people and events whose lives and happenings were prophetic perhaps of the violence and bloodshed that was to later erupt in a Civil War over the issue of slavery.

In 1800 Gabriel Prosser, a Negro slave from Virginia, secretly made plans to deliver his people from the bonds of slavery. He and his black followers (who were thought to include most of the 40,000 slaves living in the region) planned to attack the city of Richmond on August 30, just nine days after Thomas Garrett's 11th birthday.

But Prosser was betrayed, and on the very evening set for the outbreak, a great storm came up, with torrential floods and gales, and the doomed rebellion was washed away. Richmond by then was under martial law. Scores of slaves were imprisoned or hanged on the spot. Several weeks later their leader was captured. On October 7, after refusing to talk, Gabriel Prosser was publicly hanged.[7]

Born in the year of this bloodshed and rebellion was John Brown of Connecticut. He was stormy also, and his actions in the cause of delivering the slaves from bondage would also sweep across the land like a torrential flood force, and his life, too, would end in tragedy; he, too, would be publicly hanged.

In that same year, Nat Turner was born. Turner was a slave in South Hampton, Virginia. From his childhood he had what today would be called psychic experiences—visions—in one of which it had been prophesied that he was intended for some great purpose, and that he would know it by a sign. The sign came, an eclipse of the sun, and Nat Turner organized a small band of slaves..." and on the night of August 21, 1831, the night of Thomas Garrett's 42nd birthday, they forced their way into the home of his master, and killed the entire household. "Turner and his band gathered followers, as many as sixty or seventy, while they marched toward the county seat, killing slave masters and their families along the way. They killed fifty-nine people in all, before the Southhampton militia overtook them."[8] Turner escaped and hid in a swamp, but was later captured and also publicly hanged.

1803: Slavery was spreading. The United States had just purchased the Louisiana Territory from France; sugar and cotton plantations were growing in the deep South.

1812: War broke out between the United States and England, and Benjamin Lundy published an anti-slavery newspaper entitled, *The Genius of Universal Emancipation*.

In 1813 Thomas Garrett married his first wife, Mary Sharpless, of Chester County, Pennsylvania. They were married in Birmingham Friends Meeting on October 14. In William Still's book, it is stated that Thomas Garrett's first wife's name was "Sarah." This is an error. Garrett's *mother's* name was Sarah, not his wife's. This error is understandable considering the fact that both Thomas and his father had the same name.

On December 19, 1815, Thomas Garrett's first son, Elwood, was born.

Elwood Garrett became one of the first persons in America to use daguerreotype, an early photographic process. Jessie Rockwell, writing in H. Clay Reed's *Delaware: A History of the First State*, states:

> Perhaps the earliest daguerreotype machine in the United States was one sent to Elwood Garrett, In Wilmington, by English Friends. As recorded on the name-plate, it was No. 6 of those made by M. Daguerre. From reading of this invention Mr. Garrett constructed a crude camera from a cigar box, with which he took the first sun-made picture in Wilmington and possibly the United States. Mr. Garrett's enthusiasm led to the formation of an amateur Camera Club in 1891; its successor today is the Delaware Camera Club which holds an International Salon Annually at the Delaware Art Center, ranking sixth among those held.[9]

In the Garrett Manuscript at The Historical Society of Delaware, a paper on Elwood states:

> ...as there were no Daguerreotype plates in this country at that time, he improvised one by hammering out a silver dollar, and after chemically preparing it he obtained a fairly good image ... . He was for many years a member of the Board of Directors of the Wilmington Savings Fund Society, the Wilmington and Brandywine Cemetery Company, and of the New Castle Company Mutual Fire Insurance Company. He was much interested in the advent of the telephone [in Wilmington], and is said to have made many valuable suggestions in the introduction of the system there. He was also commissioned to take charge of the first train of Pullman cars sent to the Pacific coast.

Elwood also worked with his father in his hardware store on Shipley Street, but he is known mostly for his daguerreotype work. Two addresses were found for his location, probably indicating a relocation: The Wilmington Directory for 1853 lists his office as 66 Market Street, second story, while the paper on him in the Garrett Manuscript lists 720 Market Street.

1815 was the same year that Paul Cuffe, a son of a Negro father and Indian mother (who later became a member of the Society of Friends), took 38 free Negroes on board his ship, *The Traveler*, and landed them in Sierra Leone, a colony on the west coast of Africa. This was the first experiment in colonization, of transporting free blacks and settling them somewhere in Africa, and Cuffe paid most of the cost of the voyage himself. "He carried an all–Negro crew on his vessel, and concerned himself in many enterprises to improve the condition of his race. He set up a school for the colored children of the neighborhood, hoping to help them a little in their white-man's world. But he felt pretty well convinced that the lot of the Negro in the United States could never be a happy one. Africa appealed to him as a more inviting prospect."[10]

Cuffe died shortly after his first trip to Africa (in 1817), but his pioneering venture had established that colonization of free Negroes was feasible. Thus in December of 1816, the American Colonization Society was formed. This was the first attempt by white men to set up a United States colony in Africa, and it won the financial support of the federal government. The motives of those who supported the colonization movement differed. Many Quakers supported it because they sincerely believed that colonization was indeed the black man's best hope. Some Northerners saw it as a means of getting rid of free Negroes that otherwise had to be supported by the State. To Southerners, it was a means of getting rid of free Negroes who were continually stirring up unrest among the slaves.

So then, a large segment of members were Southern slaveholders. Most free Negroes, however, were against colonization. In January 1817, one month after the founding of the Society, an estimated 3,000 free blacks gathered in Bethel Church in Philadelphia to protest the colonization scheme. The chairman was James Forten, a black abolitionist who had fought in the American Revolution and later, as a sail-maker, amassed a fortune of $100,000. Forten called for a voice vote; when he called upon those in favor of colonization, only silence prevailed. But when he called upon those who opposed colonization, there went up a "No" which, according to Forten, "seemed as if it would bring down the walls of the building."

On June 1, 1818, Thomas Garrett joined the "Pennsylvania Society for Promoting the Abolition of Slavery, the Relief of Free Negroes Unlawfully Held in Bondage, and for Improving the Condition of the African Race." This was the first organization in America devoted to the abolition of Negro slavery. Benjamin Franklin served as president of this organization from 1787 until his death in 1790. During its early years, the Society devoted itself chiefly to sending petitions to Congress advocating the abolition of slavery and the protection of free Negroes from being kidnapped and carried south to be sold as slaves. The Society continued in existence until the Civil War.[11]

The following year, on April 15, 1819, Thomas Garrett's first daughter, Sarah, was born.

In the year 1820, two women were born who were to be important in Thomas Garrett's life. In Dorchester County, Maryland, Harriet Tubman was born. She was a slave. Thousands of miles away, across a great expanse of ocean, in Edinburgh, Scotland, Eliza Wigham was born. She was a free woman. In terms of their environments, their educational backgrounds, their family lives, and their positions in society, there were vast differences in these two women's lives. "A sagging cabin with buckling walls and a narrow clay-daubed chimney" was where Harriet Tubman first saw the light of day. She grew up barefooted, with no more than one dress, until she was old enough to hire herself out and earn money to buy shoes and to make her own clothes.

Eliza Wigham and her sister, Mary, were raised in a quiet, comfortable home at 5 South Grey Street, in Edinburgh. Although Eliza and her sister were raised by a stepmother, she was a woman who treated them with great kindness and affection. Harriet, on the other hand, was brutally taken away from her parents when she was five years old and hired out to work.

Eliza Wigham received one of the finest educations, while Harriet Tubman could neither read or write. The family life of Eliza Wigham was one which cultivated the growth of the intellect and an appreciation of the finer things in life, while Harriet's mother and father often had to leave her alone (when she could barely walk) while they went out to work in the fields.

Wherever she went, Eliza Wigham was regarded with well-deserved respect and admiration. Although respect and admiration would one day be accorded to Harriet Tubman, she was also hunted like an animal, and a good part of her life was spent hiding in woods and swamps and sneaking along the hidden trails of the UGRR.

But these two women had one thing in common: they both devoted their lives to the abolition of slavery and to the emancipation of all human beings. This common element dissolved all of their differences and made them sisters.

In time Eliza Wigham would write a book on the anti-slavery cause in America. About Harriet Tubman, many books would be written.

6

The Move to Wilmington

Thomas Garrett moved from Upper Darby, Pennsylvania, to Wilmington, Delaware, in 1822. The exact day he moved and the mode of transportation he used are not known. However, the Sharpless genealogy states that Thomas' second oldest daughter, Anna, was born on the second of February, 1822, in Upper Darby, and the *Delaware Gazette* carried an advertisement by Thomas Garrett of the opening of his new store on Shipley Street, in Wilmington. So Garrett obviously relocated to Wilmington between February and May of 1822.

As to the mode of transportation Garrett used we can immediately eliminate the railroad, for the development of the railroad in this country did not come until the 1830s. It would seem that travel by boat from Upper Darby to Wilmington would be the most convenient way. For one thing, both are ideally located for this. Both are located on the western shore of the Delaware River, with Wilmington being only about 25 miles south. Also, by 1810 steam-propelled vessels had demonstrated a commercial and engineering practicability on both the Delaware River, Chesapeake Bay, and the waters around New York City.[1] So steamboat travel between Philadelphia and Wilmington was fairly well developed by the time Garrett moved. However, in a letter to this writer by an authority on the Conestoga wagon (popularly known as the "covered wagon"), it was stated that "It would not be reasonable to go by boat, unless one lived right on the water and there were boats going where one wanted to go. Wagon travel was so very common in those times that I would not consider anything else."[2]

That wagon roads between Philadelphia and Wilmington were highly developed at that time is also mentioned by Benjamin Ferris in *History of the Original Settlements on the Delaware*. He reports that "About the year 1808 the attention of the capitalists (in Wilmington) was turned to the construction of turnpike roads…" and that "The popular current in their favor at that time ran so strong, that in a few years every highway leading from [the] city became a turnpike road."[3]

In 1808 The Wilmington Turnpike Company was incorporated. This company built a road through which "a communication was opened from the Susquehanna River at Columbia, through Lancaster County to Wilmington." In 1811, The Wilmington and Kennett Turnpike Company was chartered and constructed a stone turnpike from Wilmington to the Delaware-Pennsylvania state line. The object of this road was for the easy introduction of agricultural products from Pennsylvania. Ferris also reports that on the first of February, 1813, another company — which he does not name — was incorporated. This was for the "purpose of making an artificial road from Wilmington to the state line near Marcus Hook. It was made nearly the whole way on the old Philadelphia road, and was intended to facilitate the communication between Wilmington and Philadelphia."

So, we might infer from the opinion of these experts that when Thomas Garrett did move to Wilmington, he traveled by wagon. Garrett traveled with his wife, Mary, his oldest son, Elwood (who would be seven years old in December of that year), Sarah (who would be three years old in April of that year), and the baby, Anna. It is also reported that Thomas' youngest brother, Benjamin, moved from Upper Darby to Wilmington, but it is not known whether Thomas and Benjamin made the trip together, or even at the same time. Nevertheless, by May of that year the Garretts were settled in their new home at 227 Shipley Street.

The great question, of course, is "Why did Thomas Garrett move to Wilmington?" If there is only one reason, it has not been revealed, either by Garrett in any of his letters, nor by others.

And why Wilmington? Why not Chester, or West Chester, or Kennett Square, or York, or any other city in the free state of Pennsylvania? On the surface it may simply be that the decision to move to Wilmington was due to the fact that that growing city of Quakers offered many opportunities for expansion to a young man and his family. There was right at that time growing plans by the states of Delaware, Maryland and Pennsylvania to develop what would become the Chesapeake & Delaware Canal ("C & D Canal"), a close to 14-mile inland waterway that would cut the Delmarva Peninsula in half between Welch Point, Maryland, and initially Wilmington.[4] The canal would connect the Chesapeake Bay with the Delaware River, thus eliminating approximately 300 miles of travel around the Delmarva Peninsula and, at the same time facilitate the transport of goods from Baltimore and other major cities on the Chesapeake, to Wilmington and Philadelphia. The construction of the canal required iron and metal workers, as well as iron tools with which to work on the canal. When Thomas Garrett moved to Wilmington he immediately went into the iron and hardware business.[5] So there were certainly good business opportunities for Thomas Garrett to move to Wilmington.

However, we must also consider Thomas Garrett's mystical experience as a strong — perhaps the strongest — reason for him to move to a city in a slave state. With such a life's purpose revealed to him, it would be inevitable that a man of Thomas Garrett's bold character would pack up and, in today's vernacular, "be where the action is." This reason is reinforced by the fact that, although it was a slave state,

Delaware contained more free blacks then slaves, and the majority of the free blacks lived in Wilmington. It should not be surprising then to know that the city of Wilmington contained a very strong population of black UGRR workers, many of who would become Thomas Garrett's helpers. The city of Wilmington also included the African Union Methodist Church (AUM). Under the leadership of its outstanding ex-slave minister, Peter Spencer, the AUM was an active UGRR station for runaway slaves. Wilmington, Delaware, was also the home of Abraham Shadd. Although Shadd and his family would relocate to Pennsylvania, and his daughter to Canada, they were in Wilmington and were active abolitionists at the time Garrett lived there.

So, along with great business opportunities, the city of Wilmington and the state of Delaware was an ideal and practical location for Thomas Garrett to both raise a family and carry out the command he believed was given to him by the Almighty: to assist the runaway slave to freedom. We will revisit Thomas Garrett's move to Wilmington in a later chapter.

7

Wilmington

In 1822, what is now called the city of Wilmington was one of the fastest growing and most thriving towns in the state of Delaware. The town was less than a hundred years old. Its first crude plans were laid out in 1731 by Thomas Willing, for whom the town was originally named and, at that time, called, "Willingtown."

In his layout or design of the town, Willing apparently did not use much imagination. Ferris says that:

> ...the town was originally laid out in close imitation of the plan of Philadelphia, so close, indeed, that, like the Chinese painters, who carefully copy defects as well as beauties, Willing copied, most faithfully, the worst feature in that beautiful city; a feature which never entered into the design of its liberal and enlightened founder [William Penn]. As Philadelphia had a narrow and unsightly avenue, passing close to the river, called Water Street, so it was deemed proper that Wilmington should have one also, and accordingly one was laid out as narrow as its predecessor, being about one-half the width of the streets crossing it. As Philadelphia had a "Market street," with a Market house ranging along the middle of it, so was it intended that Wilmington should be accommodated in like manner; And as that city had a street called "Broad street," near the central part of it, so about the middle of Wilmington, a street running in like manner was laid out, and called "Broad Street" near the central part of it, so about the middle of Wilmington, a street running in like manner was laid out, and called Broad street. Its character, however, did not correspond to its name, for it is quite as narrow as any, except Water Street, being only forty-nine feet wide.[1]

After establishing the town, Willing did not have the means of developing it further, and the little town withered for want of settlers with sufficient capital and enterprise to give it life and growth.[2]

Then in 1735, William Shipley, a wealthy and influential Quaker from Ridley, Pennsylvania, came and bought most of the property there. According to Ferris, "On the 20th of May he purchased a lot of land situated at the easterly corner of Market and Second streets."[3] On the 9th of August in that same year Shipley purchased eight acres of land lying between Market and West Streets, above Second Street and below Fifth Street. At the same time he purchased one acre and 104 perches,[4] adjoining the same land, and lying within the aforesaid limits. On the 19th of August, Shipley bought another lot of land, containing one acre and four perches. This lot was bounded on the south by the Christiana River, and lay between Market and Tatnall Streets. He also purchased part of the church land lying above Fourth Street and west of Shipley Street.

In the fall of that same year, Shipley moved to "Willingtown," and was soon followed by many enterprising and industrious members of the Society of Friends, and, "From this period," writes Ferris, "the town grew rapidly; emigrants flocked to the settlement; and all was life and activity."[5]

Three years later, in 1738, these "industrious and enterprising Quakers" erected a Meeting House on West Street, between Third and Fourth Streets. This was the first house of worship to be erected in Wilmington. Before the Meeting House was erected the Friends held their meetings in the private dwelling of William Shipley. In the beginning the meetings were held at Shipley's house, then located between Orange and Shipley streets, later, they were held at Shipley's new home, at the corner of Fourth and Shipley streets until the Meeting House was ready for use.

Ten years after the erection of this Meeting House, the Society had become too large to be accommodated in it, and they built another one on the lot immediately opposite. This second Meeting House stood until the year 1817, "the Society having, in the preceding year, built the large house on West street,[6] which it still uses." This Meeting House was first opened as a place of worship on September 25, 1817.[7]

Approximately two months later, on November 11th, Elias Hicks, a Quaker from New York, who was destined to have a profound influence on the Religious Society of Friends, paid his first visit to the new Meeting House in Wilmington. Hicks attended both the morning and the afternoon meetings, and in his own words, "preached the gospel in the demonstration of the spirit suited ... to the states of many, or most, of the people which composed those large assemblies...."[8] Hicks' message, according to one writer, was an influence which incited discord and strife among the Friends in Wilmington.[9] Nevertheless, he returned again on the 23rd of October in 1819. His reputation by this time had spread, and he was asked to attend a large meeting which was described as a "solemn instructive season, worthy of grateful remembrance."[10]

Hicks' controversial preaching played a significant role in an eventual schism that took place in the Society of Friends in 1827. The essentials of this controversy is described by Geoffrey Hubbard in *Quaker by Convincement*:

> ...under the influence of Joseph John Gurney and other Friends, an evangelical theological outlook was gaining in ascendancy in London Yearly Meeting, and parts of America. Uneasiness at their ministry was typified by the reactions of Elias Hicks,

then an elderly and respected member of New York Yearly Meeting. His theology was centered around the inner light; he made a complete separation between the historical Christ and the Christ he described in terms of "an eternal principle in the soul, and nothing else can be Christ our Savior." For Hicks, the whole duty of man was to be still and attentive to that of God in him and by following and serving the inner light to do God's will. [Hicks'] attitude was consistent with the inherited Quaker view, but utterly in conflict with the evangelical attitude. The conflict came to a head in 1827 when the Philadelphia Yearly Meeting split. Numerically, the followers of Hicks greatly outnumbered their opponents.[11]

In a pamphlet by Hicks first printed in 1811 entitled *Observations on the Slavery of the Africans and Their Descendants* (which was revised and amplified in 1814 and 1823), Hicks "condemned slavery almost as vigorously as any which had come from a Quaker pen. [He] insisted that all men were free under the law of God; that no one had a moral right to enslave his fellows for any reason whatever. Users of the products of slave labor shared in the guilt of slaveholders, he believed they were equally culpable in the sight of God. No man made law sanctioning slavery could remove this guilt, nor could slaveholders rightfully refuse to emancipate their slaves. On the contrary, they owed their slaves wages for the work which had unjustly been required of them."[12]

When Thomas Garrett arrived in Wilmington in 1822, Wilmington was still considered a town, albeit a very rapidly growing and expanding one. In 1820 the population of the town was 5,268, and by 1845 it had more than doubled, to 10,639.[13]

This rapid growth brought with it several problems, one of which was in the process of being resolved in the same year that Garrett arrived. The nature of the problem and its resolution is described by Ferris in the following:

> The ground on which Wilmington stands is undulating, and in many places the original declivity of the streets, especially in the middle parts of the town, was too great to admit the easy passage of loaded wagons. Near the intersection of Shipley and Fourth streets, the ground descended towards the Christeen [Christiana River], the Delaware, and Orange Street by a steep decent. This place was long called "the Hill." The old houses in this neighborhood stood eight or ten feet higher than the present regulation. The house at the North corner of that intersection formerly had its door on Shipley Street, in what is now the second story, where the marks of the old doorway may still be seen. Many can yet remember the old fashion porch, and the family occupying it on a hot summer evening. Two large old buttonwood trees stood by the gutter at the gable end, whose roots grew far above the surface of the present pavement. Under their shade, in the olden time, the neighbors used to gather, in little groups, to hear the news. In Shipley street, between Second and Third streets [where Garrett's house was located], there was a very steep hill. The valley in Fourth between Orange and Tatnall Streets, has been filled up at least ten feet. These changes which extended to other parts of the town, sometimes left the houses standing high above the streets. The authority to fix or alter the ascents and descents was then vested in the Burgesses and Assistants, who were often changed at the annual elections. Different councils differed in judgment. The consequences were frequent

alterations. One year a street was taken down, the next year the same street was raised; and the owners of the property had to pay the expense, it often amounted to a burdensome charge. But a still greater grievance followed this course, they were sometimes irreparably injured by finding, after a final adjustment of the case, that the ground floors of their houses were below the pavement. These evils induced the call of a town meeting, where the subject was discussed, and it was unanimously agreed to apply to the Legislature for remedy. The Council caused the streets to be accurately surveyed, expensive instruments were purchased for determining the true levels, and the ascents and descents being accurately ascertained, a plot of the whole was laid before a town meeting, and adopted. This plot was submitted to the Legislature of the state, and in the year 1822, a law was passed confirming it, as the true map or ground plan of the borough.[14]

When Thomas Garrett arrived in Wilmington, he went into the mercantile iron and hardware business. His store was located on Shipley Street, a short distance from his house. In an advertisement placed in the *Delaware Gazette* for May 21, 1822, Thomas Garrett introduced himself to the people of Wilmington. It read:

NEW STORE
IRON, STEEL AND COAL.
The subscriber has opened a store in Shipley, between Second and Third Streets where he has for sale and intends keeping, a general assortment of iron, steel and coal.
Thomas Garrett, Jr.

William Still reports that Garrett was also a blacksmith, and Tilden, in his "Memorial Address," says that he had an occasion, while living in Wilmington, to put his blacksmith skills to good use. Tilden tells the following story of that occasion, which he says "illustrates Thomas Garrett's clear grit":

A rival house ... in the iron business, sought to run him off the track by reducing the price of iron to cost, But Friend Thomas, nothing daunted, employed a man to take his place in the store, tied on his leather apron, took to his hammer and anvil and in the prosecution of the trade he had learned from his father prepared to support his family with his own hands so long as the run lasted. Thus, by the sweat of his brow, he foiled the purpose of his rival and laid the foundation of what after many reverses became one of the permanent business houses of the city.[15]

In popular books and articles about Harriet Tubman, Thomas Garrett is referred to as a shoe merchant. This misinformation may have been gotten from Sarah Bradford who, in her book, *Harriet Tubman, The Moses of Her People*, mentions that Garrett was the proprietor of a large shoe establishment.[16] However, in his letter to Eliza Wigham (No. 4), Garrett reports that he gave Harriet Tubman money to buy shoes, and in two of his letters to William Still (Nos. 3 and 17), he reports that he gave shoes to other fugitives. But there is no mention, either by Garrett or other sources, that he was a "Shoe Merchant." In his own words, in a letter to Mary Edmundson (No. 6), he states, "I am in the mercantile iron and hardware business."

On November 22, 1824, Thomas Garrett's second son, Henry, was born. Henry Garrett became a dentist and would become a member of the first graduating class of the Philadelphia College of Dental Surgery, which was the third oldest of its kind in the United States. The school opened in 1852, and Henry graduated in 1853. The Wilmington Directory of 1853 reveals that Henry Garrett had his dental office in the same building as his brother Elwood's Daguerreotype Studio, at 66 Market Street.

In June of 1827, Mary Garrett gave birth to a girl, Margaret. In that same year 1827, the schism finally took place in the Society of Friends involving the views of Elias Hicks. This resulted in the formation of two groups: those who followed Hicks became known as "Hicksites," and the others, "Orthodox." In Wilmington the Meeting also divided between Hicksites and Orthodox, with the Hicksites being the larger of the two groups. The Hicksites retained the original Meeting House on West and Fourth Streets, while the Orthodox Friends built a Meeting House on Ninth and Tatnall Streets. After the Ninth Street Meeting House was sold (in 1915), the Orthodox Friends built a new Meeting House on Tenth and Harrison Streets. In a letter addressed to "Dear Children J&M McCollin" (Miscellaneous Letter No. 8), Garrett mentions a meeting to take place in consideration of "establishing a Boarding School for children of what are called Hicksite Friends. A Committee from New York, Philadelphia & Baltimore, are to meet," he says, "to consider the subject." In a letter to Eliza Wigham (Letter No. 3), he mentions both the Hicksite and Orthodox Quakers only briefly in connection with the support they gave to the schools for the colored children in the city of Wilmington.

Other than these two accounts, we have no written record of the position Garrett took on this important theological dispute. But the message of Elias Hicks, with its strict adherence to the doctrine of the "Inner Light" and his total condemnation of slavery, was consistent with all to which Thomas Garrett dedicated his life. At the same time, Garrett did worship at the Meeting House on West and Fourth Streets, so perhaps we can infer from these that he was "Hicksite" in his views. And, if one may be judged by the company he keeps, then Thomas Garrett's close association with other known Hicksite Quakers, such as James and Lucretia Mott and Parker Pillsbury, may also be taken as evidence that he favored the Hicksite theological point of view. Tilden tells a story from which we get the only public statement that we have by Garrett concerning his religious beliefs: "When once asked by an anxious religionist if he really believed something," said Tilden, "Garrett replied, 'Oh yes, I do believe something. I believe in doing my duty. A man's duty is shown to him, and I believe in doing it, the first duty first and so on right along every time.'"[17] With that statement Thomas Garrett summed up what was to be echoed more than a hundred years later by Geoffrey Hubbard, who said, "Every Quaker defines his position fully and clearly by his life."[18]

On Sunday, July 13, 1828, Thomas Garrett's first wife, Mary Sharpless, died. She was buried in the grounds adjacent to the Meeting House in Wilmington.

In 1828, David Walker, a Negro from Wilmington, North Carolina (who later settled in Boston), published his *Appeal* to American Negroes to organize a general insurrection. Walker's pamphlet, described as "the most articulately militant work of its time,"[19] alarmed the South: The State Legislature of Georgia, after reading Walker's *Appeal*, immediately passed a bill making it a capital offense to circulate literature that might incite slaves to revolt and offered a reward for Walker's capture: $10,000 alive, $1,000 dead. Louisiana enacted a bill that ordered the expulsion of all free Negroes who had settled there after 1825.[20] The following year Walker's *Appeal* ran through three editions, each edition containing language more militant than the preceding one.

At that time the only newspaper in the country that was concerned with the slavery issue was the *Genius of Universal Emancipation*, an irregularly published periodical founded by Benjamin Lundy, a New Jersey-born Quaker. The editorial policy of this newspaper was that emancipation of the slaves should come about gradually, and favored colonization of all black men. The paper at the time was located in Baltimore, and most of its subscribers were members of Southern Abolition and Colonization Societies. However, during a tour of New England to solicit subscribers, Lundy met a young man admirer who was to affect the future of his newspaper, as well as the whole anti-slavery movement—William Lloyd Garrison.

Garrison accepted an invitation by Lundy to come to Baltimore and co-edit the *Genius of Universal Emancipation*. But the two men had widely different ideas about emancipation. Garrison's position was that of immediate emancipation. And, rather than colonization, he advocated the assimilation of the Negro into American society. Lundy, on the other hand, "feared the consequences if emancipation took place suddenly, and he knew that the very idea would infuriate slave-holders.... He believed that slavery would be abolished only through the employment of all the various plans and methods which had been or might be suggested. He intended to publicize all anti-slavery schemes in the columns of his paper, not to promote any one exclusively."[21] To Garrison's position, he stated, "Thee may put thy initials to thy articles, and I will put my initials to mine, and each will bear his own burden." Apparently Lundy had no idea whom he was dealing with. Although Garrison himself was a professed advocate of nonviolence, he was to later earn a wide spread reputation of being a "disturber of the peace" and a "promoter of rebellion." His style of writing was called "inflammatory." In his editorials Garrison launched blistering attacks on slaveholders, and almost every article he wrote brought about subscription cancellations. In one issue he attacked the owner of a slave-carrying vessel as a "highway robber and murderer." For this he was prosecuted for libel and fined $50.00. He refused to pay the fine and was thrown in jail. Quaker poet John Greenleaf Whittier and New York merchant and philanthropist Arthur Tappan interceded and paid the fine for him, and Garrison was released, after serving seven weeks in jail. It was during this incident that Lundy decided to resolve the partnership with Garrison, and moved the paper to Washington, D.C. The partnership lasted only six months.

Garrison's experience in jail, rather than humbling him, had only fired him with new enthusiasm. He went back to Boston, but he took with him Isaac Knapp, the printer who had worked on Lundy's paper. In Boston, Garrison would start his own paper, *The Liberator*.

8

Rachel (Mendinhall) Garrett

On Thursday, January 7, 1830, Thomas Garrett married Rachel Mendinhall in Wilmington Meeting.

Rachel Mendinhall was the third oldest of nine surviving children. Her father, Eli Mendinhall, also a Quaker, was a merchant and one of the directors of the National Bank of Wilmington & Brandywine. He also kept both a dry goods store and a grocery store. In 1803, 1805, 1806, 1807, 1810 and 1811, he was Assistant Burgess of the city of Wilmington. In 1802 he joined the Delaware Abolition Society.

Eli Mendinhall's first wife was Phoebe Pritchett, by whom he had six children, Joseph, John, Rachel, Hannah, Benjamin and Jesse. Two other children by this marriage died in infancy — Lydia, who died when two years old, and Phoebe, who died at ten months old. After the death of his first wife, Eli Mendinhall married Mary (Jackson) Wayne, and by her had three children, Lydia, Mary, and Samuel.

Rachel's grandfather, Benjamin, and his brother, Isaac, are credited with changing the spelling of the family name. Originally the name is spelled, "Mendenhall," but Benjamin and Isaac "both spelled their name with an 'i' in the middle syllable. It is said they dropped the 'e' for an 'i' in the middle syllable to make that distinction in their families."[1]

Apparently this change was not a legal change. On Thomas and Rachel's wedding certificate the printed material carries the original spelling, "Mend[e]nhall." Just below the printed material are Rachel's and Thomas' signatures and the signatures of those who attended the wedding, among whom were members of Rachel's family — her father, Eli, her brother, Jesse, and her sisters, Mary and Lydia, and every one of them signed their name with the "i" in the middle syllable. The wedding certificate is located at The Historical Society of Delaware.

The distinction in the two spellings of the name, Mend[e]nhall, is important for future Garrett researchers to bear in mind. Many who have written sketches of Thomas Garrett's life confused the two spellings. *Dictionary of Quaker Biography*

8. RACHEL (MENDINHALL) GARRETT

uses the original spelling, as does also A *History of Upper Darby* (p. 119). Thomas Garrett, of course, uses the family spelling (with the "i" in the middle syllable). For example, see his letters to J. Miller McKim, Nos. 21 and 29.

The 38 years that Rachel was married to Thomas Garrett (she died in 1868) encompasses the most active period of his life as a station master on the UGRR. Yet we hear very little of Rachel Garrett in connection with it. There were other husband and wife teams who distinguished themselves as UGRR workers: Isaac and Dinah Mendinhall, John and Hannah Cox, Benjamin and Hannah Kent, William and Phoebe Wright, and Daniel and Hannah Gibbons, to name a few. But all we know of Rachel Garrett is that she was the wife of Thomas Garrett. She remained in the background. From several letters Garrett wrote to his children (not in this book), we get the impression that Rachel was of poor health. If so, this may account for her not being as openly involved in UGRR activities as was her husband. But in her outlook and temperament, at least, Rachel Garrett seemed to be very much like Thomas. Among the Garrett papers at the Historical Society of Delaware is one which states that, in the same year Rachel and Thomas were married, she was expelled from the Wilmington Meeting. The reasons given were that she did not attend the meetings, and that she attended those meetings contrary to the established order and discipline of the Society of Friends. What those latter meetings were is not mentioned, but the statement does suggest that Rachel, like Thomas, acted first with regard for her own convictions, her religious affiliations notwithstanding. Those convictions were apparently the same as her husband's. For example, in 1852, when anti-slavery feelings in the North were running high as a result of the passing of the Fugitive Slave Law, and exacerbated by Harriet Beecher Stowe's anti-slavery novel, *Uncle Tom's Cabin*, the Pennsylvania Meeting of Progressive Friends was formed. This organization invited "every one who recognized the equal brotherhood of the human family, without regard to sex, color or condition" to join them.[2] The following year, Thomas Garrett and other staunch anti-slavery Quakers founded the Progressive Meeting of Friends at Longwood, near Kennett Square, Pennsylvania. Their meetings were attended by prominent anti-slavery individuals, among them Sojourner Truth, Frederick Douglass, William Lloyd Garrison, John Greenleaf Whittier and Susan Anthony.[3] Rachel Mendinhall Garrett reg-

Rachel (Mendinhall) Garrett, 1792–1868, second wife of Thomas Garrett. (Courtesy of the Historical Society of Delaware.)

ularly attended these meetings, as well. So she apparently supported Thomas Garrett in all that he did, and in his letters he always speaks fondly of her.

If Thomas Garrett followed in the footsteps of his father — and it seems that he did — then his relationship with his wife, as well as with his children, was one in which he regarded them as equals. *A History of Upper Darby* reports that Thomas' father "paid his wife a compliment in [the house in which they lived in Upper Darby], and a rare compliment it was. For on the front gable were the initials 'T. & S. G.,' arranged in a triangle. This was an admission that was seldom made."[4]

This tendency to regard wife and children as equals is also in the best Quaker tradition. We note an advertisement in the *Wilmington Directory* for 1845 which reads "T&H Garrett's New Hardware Store," not "Garrett & Son," as might be expected in the average father-and-son business relationship.

In the same year of Thomas' marriage to Rachel (in April), Benjamin Lundy denounced David Walker's *Appeal*, labeling it as "a labored attempt to rouse the worst passions of human nature, and inflame the minds of those to whom it is addressed."

On the second day of the following December, Rachel gave birth to a baby boy. He was named Eli.

In Boston, on January 1, William Lloyd Garrison published the first edition of *The Liberator*, a newspaper which was to become the most important reform journal of its time in the United States. In the first month of the paper's publication, Garrison printed his own opinion of Walker's *Appeal*: "we deprecate the spirit and tendency of this Appeal," wrote Garrison, "Nevertheless, it is not for the American people, as a nation, to denounce it as bloody or monstrous.... We say that the possibility of a bloody insurrection at the South fills us with dismay; and we avow, too, as plainly, that if any people were justified in throwing off the yoke of their tyrants, the slaves are that people. It is not we, but our guilty countrymen, who put arguments into the mouths, and swords into the hands of the slaves." Seven months later, on August 21, 1831, the Nat Turner revolt took place.

In 1833 a group of abolitionists, consisting mostly of Quakers, met in Philadelphia for the purpose of freeing the Negroes from slavery and discrimination, and they proposed to do this without violence. They believed that violence was not only contrary to Christian principles, but to resort to violence, even to defend oneself, was to countenance the slaves to do the same thing. Violence, therefore, was harmful to the anti-slavery cause. William Lloyd Garrison and the majority of Quakers present (including many who did not attend the meeting) held to this belief. This belief, and several other sentiments of nonviolence, were drawn up at this meeting under the title "Declaration of Sentiments," and the adherents of these sentiments were called "Non-resistants."

As the belief in the principles of non-resistance developed, some non-resistants would not vote, because to vote was to participate in a government upheld by the sword. They also tried vegetarianism because it reduced the bloody slaughter of animals. They believed that national flags were symbols of barbarism. They tried to

Dr. Henry Garrett, 1824–1903, one of Thomas Garrett's five children from his first wife. (Courtesy of the Historical Society of Delaware.)

collect debts without violence and refused to do military duty. They also refused to do jury duty, because to do so might involve helping to imprison someone. These non-resistants extended their principles to include the world, and not only one country.

There were other abolitionists, however, who were advocates of a more limited non-resistance. These were led by Arthur and Lewis Tappan, two merchants from New York. The philosophy of the Tappan brothers was that one should attempt by every peaceful means to achieve emancipation of the slaves, but one should not fail to use violence oneself, if necessary. The following year (1834), during a riot in New York, Lewis Tappan's house was burned by a number of pro-slavery rioters. After this, Arthur Tappan armed himself and his employees with guns and ordered them to fire at any of the pro-slavery rioters who entered his warehouse. It is reported that none did.

Margaret Garrett, 1827–1863, one of Thomas Garrett's five children from his first wife. (Courtesy of the Historical Society of Delaware.

Elijah P. Lovejoy, however, was not quite as successful (or lucky) with the practice of non-resistance. "When a hostile ... crowd surrounded him, threatening to tar and feather him, Lovejoy replied, 'I am in your hands, and you must do with me whatever God permits you to do.'" However, when his press was destroyed several times, and his house invaded several times, Lovejoy decided to defend himself. "When a mob arrived to seize his press again (for the 4th time), there was an exchange of gunfire, between Lovejoy and his defenders and the mob, and one of the mob was killed."[5] In a later incident resulting from this, Lovejoy himself was killed.

Lovejoy's decision to use violence — even to defend himself — was denounced by the advocates of non-resistance. Shortly after his death a group of Quakers called at the American Anti-slavery Society's office in New York to issue a repudiation of Lovejoy's use of violence.[6] The Massachusetts Quaker schoolteacher, Abby Kelly, learned that Lovejoy defended himself — he had better died as our Savior, saying, "Father, forgive them, they know not what they do."[7]

Henry Highland Garnet, a Negro pastor of a black Presbyterian church in Troy, New York, whose family Thomas Garrett helped escape from slavery in Maryland,[8] went a little further than limited non-resistance. He urged the slaves not to hesitate to use every means, both moral, intellectual, and physical, to help attain freedom.

Garnet was well aware that such acts would bring about violence, but he believed that there was not much hope of the slave attaining freedom without bloodshed — the opinion of Abby Kelly notwithstanding.

As a friend and admirer of William Lloyd Garrison, Thomas Garrett professed to be a non-resistant, but he knew, and openly confessed, that he fell short of living up to its principles. In a letter to William Still, for example, (No. 33), Garrett reports that he is sending to Still a young runaway slave who desires to join the Army and fight for the North, and requests Still to inform him when the young man was "snugly fixed in his regimentals, so that [he] may send word to the young man's wife." Then in a postscript to this letter Garrett asks: "Am I not naughty, being a professed non-resistant, to advise this poor fellow to serve Father Abraham [Lincoln]?"

Elwood Garrett, 1815–1910, Thomas Garrett's eldest son. (Courtesy of the Historical Society of Delaware.

There are also other accounts of Garrett's life (which we will cover later) which indicate that, if he was a non-resistant, he was a very "limited" non-resistant.

In 1833, on October 30, The Edinburgh Ladies Emancipation Society was formed. Eliza Wigham was chosen Secretary.

On June 10, 1834, Rachel's father, Eli Mendinhall, died.

1837, November 9th, Edward Garrett, Thomas' youngest brother, married Abigail Sellers.

In 1839, Thomas Garrett's mother and father died.

1841, Sarah Garrett married Edward Hewes, September 9th. In 1842, Elwood Garrett moved to Baltimore.

1846, May 7th, Henry Garrett married Catherine Ann Canby.

9

The Trial of 1848

I should have done violence to my convictions of duty, had I not made use of all the lawful means in my power to liberate those people, and assist them to become men and women, rather than leave them in the condition of chattels personal.
— Thomas Garrett, after his trial in 1848

Throughout his life Thomas Garrett made no effort to hide, or even be discreet about, his giving assistance to runaway slaves. That he continued in such a manner without personal harm is little short of amazing! For running the UGRR was a dangerous business; this was particularly true in those states that occupied the borderline between the free states (Pennsylvania, Ohio, Indiana and Illinois on the North), and the slave states (Delaware, Maryland, Virginia, West Virginia and Kentucky on the South), for, from the southern borderline states, the runaway slave did not have far to go to obtain his freedom. Hence, pursuit by the slave owner in the southern borderline states was often hot and ruthless, "and in some parts of southern Illinois and Indiana those suspected of harboring runaways were apt to have their houses burned and their persons tarred and feathered."[1] Garrett tells of a single incident in his life when "two or three" southerners took hold of him to throw him off the train in Wilmington when he entered to save a free black woman from being carried south (see Miscellaneous Letters No. 4). During this incident he says he was only "slightly bruised by the railing of the cars, but well in a few days." Other than this, Garrett was never a victim of violent reprisals from Southern slaveholders, in spite of his open opposition to the slave system and general lack of secrecy in giving assistance to runaway slaves: Although Garrett attributed his relative freedom from harm to either his age (he was 64 at the time of the above incident), "plain Quaker garb," or "cool impudence," others believed it was due to his absolute fearlessness—it totally disarmed his opponents.

In 1848, however, two slave owners from Maryland did manage to achieve some measure of revenge. They brought Thomas Garrett and John Hunn (a fellow

9. The Trial of 1848

Delawarean) to trial on charges of harboring and aiding fugitive slaves. John Hunn was also a Quaker, and lived in Middletown, Delaware, a distance of approximately 25 miles south of Wilmington.

The trial took place in the United States Circuit Court at New Castle, Delaware. The judges of the case were Willard Hall, District Judge, and Chief Justice Roger B. Taney. This was the same Judge Taney who was to render the famous decision in the "Dred Scott" case of 1857, in which he ruled that, "from the founding of the country, Negroes had been considered as a subordinate and inferior class of beings, who therefore had no rights which the white man was bound to respect."

The plaintiffs in the case were Elizabeth N. Turner and Charles W. Glanding, both from Queen Anne's County, Maryland. The lawyer for the plaintiffs was James A. Bayard, and the lawyer for the defendants was Senator John Wales—who was also a personal friend of Thomas Garrett.

Both Garrett and John Hunn gave separate accounts to the local newspaper, *The Blue Hen's Chicken*, of the events that led to the trial. At later dates they also gave separate accounts to different writers. Garrett gave an account to Harriet Beecher Stowe, which she published in her book, *The Key to Uncle Tom's Cabin,* and John Hunn gave an account to William Still, which Still published in his book, *The Underground Railroad*.

These accounts by Garrett and Hunn have many inconsistencies. For example, John Hunn added many more details (and at some points tells an entirely different story) in his account to William Still, some 24 years later, than he did in his letter to *The Blue Hen's Chicken* right after the trial. A comparison of Hunn's two accounts certainly lends support to Professor Gara's assertion that much of the reminiscences of aged abolitionists are exaggerations.

However, Garrett's two accounts vary mostly in the exact dates of the happenings. He apparently just sent a copy of his previous letter to *The Blue Hen's Chicken* to Harriet Beecher Stowe, and she, in turn, reprinted an extract of it in her book. A brief word about Mrs. Stowe's book is in order.

After *Uncle Tom's Cabin* was published in 1852, the book was credited as being the single work of literature responsible for promoting the feelings that led to the Civil War. There is the popular story that Abraham Lincoln, upon meeting Mrs. Stowe, made the statement: "So you're the little woman

Harriet Beecher Stowe, 1811–1896, author of *Uncle Tom's Cabin.*

who wrote the book that made this big war." Naturally, because of the strong antislavery feelings that this book evoked, it received strong criticism from the South and pro-slavery advocates. The criticisms were chiefly that the life of the slave, and slavery, as told by Mrs. Stowe was mostly a product of her imagination, and wholly lacking in fact. Mrs. Stowe felt it her obligation to answer her critics and defend her work. She started out with what was to be nothing more than a 25-page brief document that would be appended to the next edition of *Uncle Tom's Cabin*, but she became quite consumed in the work, and finished with more than 500 pages of "documentation," which she entitled *The Key to Uncle Tom's Cabin*. In the beginning of this work, Mrs. Stowe declared *Uncle Tom's Cabin* to be "a collection and arrangement of real incidents, of actions really performed, of words and expressions really uttered...."[2] And, in a letter to the Earl of Shaftesbury, she said of this work, "It contains, in an undeniable form the facts which corroborate all that I have said. One third is taken up with judicial records of trials and decisions and with statute law.... If they [her critics] call the fiction [*Uncle Tom's Cabin*] dreadful, what will they say of the facts, where I cannot suppress, deny, or color."[3]

Among those "trials and decisions" which Mrs. Stowe calls "facts," is an extract of Thomas Garrett's letter to *The Blue Hen's Chicken*. Before she presents Garrett's letter, however, Mrs. Stowe confesses to having in mind at the time she wrote *Uncle Tom's Cabin*, "scenes in the trial of Thomas Garrett of Wilmington, Delaware." Garrett's trial and conviction gave Mrs. Stowe the idea for her character, Simeon Halliday.[4]

Later accounts of the trial, by Smedley, Tilden and Drake, do more to confuse than enlighten through inaccurate reporting and exaggerations. There is not much consolation to be gotten from an examination of the court record (which this author has examined) for most of it is written in a handwriting that is so illegible as to be next to impossible to decipher. Nevertheless, from all this I have constructed what is, hopefully, a consistent account of what took place. Part of Garrett's account will be found in Appendix II. In Appendix II will also be found both of John Hunn's accounts.

• • •

Samuel Hawkins was a free Negro. His wife, Emeline, was the slave of a Mr. Glanding, of Queen Anne's County, Maryland. While she was owned by Mr. Glanding, Emeline had two sons, Chester and Samuel, who, at the time of the incident, were 16 and 14 years old, respectively. We do not learn how, or by what process, but "Em" (as she was called) became the slave of Elizabeth N. Turner, a widow, also from Queen Anne's County.

While she was owned by Mrs. Turner, Em had four more children, described as Sally Ann, seven or eight years old, a boy named Washington, then another boy (no name given) and an infant, estimated to be 18 months old at the time of the incident. Em's two sons, Chester and Samuel, however, were *still* the property of Mr.

Glanding and, after his death, became the property of his son, Charles Wesley Glanding.

Mrs. Turner allowed Sam and Em to live together in a rented house. Charles Glanding, in his testimony said at first that the house was half of a mile from where Mrs. Turner lived, but later in his testimony said Mrs. Turner lived about 20 miles from Sam and his wife.

Sam often tried to buy his wife from Mrs. Turner, but she was unwilling to sell. She allowed Sam and Em to live together because, as one witness testified, "they had more people about the house than was wanted." This witness also testified that Mrs. Turner furnished the children with clothes. However, Garrett said that Mrs. Turner never contributed one dollar to their support or came to see them.

Eventually Sam Hawkins decided to take his wife and all of his six children and strike out for freedom. He sought the services of Samuel D. Burris, a Negro conductor in the vicinity of Camden, Delaware, to show them the way. While in Camden they also received assistance from Ezekiel Jenkins, a Quaker, who gave Burris a letter to present to either Daniel Corbit, or to John Alston, or to his cousin, John Hunn, of Middletown, Delaware.

When they reached John Hunn's house on Friday, the 5th of December in 1845, Hunn reports that there were four other Negro men with them, making a party of 13 in all. They had been traveling all night through a heavy snowstorm. Sam drove Em and the four younger children in a covered wagon pulled by a single horse (which he owned), while the others walked.

After receiving the letter, John Hunn took them in and gave them breakfast. Hunn reports that this was his first acquaintance with assisting runaway slaves.[5] If so, then his intention was probably to do no more than to provide the runaways with temporary food and shelter. In his letter to *The Blue Hen's Chicken,* right after the trial, he said, "In consequence of the deep fall of snow, they concluded to tarry with me until the roads should be open, and recruit both themselves and their horse." He then put up the woman and the four children in the house, and the rest of the fugitives in the barn.

About two o'clock of the day on which the fugitives arrived at his house, a neighbor drove up with his daughter in a sleigh, apparently on a friendly visit. Hunn says he noticed that the neighbor appeared restless and was frequently looking out of the window fronting the road. But he did not know that the man had already seen the wagon and the fugitives walking with it from his house and reported this fact in Middletown, and he had now came to "spy out the land."

Later on that afternoon several men showed up at Hunn's house. The exact number cannot be given, as Hunn gives two different accounts of this. In his letter to *The Blue Hen's Chicken,* he names five men: Thomas Schee Merritt, Robert A. Cochran, and his son, Robert T. Cochran, Richard C. Hays, and William Chesney. Later, in his account to Still, Hunn mentions only three men: "a constable of Middletown" (who was Richard C. Hays), William Hardcastle (whose name is listed as *Robert Hardcastle of Queen Anne's County* on the court records) and William "Chestnut," who is probably the same William *Chesney* he mentioned in his letter to *The Blue Hen's Chicken*. This discrepancy — whether the person is William Hardcastle, as Hunn says, or Robert Hardcastle, which is on the court records — is an extremely important one, for Siebert, considered the 19th century authority on the UGRR, lists a William Hardcastle of Queen Anne's County as an *agent* on the UGRR. If it is the same man, was he an agent on the UGRR or a slave hunter?

The men were looking for runaway slaves. One of the men asked Hunn if there were any strange blacks in his house, and again Hunn comes up with two different stories. In his letter to the *Chicken* he says:

> Robert A. Cochran asked me if any strange blacks were in my house. I told him yes, and he said he guessed they were runaways. I asked him why so? and he pulled out an advertisement for some, in which a reward was offered for their apprehension. I told him he could walk around and see them.

Later, in his account to William Still, Hunn says:

> I met them at the gate, and the constable [Richard C. Hays] handed me an advertisement, wherein one thousand dollars reward was offered for the recovery of three runaway slaves, therein described. The constable asked me if they were in my house? I said they were not: He then asked me if he might search the house? I declined to allow him this privilege, unless he had a warrant for that purpose.

Which of these stories is the correct one is anybody's guess. Whatever the case, while Hunn and the men stood there talking, the men caught sight of Sam Hawkins coming out of a house near the barn. Sam, apparently realizing that he was recognized by the slave hunters, began to flee. The hunters gave chase. Sam, perhaps not wanting to leave his family, doubled back to Hunn's house, where he decided to stand and fight to the death — though it would not have been much of a fight, for even Sam's butcher knife (or *two* knives, depending on which one of Hunn's accounts is read) would be no match for the pistol with which the constable was threatening to shoot him. The constable requested Hunn to take Sam's "knife" from him. Hunn said he refused to do so unless the constable first gave him his pistol. The constable agreed, and Hunn persuaded Sam to give him his knife. Sam then showed the men his pass, which Hunn says was "properly authenticated, and signed ... by a magistrate of Queen Ann's [sic] county, Maryland," certifying that Samuel Hawkins was a free man.

The slave hunters pronounced the pass a forgery, but William Hardcastle came forward "and said that he knew the man to be free; but that he was accused of running away with his wife and children, who were slaves. He also said that [Sam] had two boys with him, who belonged to a neighbor of his, named Charles Wesley Glanding, and that the four other children and the mother belonged to Catherine Turner, of Queen Ann's [sic] county, Maryland." (The court records and other accounts state that the woman's name was Elizabeth N. Turner) The slave hunters insisted that Samuel Hawkins should go before a magistrate in Middletown. "As there was no other course to pursue under the circumstances," says Hunn. "I had my sleigh brought out, and we all went to Middletown, before my friend, William Streets, who was then in commission as a magistrate." He continues:

> Soon after our arrival at the office of William Streets, Hardcastle put his arm lovingly around the colored man, Samuel Hawkins; and drew him into another room. In a short time Samuel came out and told me that Hardcastle had agreed, that if he, Hawkins, would give up his two older boys, who belonged to Charles Wesley Glanding; then he might pursue his journey with his wife and four children. I asked him if he believed Hardcastle would keep his promise? He replied: "yes! I do not think master William would cheat me." I assured him that he would cheat him, and that the offer was made for the purpose of not only getting the two older boys ... but his wife and other children to the office when all of them would be taken together, to the jail, in New Castle.

This must have been a difficult time for Samuel Hawkins. Just a short period before he was willing to fight to the death to insure that his family would be free. Now he was being asked to let two of them go back into slavery. He agreed to let them go back. Perhaps he thought he could go back and get them later, or that it would be better to have at least some of them if he could not have them all. Whatever his reasons, as Hunn was quick to point out, Samuel Hawkins' agreement with Hardcastle was nothing less than a bargain with the devil, and "at his request," says Hunn, "I wrote to my wife for the delivery of the family of Samuel Hawkins to the constable. They were soon forthcoming, and on their arrival at the office, a commitment was made out for the whole party. Samuel and his two older sons were handcuffed, amidst many tears and lamentations, and they all went off under charge of the man-hunters, to New Castle jail, a distance of eighteen miles."

As they left for New Castle, John Hunn says he returned home, where he found S. D. Burris and the four other men. Hunn sent a letter by Burris to Thomas Garrett, detailing the arrest and commitment of the Hawkins family. Burris and the four men left for Wilmington about nine o'clock that night and arrived shortly before daylight the next morning [Saturday].

Meanwhile, the slave hunters and the Hawkins family arrived at the jail in New Castle around midnight, where they were joined by John Hunn. Sheriff Jacob Caulk was aroused and the commitment was shown to him. "After reading it he asked Samuel if he was a slave? He said no, and showed his pass ... the sheriff hereupon told the slave hunters that the commitment was not legal, and would not hold them lawfully." It was now Saturday and, as Hunn put it, "the man hunters were in a quandary." What were they to do now? William Streets, the Magistrate of Middletown (and John Hunn's friend), had given them a commitment that was not legal, which meant that the runaways were free, and that the sheriff could not hold the slaves. The question is, did William Streets do this purposely, as a favor to his friend, John Hunn, in order to help Hunn gain the time needed to get legal help, or help from someone more experienced in assisting the runaway slave, such as Thomas Garrett? Although in his account of this to William Still, some 23 or 24 years later, John Hunn does not mention that there was collusion between himself and William Streets, it *is* possible there was. Perhaps while Hardcastle was busy betraying Samuel Hawkins' trust in order to get his family back into slavery, John Hunn and William Streets were making plans to see that they remained free.

Whatever the case, with nothing further that could be done, Constable Hays agreed to go back the 18 miles (through the snow) to Middletown to get another commitment from William Streets, if Sheriff Caulk "would take the party into the jail until his return." Hardcastle also urged the sheriff to adopt this plan, and Samuel Hawkins and his family were taken into jail.

The sheriff's daughter overheard her father's conversation with the constable, and she, too, sent word that morning to a lady friend in Wilmington to request Thomas Garrett to come to New Castle and inquire into the case, "as her father and self really believed they were, most of them, if not all, entitled to their freedom."

The next morning (Sunday), Garrett went to New Castle and took Edith Pusey along. Why he took Edith Pusey along, Garrett does not say, but perhaps it was because she was the "lady-friend" in Wilmington who received the message from the sheriff's daughter. Upon arrival in New Castle, Garrett interviewed Samuel Hawkins and his wife and some of the children in a private room, in the presence of Sheriff Caulk and Edith Pusey. He says, "Hawkins and wife admitted to us that two of their sons claimed by Glanding were slaves; but assured us, in the most positive manner, that themselves and four small children were entitled to freedom; that himself and wife had been keeping house and living together as free persons" previous to the birth of the eldest of the four children. "Neither the Sheriff, or myself, had the slightest doubt of the truth of their statement."

Garrett then asked Sheriff Caulk if he could see the commitment the slave hunters received from William Streets. Upon examining the commitment Garrett reported he found it "was defective, and not in due form according to law," and he had no doubt that if the runaways were taken before Judge Booth (Chief Justice of the state of Delaware), they would be legally set free. So he procured a copy of the commitment from the sheriff and returned home. He then called on his friend and attorney, Senator John Wales. Garrett said he stated the "facts" of the case to Wales and requested Wales to return with him to New Castle in order to take the fugitives before Judge Booth for examination.

They returned the next day (Monday) with a petition to obtain a writ of *habeas corpus* from Judge Booth. This was around nine o'clock in the morning. Judge Booth testified later that the only persons present in his office were "Garrett and Wales, and Mr. Caulk, or his deputy." "The investigation lasted about one hour," says Garrett. "The business was conducted by Attorney Wales in such a manner that the judge was induced to discharge the whole family, and with his decision I was well pleased." Smedley says, "Judge Booth decided that there was no evidence on which to hold them and that, in the absence of evidence, *the presumption was always in favor of freedom,* and discharged them."[6] Judge Booth testified that the warrants or commitments issued (by William Streets) were not supported by oath or affirmation, and therefore were illegal, hence he had no right to hold them, and so ordered their immediate discharge. The judge also testified that he had known several blacks who were imprisoned and carried off by claimants who had no right to them, and he had known persons illegally carried off and sent into slavery. So apparently Judge Booth was sympathetic to the plight of the Hawkins' family, and no doubt this influenced his decision and quick action in their favor. Although there is no information that Garrett and Judge Booth were friends or associates, it is probable that Garrett *was* aware of the judge's sympathies and therefore felt confident in bringing the slaves before him.

After the judge's decision, Garrett inquired of the judge if he could employ a hack to take the fugitives to Wilmington. Judge Booth permitted it, and Garrett asked Sheriff Caulk to procure a carriage. The sheriff sent his son, Alfred. This incident is also related by Smedley, who writes that Garrett said to the judge:

> Here is a woman with a babe at her breast, and the child suffering from white swelling on its leg; is there any impropriety in my getting a carriage and helping them over to Wilmington? Judge Booth responded, "certainly not." Mr. Garrett then hired the carriage, but gave the driver distinctly to understand that he only paid for the woman and the young children; the rest might walk; they all got in, however, and finally escaped; of course the two children born in slavery among the rest.[7]

One of the witnesses (Dave R. Wolfe) testified that, after Judge Booth discharged the fugitives and they came back to the jail to get their clothes, he "observed Garrett *rubbing* his hands together" and saying to the fugitives "that he would have them over the State line as soon as a carriage could be procured." However, this statement conflicts with Judge Booth's testimony that procuring the hack, and its arrival, all took place in his office.

Joseph Bartlett was the owner of the hack, and he testified that he transported the family to Wilmington (Garrett did not ride with them). They arrived the same day (Monday), and Bartlett deposited the Hawkins family at Garrett's store, and says, "they got out and went in there." For this he received one dollar and a half from Garrett.

Also in Wilmington at that time was Samuel D. Burris, the Negro conductor who originally brought the Hawkins family up from Queen Anne's County. He now had the pleasure of seeing them all arrive safely in Wilmington.

Soon after the Hawkins family left the New Castle jail for Wilmington, Constable Richard D. Hays returned with new commitments from William Streets and presented them in due form to Sheriff Caulk. The sheriff informed Hays that the slaves had been liberated by order of Judge Booth. Although John Hunn did not say so, apparently Hardcastle had gone to Philadelphia from New Castle, for he says that a few hours after Hays returned from Middletown, Hardcastle returned from Philadelphia to take Sam Hawkins and his family back to Queen Anne's County—

back into slavery. "Judge of his disappointment," says Hunn, "at finding they were beyond his control — absolutely gone!"

"Hays and Hardcastle returned to Middletown in great anger," says Hunn, "and threatened to prosecute William Streets for his participation in the affair." We do not learn whether they ever did prosecute William Streets, nor does Hunn tell us specifically what they were going to charge him with. My guess is that Hays and Hardcastle believed, as I asserted earlier, that William Streets *purposely* gave them commitments that were not legal.

Early Tuesday morning, Samuel D. Burris arrived back at John Hunn's house in Middletown with a letter from Garrett, giving a description of all that took place. "My joy on this occasion was great," says Hunn, "and I returned thanks to God for this wonderful escape of so many human beings from the charnel house of slavery."

As to the ultimate fate of Samuel Hawkins and his family, one witness — Zenor B. Glasier — testified that he overheard Garrett say that "they were placed twenty five miles out of reach." In his account to William Still, Hunn said that the Hawkins family "went from Wilmington to Byberry (Pennsylvania), and settled near the farm of Robert Purvis," a member of the Pennsylvania Anti-slavery Society. "Samuel Hawkins and his wife have since died," said Hunn, "but their descendants live in that neighborhood under the name of Hackett."

After the trial, Garrett sent the following letter to the editors of *The Blue Hen's Chicken,* Jeandell and Vincent, which they printed in that paper on June 28, 1848. In his letter Garrett presents a letter he received from an unnamed person, telling of assistance he gave to the Hawkins family on their way to freedom:

> For the Blue Hen's Chicken.
> Wilmington, 6th mo 14th 1848
> Respected friends, Jeandell & Vincent: — I have received a letter by mail, dated 6th mo. 9th, 1848, from which I propose to make a few extracts for the benefit of those most interested in the family of Samuel Hawkins, on whose account I have lately been mulcted in a heavy sum by a Jury in the State of Delaware. "I see by the Pennsylvania Freeman [an Anti-slavery newspaper], that thou has been mulcted in a very heavy sum for the charge of speeding the flight of the oppressed from out of the hands of the cruel spoiler; I stand equally censurable, if the benevolence of our day so construes the doing unto others, as we would they should do unto us, as to controvert the order of God, so as to inflict pains and penalties for doing good. But such is the base morality of our praying, preaching, psalm-sing republican, slave-holding Union, like Milton's devils, who were to vice industrious, but to noble deeds timorous and slothful. The constituted authorities that imposed the penalties on thee for that noble act of sympathy, on behalf of suffering humanity, would the next hour bring in a verdict of acquittal to a slave' holder for moderately whipping a colored female to death. But after all I wish my friend to keep of good cheer, for it is evident that the spirit of God is moving upon the waters, or in other words, the same light that shone round about Paul ... is now in like manner shining round about the cruel savagism of slavery. Resolving thus far, shalt thou go, but no further, and here shall thy proud waves be stayed. The same family, a man and his wife and six children, for

which thou hast been brought into difficulties, was at my house. On the evening of their arrival; I had retired to bed, and about 11 o'clock my dog aroused me up, and when I opened the door, lo and behold, the family above alluded to. Two of the children was quite small and sickly, the one at the breast nearly perished with cold; in fact they were all in a suffering condition from the inclemency of the weather, and great destitution of clothing; the mother kept the infant warm by her breast on one side, and an old rag carpet held to its back by the mother. If thou should ever have it in thou power, thee may inform those hardened impenitent claimants, that the two eldest were bound out till they arrived at the age of 21 years, and the man, his wife and four young children are comfortably provided for."

This news may be satisfactory to their former claimants, more especially the owner of the mother and four young children, as it was given in testimony by her Attorney, that she was so desirous that the woman should be free for that purpose, she would sell her time to her husband for one hundred dollars cash, although she could get three hundred dollars for her, to sell her as a slave.

— Thomas Garrett

On May 23, 1846, both Thomas Garrett and John Hunn received summonses, and were brought to trial in May of 1848. Tilden, Still, and Smedley all report that there were four trials, and that they ran for three days. They were probably referring only to Thomas Garrett's trials. There were six cases in all, two against John Hunn and four against Thomas Garrett, and the whole procedure took five days, beginning on Wednesday, May 24th, and ending on Monday, May 29th, with no trial on Sunday, May 28th.

The first two cases were against John Hunn. In Case No.1 (which was on the 24th), Hunn was sued by Charles Glanding for debt, for the amount of $1,000, and the jury found for the plaintiff.

In Case No.2 (which took place the following day), Hunn was sued by Elizabeth Turner for debt, for the amount of $2,000. There was no trial in this case. Hunn confessed a judgment to the agreement of $1,500. Hence John Hunn was fined a total of $2,500.

On Friday, May 26th, in Case No.3, Charles Glanding sued Thomas Garrett for debt, for the amount of $1,000, and the jury found in favor of the plaintiff.

The following day, in Case No.4, Elizabeth Turner sued Garrett for debt, for the amount of $2,500, and again, the jury found in favor of the plaintiff.

On Monday, the 29th, two trials took place, Cases Nos. 5 and 6. In No. 5 Charles Glanding sued Garrett for trespass, for the amount of $2,000. The jury found for the plaintiff but assessed damages for only $1,000. In Case No.6, Elizabeth Turner sued Garrett for trespass, for the amount of $5,000. The jury found for the plaintiff but assessed damages of only $900.

After one of Garrett's trials The Delaware *Republican* printed the following extract of Judge Taney's charge to the jury:

> To entitle the plaintiff to a verdict in this case, it is necessary for him to have proved property in the slaves. This has not been contradicted by the defense. It only remains

then to prove that they escaped, and that the defendant harbored them, knowing them to be slaves. It does not require absolute knowledge on the part of the defendant that these persons were slaves. If, at the time, or before he harbored them, circumstances came to his knowledge sufficient to put a prudent man upon his inquiry, [then] it is "knowingly harboring" within the meaning of the act of Congress, and makes him liable to the penalty. If, therefore, you believe that these persons were the property of the plaintiff, and that the defendant carried them from New Castle to Wilmington, or caused them to be carried there, and taken to his store, with the knowledge that they were slaves, or under circumstances sufficient to excite the suspicion of their being slaves, and that they were taken away for the purpose of avoiding pursuit, and of preventing their owner from recovering them, you must find a verdict for the plaintiff; if you believe otherwise, your verdict will be for the defendant.

The news of Garrett's conviction undoubtedly spread throughout the Peninsula, to the Virginia and Maryland mainland and into the northern states of Pennsylvania, New Jersey and New York. Thomas Garrett, the fearless abolitionist and friend of the runaway slave, was finally tried and convicted in an apparent victory for southern slaveholders.

Drake, in *Quakers and Slavery in America,* reports that many people in the slave state of Delaware disagreed with Garrett's giving assistance to runaway slaves, and that "many Wilmingtonians censured [his] activity as dangerous to the community and destructive to the Union."[8] After the trial, however, *The Blue Hen's Chicken* printed letters in which strong support was given to Garrett for the action he took on behalf of the Hawkins family, suggesting that there were also many who, tacitly at least, joined him in his cause of helping the runaway slave. The following letter appeared in the paper's June 2, 1848, edition:

> MESSRS. EDITORS:—I am informed from good authority that John Hunn, near Cantwell's Bridge, and Thomas Garrett, of your city, have been sued by certain persons from Maryland, in the District Court of the United States for the District of Delaware, and mulct into fines, the former $2,500 and the latter $5,400, one for humanely giving some five negroes something to eat and a place to sleep, and the other after said negroes were discharged by Chief Justice Booth, because of there being no testimony against them, for affording them a ride over to Wilmington from New Castle. It is said and believed that certain kidnappers, negro-catchers, and slave dealers of Maryland, and our own state, have united their friends to fee lawyers, and not bribe but pay officers, to bring about this result. The jury summoned by the Marshal smells strongly of packing if not salting. These two men are among the most humane and orderly and exemplary of our citizens. When such a result can be brought about there is something rotten either in the laws or in the manner of their administration. I venture to affirm that no jury chosen indifferently from the citizens of New Castle County could have been found to condemn the estimable citizens under the circumstances. What shall be done? Shall such laws exist by which the worst of men may ruin our best citizens?
>
> JUSTICE.

The reports of the trial, itself, were inconsistent. For example, on June 1, 1848, the Pennsylvania *Freeman,* an anti-slavery newspaper, in an apparent attempt to make Garrett the hero in the case, stated that:

> An offer of compromise was made to Thomas Garrett by the kidnappers, but he replied that he would make no compromise with slaveholders. Finding him firm, his persecutors pressed the case to a decision.

However, the court records indicate that there were indeed several compromise settlements made in Garrett's cases. At the same time, the much-quoted figure of $5,400 is only what the court assessed as the damages. The actual amount of money Garrett had to pay after compromise was $1,500. This is not to minimize the amount of money Garrett had to pay, but to point out that there is a significant difference between what his biographers *said* he paid and what he actually did pay. But Garrett's biographers probably never really knew just what he did pay, for it is only in the court records that this information can be found, and it appears that Garrett, himself, never told the whole story. In his letter to William Lloyd Garrison, for example (see Letter No.1), although he said that he lost $40,000 (all that he accumulated for 40 years) to unprincipled slaveholders, he also said that part of it was due to the imprudence of his business partners.

Smedley, in retelling the story (some 35 years later), comes up with a figure that is entirely out of line with the facts. He states that the amount of money Garrett lost was $8,000, "all he was worth," and Siebert apparently copied this misinformation from Smedley, for he writes the same thing.[9] Tilden, on the other hand, does say that Garrett met with business reverses and therefore did not have much property at the time of the trial. He also reports that the heavy fines from the trial swept all of Garrett's property away, and that he had to sell all of his household goods to pay the awards of the court.[10] This report by Tilden is unsubstantiated. There is no evidence that Garrett lost all of his property, household goods, etc. What did happen was that, on June 6, 1848, the Clerk of the U.S. Circuit Court of the District of Delaware issued a writ of *habeas corpus,* which authorized the marshal of that district to attach all of Garrett's "Goods and Chattels, Rights and Credits, Lands and Tenements...." This was to assure that Garrett appeared before the U.S. Circuit Court (on Tuesday, October, 17th of that year) to pay his fines to both Glanding and Turner.[11] In other words, had Garrett not shown up to pay his fines, *then* the court would have seized all of his property, household goods, etc.

Did Thomas Garrett receive a fair trial? According to the Wilmington *Daily Commercial,* "Garrett's friends claimed that the jury was packed to secure an adverse verdict."[12] Smedley repeats this statement. Drake, in *Quakers and Slavery in America* also says that the court was "obviously" pro-slavery, and adds that, "local rumors had it that the jurors were equally so, and blamed the federal marshal for packing the jury."[13] In Still's book, a writer who signed his name as "W" said, "It is hardly true to say that anyone of the juries was *packed,* indeed, it would have been a difficult matter in that day *for* the Marshal to summon thirty sober, honest, and judicious men, fairly and impartially chosen from the three counties of Delaware, who would have found verdicts different from those which were rendered. The jury must have been fixed for the defendant to have secured any other result, on the supposition that the testimony admitted of any doubt or question, the anti-slavery men in the state being like Virgil's ship-[wrecked mariners, very few in number and scattered over a vast space."[14]

From these reports we may infer that many members of the juries were pro-slavery, or at least were out to put a stop to Thomas Garrett's "dangerous and destructive activities." Yet, on the other hand, we learn that there were some people in the slave states who did not support the slavery cause. Robert Wright, one of the witnesses, gave testimony that he was at a meeting in Queen Anne's County, Maryland, when a committee was raised to procure funds to carry on the suit against Garrett and Hunn, "but no money was collected," he says, and that even he, himself, contributed nothing.

At the end of his trial Thomas Garrett gave a speech. He sent copies of what he said to *The Blue Hen's Chicken* and to Harriet Beecher Stowe. In it he gave a detailed account of the events that led to the trial (why and how he helped the Hawkins family escape), what his intentions were regarding the fugitive slave (he would continue to help more to escape), and his opinion of the current political and military actions regarding expansion and slavery. In writing of Garrett's post trial speech, later writers focused only on Garrett's open defiance of the verdict against him, and they varied in telling it. For example, the author of the article in William Still's book writes:

> When the trials were concluded, Mr. Garrett arose, the court being adjourned, and made a speech of an hour to the large crowd in the court-room, in the course of which he declared his intention to redouble his exertions, so help him God. His bold assertion was greeted with mingled cheers and hisses, and at the conclusion of his speech one of the jurors who had convicted him strode across the benches, grasped his hand, and begged his forgiveness.[15]

According to the next account by Smedley, Garrett addressed his words to the "judge"; however, in his letter to *The Blue Hen's Chicken* (see Appendix III), Garrett, himself, reported that both the judges had left the court room when he gave his speech:

> After sentence, he arose in open court and said, "Now Judge, I do not think that I have always done my duty, being fearful of losing what little I possessed; but now that you have relieved me, I will go home arid put another story on my house, so that I can accommodate more of God's poor." Then turning to the large crowd in the court-room he addressed them. He was listened to throughout with the closest attention. Sometimes profound silence prevailed. Sometimes his bold assertions were applauded, while some who felt the keenness of his remarks tried to relieve themselves by hissing. But those who prosecuted him, were so impressed with his candor and honesty, that one of them came forward and shook him by the hand and asked

his forgiveness and desired his friendship, which was fully promised on condition of the person's ceasing to be an advocate of the iniquitous system of slavery.

Six years after Smedley's book was published, Tilden gave his "Memorial Address," commemorating the 100th anniversary of Garrett's birth. Although Tilden gathered much of his material from interviews with those who knew Garrett personally, he apparently copied Garrett's post trial speech from the article in William Still's book, for he writes, almost verbatim, the same thing (see pages 12–13).

Thomas E. Drake, in *Quakers and Slavery in America,* does not give Garrett's speech. Instead, he describes the speech as Garrett wrote it, to *The Blue Hen's Chicken.*

Siebert, taking his information from an article by Lillie B.C. Wyman in *New England Magazine,* states:

> There is a tradition that the presiding judge admonished Garrett to take his loss as a lesson and in the future to desist from breaking the laws; whereupon the aged Quaker replied: "Judge, thou hast not left me a dollar, but I wish to say to thee, and to all in this court-room, that if anyone knows a fugitive who wants a shelter and a friend, send him to Thomas Garrett, and he will befriend him."[16]

Tilden's account varies a little from Siebert's. He reports:

> It is told that at the Sheriff's sale of his household goods to pay the awards of the court the officer said to him: "Thomas, I hope you will never be caught at this business again..." "Friend," was the reply, "I haven't a dollar in the world, but if thee knows a fugitive who needs a breakfast, send him to me."[17]

However, in his letter to Eliza Wigham (No.1), Garrett says it was not the sheriff (or the judge) but the *marshal* who admonished him, and that his reply was not at all what the above writers say.

Finally, Garrett, himself, in a letter to Harriet Beecher Stowe, said that, after his speech, "a young man who had served as jury-man came across the room, and taking him by the hand, said:

> Old gentleman, I believe every statement that you have made. I came from home prejudiced against you, now I acknowledge that I have helped to do you injustice.

But the full text of Garrett's speech was more than just his reasons for helping a family of slaves escape. Nor was it strictly of his commitment to continue to assist runaway slaves. It was also of his belief that the issue of slavery was at the root of the political wrangling and infighting over the country's present rapid expansion, which carried with it the expansion of slavery, annexation of Texas and the war with Mexico. For example, by the turn of the 19th century the United States was expanding territorially and economically, and increasing in population, more rapidly then any country in the world. In 1803 the country doubled its territory by purchasing the Louisiana Territory from France. This was a tract of land 828,000 square miles that stretched from the west of the Mississippi River to the Rocky Mountains, and from the Gulf of Mexico to the Canadian Border. From this territory the country would eventually create 13 new states, among them, Missouri, which would figure significantly in the controversy over the expansion of slavery.

Spain, meanwhile, possessed all the territory consisting of what is now Mexico, Texas, New Mexico, Arizona and California, as well as Florida. Mexico, known officially as "La Nueva España" (New Spain), was the most important Spanish colony in the New World. However, on September 16th, in 1810, Miguel Hidalgo, a Catholic priest in the village of Dolores, called the Indians and Mestizos (the latter a mix of Spanish and Indian) to retaliate against the native Spaniards who had exploited and oppressed them for ten generations. He would start a bloody insurrection from which Mexico would eventually win its independence from Spain, giving that new country all that territory.

That same year (1810), the United States purchased part of Florida from Spain — "East Florida." However, that territory was the source of much annoyance to the Southern States. "Fugitive slaves — mostly from Georgia — took refuge there, trying to reach a place where their owners had no authority and effectively could not reach them."[18] Many of the runaways joined with the Seminole Indians to later fight against the United States Army, led by then General Andrew Jackson, in what became known as the Seminole Wars.

Finally, in 1819, Spain, realizing it could no longer keep the territory, signed a treaty with the U.S. formally ceding the remaining part of Florida to the United States — "West Florida" — further increasing the territory of the United States and further expanding slavery.

That year (1819), the Missouri Territory applied for statehood. This set off a bitter debate in Congress over the issue of slavery in the new territories, the issue being whether or not slavery be allowed in the new state of Missouri. Admitting Missouri as a slave state would give a political advantage to the South — i.e., the slave interest — by having greater representation in Congress. The issue was resolved by a two-part compromise known as the "Missouri Compromise":

> First, Missouri gained admission to the Union as a slave state, with a provision that portions of the Louisiana Territory lying north of 36' 30' north latitude would be free .... Second, Maine was simultaneously admitted to statehood, which enabled the Senate to maintain the balance between slave and free state representation — twelve of each. The enabling act of March 6, 1820, made it clear, however, that fugitive slaves could be apprehended north of the compromise line and returned to their owners.[19]

Representative Henry Clay of Kentucky was the architect of the Compromise.

In 1825 Tennessee Democrat, James Polk, was elected to the United States House of Representatives. Polk was a lawyer — admitted to the bar in 1820 — but rose steadily within the ranks of the Democratic Party in Tennessee. He served in the Tennessee legislature, as well as in the United States House of Representatives, and became

Speaker of the House during the last four years of his congressional term. He left the House to become Governor of Tennessee in 1839. That year Texas broke away from Mexico to became an independent republic. Texas becoming independent would play a major role in Polk's political career. Meanwhile, as governor, Polk served a two-year term, from 1839 to 1841. That year (1841), William Henry Harris, died after serving only one month as president. His vice president, John Tyler, assumed the office on April 6th.

With the country caught up in the idea of "Manifest Destiny," the belief that Americans had a right to settle in the West. President Tyler quickly moved to further that cause by concentrating his efforts to achieve the annexation of Texas. On April 22, 1844, Tyler submitted a "Texas Annexation Treaty" to the Senate. The treaty was met with controversy. Although it was popular in the South and Southwest, the North objected to it on the grounds that the entry of Texas would not only add a new slave state to the Union, but it would also lead to war with Mexico. Kentucky Senator Henry Clay and former president Martin Van Buren opposed statehood for Texas.

The following month (May, 1844), the Democratic National Convention met in Baltimore, Maryland, where they nominated Polk for president and George M. Dallas of Pennsylvania for vice president. Tyler was originally renominated for president and did accept, but then he decided to withdraw from the campaign and throw his support behind Polk with the expectation that Polk would support the immediate annexation of Texas. On December 4th Polk achieved a narrow victory in the general election over the Whig Party candidate, Henry Clay. However, on just the day before, Tyler had recommended annexation by a joint resolution of Congress. On March 1, 1845, three days before Polk's inauguration, President Tyler signed a joint resolution of congress authorizing the annexation of Texas.

> Begun and held at the city of Washington, in the District of Columbia, on Monday the second day of December, eighteen hundred and forty-four. Joint Resolution for annexing Texas to the United States. Resolved by the Senate and House of Representatives of the United States of America in Congress assembled, That Congress doth consent that the territory properly included within, and rightfully belonging to the Republic of Texas, may be erected into a new state, to be called the state of Texas, with a republican form of government, to be adopted by the people of said republic, by deputies in Convention assembled, with the consent of the existing government, in order that the same may be admitted as one of the states of this Union.

The United States Congress passed the annexation resolution on February 28, 1845. With that, the United States had further expanded, and with it, the expansion of slavery, and with that the prospect of war with Mexico loomed larger. On March 6, 1845, three days after Polk's inauguration, Mexico broke relations with the United States in protest against the annexation of Texas.

Almost from the beginning Polk's administration was marked with controversy. "While winning congressional support for policies he favored, he effectively used his power of the veto to block those to which he opposed. [However] The wisdom and morality of his major policies were questioned by many,"[20] among them, Thomas Garrett.

> Intent on also acquiring California, which belonged to Mexico, Polk was prepared in early May 1846 to make war on Mexico. Polk sent an envoy, John Slidell, to offer Mexico up to $20,000,000, plus settlement of damage claims owed to Americans, in return for California and the New Mexico country. Mexican leaders knew that they could not cede half their country and still stay in power. Thus Slidell was not received. To strengthen his position, Polk sent General Zachary Taylor to the disputed area on the Rio Grande. The Mexican troops fired on the American soldiers. In May 1846, Congress declared war and supported the military operations, despite northern opposition. Alexander H. Stephens and some southerners joined with Abraham Lincoln and northern Whigs, to condemn what they believed were dishonest methods used by Polk in provoking the hostilities.[21]

Polk also moved to settle the boundary of the Oregon Territory which stretched from the Pacific coast to the Rocky Mountains, encompassing the area including present-day Oregon, Washington, and most of British Columbia. Originally Spain, Great Britain, Russia, and the United States claimed the territory. However, Spain had previously ceded its claims to the territory to the United States in 1819, and in 1823 President Monroe denied any Russian claims to the territory by invoking The Monroe Doctrine which left only Britain. President Polk proposed a settlement on the 49th degree line to Great Britain. Along with Secretary of State James Buchanan, and South Carolina Senator John C. Calhoun, he worked out a compromise with the British. By June 18, 1846, the Senate ratified the treaty by a vote of 41–14. United States had now tripled its territory.

Meanwhile, as a result of repeated victories by American Forces, in 1848, Mexico ceded New Mexico and California in return for $15,000,000 and American assumption of the damage claims. Although Polk had succeeded in adding a vast area to the United States with this military victory, questions were raised about the nation's honor.

Mexico's ceding of the California and New Mexico territories took place at the very time of Thomas Garrett's trial. Garrett was acutely aware of this decision's impact on slavery, as well as what he believed was this government's unethical actions—to expand slavery—which brought about the decision. The following is an excerpt from his letter to Jeandell and Vincent, editors of *The Blue Hen's Chicken*, following his trial. In it, Garrett expresses his disdain for the political maneuvering by the slave power and the weakness of the North that brought about the annexation of Texas and war with Mexico. He believed that the result of this, along with growing anti-slavery feelings, would ultimately result in the dissolution of the Union:

> I am sorry to have to admit this truth, that the slave states and slave interests have ruled this nation from the Declaration of Independence till the present time. They have kindly taken the North and West under their care and keeping. [They] have

9. THE TRIAL OF 1848

provided a large majority of our Presidents, Cabinet officers, Foreign Ministers and Judges of our Supreme Courts from the slave states. They have made our laws to suit their peculiar institutions. It was slave holders that demanded the Admission of Texas into this union, with her mix'd breeds and degenerate race of inhabitants of all nations. They knocked at the Halls of Congress for admission into our glorious Union. The North blustered a while, but were soon whipped into the traces by their masters; they knew it would be contrary to law to admit them; they also know there was no use to contend about that, as the south always managed to have it their own way. They consented, and Texas was admitted in a day with the dash of a pen, with her mixed and motley crew of inhabitants as good and loyal subjects of these United States; when at the same time the most foreigners coming amongst us and adopting this country as his future home, must knock for years for admission as a citizen before they can be admitted. They must then swear to support the constitution, and pay a fee for admission.

Surely the slave power is omnipotent. No other power in this land could have produced the same result; and what has been the legitimate fruits of the admission of Texas into the Union? We have the admission of some of the strongest minds, even at the south [J. C. Calhoun of that number] that the admission of Texas was the cause of the Mexican War; where hundreds of millions of the peoples' money has been wasted, and thousands of valuable lives sacrificed by sword and climate, all for the slave interest. No intelligent man doubts this fact, that it was the slave interest, cruel, disgraceful and unrighteous war.

But all those things are producing their legitimate fruits. A few years since, a Senator that would speak his mind freely on the subject of slavery, in Congress, was in danger of being expelled; now it is the all engrossing subject. It enters more or less into every subject brought before either House at Washington. It is an institution that cannot bear investigation. This subject is now fairly before the people. This is what Abolitionists have been laboring for, to have the subject fairly canvassed by the people. Then I fear not their verdict. Look at the nations around us. The cause of freedom is progressing with railroad speed. Their object is about to be accomplished. I have not correctly read the signs of the times if the days of slavery are not numbered in this country. The south will have to yield to the growing anti-slavery feeling of the north and west; or before ten years from this date there will be a dissolution of this Union. There is a point of forbearance beyond which the north, and rapidly growing west, will not submit.

I have done, and thank you for your time.

The country became increasingly divided over the issue of the expansion of slavery. To be expected, the Mexican War was popular in the southern states while the opponents of slavery viewed it as—once again—a way of bringing additional slave states to the Union. Meanwhile, Polk had vowed that he would serve only one term as president. His general, Zachary Taylor, now the Whig Party candidate, defeated the Democratic Party candidate, Lewis Cass, in the presidential election of 1848 to become the 12th president of the United States.

During Polk's single term, however, he increased the boundaries of the country by the "Oregon Treaty," and the victorious Mexican War. Under his administration America truly became the land that stretched from "sea to shining sea." Polk died on June 15, 1849, in Nashville, Tennessee, three months after leaving office.

Meanwhile, in Dorchester County, Maryland, while recovering from a serious injury to her head, Harriet Tubman had a vision that God had chosen her to be an instrument to help free her people from slavery. She also overheard her young master, Edward Brodess, say he was going to sell her and her sisters into the deep South. The thought of it was so disturbing to Harriet that she prayed to God to kill him. In March of that year, 1849, Edward Brodess died. Believing that she herself had brought on Brodess's death, Harriet became remorseful and asked God for forgiveness. She then decided it was time to run away from slavery. She told her biographer, Sarah Bradford, she remembered the year, for it was the last year of Polk's presidency.

On July 9th of the following year (1850), president Zachary Taylor died in office, having served only 16 months. His vice president, New York Representative Millard Fillmore, assumed the office the following day, becoming the 13th president of the United States.

Meanwhile, the vast territory recently acquired by the United States as a result of the Mexican War became, once again, the focus of the slavery controversy. The questions that arose were: "Should the territory allow slavery, or should it be declared free? Or should the inhabitants be allowed to choose for themselves?" The decisions made would affect the balance of power between the States that existed since the Compromise of 1820. Kentucky Representative Henry Clay, once again, presented a compromise. The Compromise was debated from mid–August to mid–September of 1850. Congress passed five separate bills: 1) California would be admitted as a free state, 2) the border of Texas—still in dispute—would be adjusted, 3) the territories of New Mexico, Nevada, Arizona, and Utah would be organized without mention of slavery (the decision would be made by the territories' inhabitants later, when they applied for statehood),[22] 4) the enactment of a rigorous "Fugitive Slave Law," and 5) the abolition of slavery in the District of Columbia. The bills were signed into law separately between September 9th and 20th.

Of all the bills that made up the Compromise, the Fugitive Slave Law was the most controversial. It not only required citizens to assist in the recovery of fugitive slaves, it also denied the fugitive the right to a jury trial. It assumed his "guilt rather than his innocence" by which some argued it was unconstitutional and gave unbridled authority to slave owners to retrieve a runaway. Neither runaway slaves nor free blacks felt safe.

The reaction to the law was immediate. Many blacks—free and runaway—decided to flee to Canada. Many decided to stay and fight rather than be returned to slavery. They formed Vigilance Committees, organizations, associations and societies to be on the lookout for slave catchers, to protest the law, and to give succor to runaways. Some even snatched captive fugitives directly from the arms of law enforcers and rushed them to places of hiding and ultimately to safety and freedom. Still others raised money to purchase the freedom of those runaways who were claimed by their owners. For those who were arrested, "Negroes throughout the country held meetings to raise money for their legal counsel, to make their stay in prison more comfortable, and to provide relief for their families."[23]

In October of that year (1850) a Boston Vigilance Committee of white and black abolitionists spirited to safety escaped slaves William and Ellen Craft.[24] In December, Thomas Garrett, though optimistic, underestimated the serious impact of the law on the Negro. He wrote to William Lloyd Garrison:

> The slave population who have escaped to the free states have been very much alarm'd by the passage of this infamous bill, but I very much doubt whether on the whole there will be more arrested under the new law, than the law as it stood for years past. There are so many more who feel an interest in affording them shelter, and protection. May this feeling increase till not a soul can be found in the free states mean enough to assist the master in reclaiming them.[25]

Harriet Tubman, however, saw clearly the dire consequences the new law would have, not only on the Negro population in general, but on those already in bondage, particularly her own family. Still shaken perhaps by the thought of her sisters being sold into the deep South, and with the hope that existed in running away now greatly diminished, Harriet Tubman realized she had to act quickly. At the very time that Thomas Garrett was writing to William Lloyd Garrison expressing his view of the Fugitive Slave Law, Harriet Tubman went right back to the Brodess plantation and rescued one of her sisters and her sister's two children.[26]

Ironically, because the Fugitive Slave Law "required citizens to assist in the recovery of fugitive slaves," it now made slave catchers out of anyone who may have originally been apathetic to slavery. They were now bound, by law, to assist slaveholders to retrieve runaways. Feeling the law to be an affront to their own liberty, many among the general white populace now joined with abolitionists in the cause. In Boston — which became known as "The Cradle of Liberty"— a runaway named Fred Wilkins— also known as "Shadrach"— was seized on February 15, 1851, and rushed to the court house. Although five lawyers had succeeded in obtaining a delay while they prepared his defense, some 50 Negroes in the town took matters into their own hands. They rushed into the courthouse, "lifted Shadrach into the air and bore him to the street. His clothes half torn off, Shadrach was placed in a carriage..." and rushed off to Canada. "There was no pursuit, the seizure having been so sudden and unexpected."[27] In April, in that same city, the government had to turn out 300 soldiers to guard runaway slave Thomas Sims to prevent him from being rescued by abolitionists.

On September 11th, in the city of Christiana in Lancaster County, Pennsylvania, the first armed resistance to the Fugitive Slave Law took place. Led by the militant runaway slave, William Parker, and a number of free blacks in that neighborhood, they shot and killed slave owner Edward Gorsuch. Historian Charles L. Blockson writes:

> Blood was first shed in resistance to the Fugitive Slave Law of 1850 when slaves of Edward Gorsuch, a prominent Maryland farmer, were discovered in Christiana,

Pennsylvania, in 1851 in the home of fugitive William Parker. They had fled to Lancaster County by means of the Underground Railroad. Gorsuch expressed his intention of "getting his property, or breakfast in hell." Threats were exchanged, shots were fired, the cry of "kidnappers" was raised, and neighbors arrived in numbers. Gorsuch was killed in the exchange and his son was wounded. Parker and thirty others were tried for treason, but [Pennsylvania Congressman] Thaddeus Stevens so ably defended them that the jury returned a "not guilty" verdict in fifteen minutes. Parker, the subject of a national manhunt, made a daring escape to Canada with assistance from his boyhood friend Frederick Douglass and others. He was never apprehended. The Christiana Riot became one of the most famous events in the annals of the Underground Railroad.[28]

On the morning of October 1st, a group of black and white abolitionists in Syracuse, New York, performed a spectacular rescue of fugitive William ("Jerry") Henry, an escaped slave from Missouri. Historian Milton Sernett recounts, in full, this celebrated case in *North Star Country, Upstate New York and the Crusade for African American Freedom*.[29] The story, in brief, is that "Jerry," as he was known, was arrested under the ruse that he was wanted for theft. "Only when he reached the office of the Commissioner was he told that he was being apprehended as a fugitive slave." As in the case of Shadrach, a crowd of 52 known rescuers, 40 of them white, stormed the office. They lifted Jerry over their heads and rushed him out the door, down the stairs and into the street. However, the authorities recaptured Jerry, put him in leg irons and took him to the police office. Undaunted, the rescuers tried again later that evening:

> Picking up clubs, iron bars and axes ... a band of men, some with burnt cork smeared on their faces, rushed the building. Doors and windows were smashed. The gas-jet lamps of the front office went out. A stone knocked down one of the deputies. Within minutes, the rescuers had forced their way into the police station ... charged the door [of the room where Jerry was kept] with a ten-foot pine beam.... They carried Jerry out through the streets — to the hurrah of others.[30]

Jerry was eventually carried to Oswego, New York, where he boarded a British schooner bound for Kingston, Canada — and freedom. The case became nationally known as the "Jerry Rescue." Today, a monument to the Jerry Rescue stands on the west end of Clinton Square in downtown Syracuse, New York, a lasting monument to when, in defiance of the Fugitive Slave Law, that city achieved what is believed its "proudest moment."

Meanwhile, still determined to fulfill the command given to her by God, Harriet Tubman, once again, journeyed into slave territory, and in December of that year (1851) she brought away a party of 11 slaves and took them all the way to Canada, hiding them for a period of time in the Rochester, New York, home of black abolitionist Frederick Douglass. "Holding steady on to God," she returned to the South in May the following year (1852) and rescued nine more and took them also to Canada. She would later tell her biographer, Sarah Bradford, "I wouldn't trust Uncle Sam wid my people no longer. I brought 'em all clear off to Canada."[31]

That year, the simmering pot of controversy over the issue of slavery was further heated by the publication of Harriet Beecher Stowe's *Uncle Tom's Cabin*.

In Philadelphia, a self-educated son of slaves, under the auspices of the Pennsylvania Abolition Society, began to compile what would become the most authentic body of runaway slave data known to date. He was, of course, William Still, and his most popular collaborator was Thomas Garrett.

In March of 1852, the Democratic Party nominated New Hampshire Senator, Franklin Pierce for president. Despite his Yankee heritage, Pierce was pro-slavery. He was openly against abolitionism and endorsed the Compromise of 1850, which included the Fugitive Slave Law. With a pro-slavery voting record, he won favor with the pro-slavery South in Congress. He won the election over his Whig opponent, General Winfield Scott, who was his commander under President James Polk during the Mexican War. Pierce assumed the office of the president on March 4, 1853, becoming the 14th president of the United States.

That year (1853), the Friends at Kennett Monthly Meeting, in Chester County, Pennsylvania, developed profound differences over the slavery issue. One matter of contention was the Underground Railroad. Quakers on the whole denounced slavery, but not all Quakers approved of the UGRR. To them, personally helping slaves escape was illegal. They wanted no part of it. However, with the passage of the Fugitive Slave Law, and the increasing widespread reaction to it—fueled by the publication of *Uncle Tom's Cabin*—the issue of slavery and participation in assisting runaway slaves became more intense in both the North and the South, as well as in the minds and hearts of the Society of Friends at Kennett Monthly Meeting. And so they divided. Thomas Garrett's brother-in-law, Isaac Mendinhall, was disowned by the Meeting. Joined by some members of the nearby Marlborough Meeting he, along with like-minded Quakers and non–Quakers, decided to form the "Progressive Friends at Longwood." Priscilla Thompson says that Thomas Garrett was one of the founders of the Progressive Friends Meeting and was on the committee which was to outline the purposes of the new meeting.[32] William C. Kashatus writes:

> Quakers who left the Kennett and Marlborough Meetings joined with non–Quaker reformers to establish a "Progressive Friends Meeting" at Longwood. On May 22 1853, the Progressives—a total of 56 Friends—met at the Old Kennett meeting-house near Hamorton and opened their membership to all those who recognized the "brotherhood of the human family, without regard to sex, color or condition. No issue was "too sacred for examination and discussion," and all issues would be addressed in a manner "free of clerical restraint" that they once felt as members of the Kennett and Marlborough meetings. Among the most pressing issues identified were women's rights, Negro slavery, war, capital punishment and temperance
>
> While neither side associated the split with the Underground Railroad, many of the Progressive Friends were agents on the clandestine route to freedom. Others were non–Quakers, some of who had already established a prominent national role in abolitionism, including: Sojourner Truth, a former slave and conductor on the Underground Railroad; Lucretia Mott, a leading Philadelphia Quaker reformer; and Thomas McClintock, a founder of the Waterloo, New York Progressive Friends.[33]

Tragedy struck the Garrett family that year: On August 23rd, one year after her marriage to doctor James Edwards, Thomas Garrett's daughter, Anna, died. A little later (September 3, 1853), Thomas's oldest daughter, Sarah, died. Despite his personal tragedies, Thomas Garrett's commitment to the anti-slavery cause did not diminish. In June of 1854 he appeared in Boston at the time of the trial and conviction of the slave, Anthony Burns.[34]

That year (1854), the Progressive Friends at Longwood purchased land from Quaker UGRR worker, John Cox, and built their own Meeting House, which came to be known as the "Longwood Meeting of Progressive Friends." It

> quickly became a center of radical abolitionism. "In dealing with such a sin as slavery, we can adopt no half-way measures," they stated, echoing the immediatist philosophy of Garrison. "The whole truth must be proclaimed, 'without concealment and without compromise.' No Church, no Government, no Constitution, no Union, which requires us to support or sanction such a crime, can have any binding force upon our consciences. We seek not alone to prevent the extension of slavery, but to exterminate it from every part of the land...." On many occasions, Longwood Meeting House was a gathering site for nationally famous leaders of the abolitionist movement, who traveled from all over the country to speak there, including Frederick Douglass, William Lloyd Garrison, Thomas Garrett, John Greenleaf Whittier, Sojourner Truth, and Susan B. Anthony.[35]

In January of 1854, Senator Stephen Douglas, Democrat from Illinois and chairman of the Senate Committee on Territories, introduced a bill that provided for the creation of two new territories—Kansas and Nebraska. The bill

> contained the provision that the question of slavery should be left to the decision of the territorial settlers themselves. This was the famous principle that Douglas now called "popular sovereignty." The Kansas-Nebraska Act flatly contradicted the provisions of the Missouri Compromise [under which slavery would have been barred from both territories]; indeed, an amendment was added specifically repealing that compromise. This aspect of the bill in particular enraged the anti-slavery forces.[36]

Abolitionists denounced the bill as a Southern device to open the new territories to slavery. However, President Franklin Pierce supported the bill and lobbied for its passage. By February, the opponents of the bill met at Ripon, Wisconsin, and formed a new party—the Republican Party. After three months of bitter debate in Congress, the bill became law on May 30th.

The provision of "popular sovereignty" in the bill was the bone of contention. It was settled easily by Nebraska, for the majority of the settlers there opposed slavery. So Nebraska became a free state. The matter was very different in Kansas, however. There, the issue was bitterly and violently contested by both the North and South over who would control the territory. In the North, the New England Emigrant Aid Company was formed, which sent settlers to Kansas to secure it as free territory. They were armed with rifles given to them by the abolitionist minister, Henry

9. The Trial of 1848

Ward Beecher (Harriet Beecher Stowe's brother). The South reacted by sending thousands of armed Southerners, mostly from the neighboring state of Missouri. These became known as the "Border ruffians." The two factions struggled, often violently, for control of the territory; to decide whether Kansas would become a free or slave state. By 1856 they had set up two different governments. The pro-slavery government chose the town of Lecompton as its capital. The "Free Staters," as they became known, chose Lawrence as its capital. Pro-slavery president Franklin Pierce recognized only Lecompton as a legitimate government.

On May 19th to 20th, Massachusetts Senator Charles Sumner, the Senate's leading opponent of slavery and considered one of the Radical Republicans in Congress, delivered a scathing speech entitled *Crime Against Kansas* in which he ridiculed South Carolina Senator Andrew Butler:

John Brown, 1800–1859, intense abolitionist and leader of the uprising at Harpers Ferry.

> The Senator from South Carolina has read many books of chivalry, and believes himself a chivalrous knight, with sentiments of honor and courage. Of course he has chosen a mistress to whom he has made his vows, and who, though ugly to others, is always lovely to him; though polluted in the sight of the world, is chaste in his sight. I mean the harlot, Slavery. For her, his tongue is always profuse in words. Let her be impeached in character, or any proposition made to shut her out from the extension of her wantonness, and no extravagance of manner or hardihood of assertion is then too great for this Senator.[37]

The following day, pro-slavery men in Kansas entered Lawrence, the Free State capital, and burned the Free State Hotel. They also destroyed property, and ransacked homes and stores. The next day (May 22nd), Congressman Preston Brooks of South Carolina, a cousin of Senator Andrew Butler, beat Sumner unconscious with his cane on the floor of the Senate for Sumner's remarks about his cousin. These two incidents were the last straw in the mind of the man who would once and for all change the course of the country's history regarding slavery. He was John Brown.

Brown was a deeply religious, fiery abolitionist with an intense hatred for slavery. He related completely with Negroes early in life, at one time living with them in the Freedman's Community in North Elba, New York. He worked as a conductor on the Underground Railroad and is known to have raised a young Negro boy as his own. Historian Benjamin Quarles writes:

Brown's relationship with Negroes had been close, continuous and on a peer basis, a pattern which no other white reformer could boast. Apparently, no Negro who ever knew Brown ever said anything in criticism of his attitude or behavior toward colored people. Brown's attitude toward slavery, and his grim and forceful response to it were shaped by many things, of which his own experiences with Negroes was not the least.[38]

Brown believed that slavery could only be ended when the "land was purged with blood." Hence his attitude toward the proponents of slavery was akin to the Laws of Hammurabi: "An eye-for-an-eye." "To Brown, slavery itself was a species of warfare, demanding a counter resort to arms."[39] Shortly after the passing of the Fugitive Slave Law in 1850, Brown had formed the United States League of Gileadites, a group of Negro men and women who pledged themselves to "go armed and to shoot to kill." Throughout the 1850s, Brown and his sons would fight numerous bloody battles against pro-slavery forces in Kansas and Missouri. Incensed now by the ransacking of Lawrence and the attack on Charles Sumner, Brown decided it was time to extract retribution and strike terror in the hearts of the pro-slavery people. On May 24, two days after the attack on Sumner, Brown and four of his sons led a group of men in an attack at Pottawatomie Creek, in Kansas. There he dragged five pro-slavery men from their homes and hacked them to death, after which Kansas became a powder keg that exploded into a State Civil War. The next four months were "characterized by lynching, bushwhacking, and burning — a continuous stream of violence that could not be contained by federal or territorial authorities." About two hundred men were killed, including one of John Brown's sons. The bloody fighting became known as "Bleeding Kansas."

> President Pierce finally replaced the ineffective governor Shannon [of Kansas] with John Geary, a tough but fair-minded Pennsylvanian, who had won his spurs as a captain in the Mexican War, and as San Francisco's first mayor. Combining persuasion with a skillful deployment of federal troops, Geary imposed a truce on the two sides and brought an uneasy peace to Kansas in the fall of 1856. By this time the larger question of which Kansas was a part — slavery in the territories — was the focus on the coming presidential election.[40]

President Franklin Pierce either did little to control the violence in Kansas, or by his pro-slavery bias simply made matters worse — though some say he probably could not have done much to prevent it in the first place.[41] On the whole, however, Pierce was considered an "accidental president" and is "generally ranked among the least-effective chief executives."

> [He was] viewed as an attractive, charming, but indecisive politician, easily influenced by such dominant figures as his secretary of war, Jefferson Davis. While historians have generally recognized that Pierce's endorsement of the Kansas-Nebraska Bill contributed to the disruption of his party and of the Union, they have been less successful in indicating what course of action he might have taken that would have prevented such an outcome.[42]

9. The Trial of 1848

Pierce was not re-nominated for president. Instead, James Buchanan, who was Secretary of State under James Polk, was the front-runner for the Democratic Party at their convention in June of 1856. "The Democratic platform, among other things, supported the compromise of 1850 [which repealed the Missouri Compromise], opposed federal interference in slavery and supported the building of the transcontinental railroad." Buchanan had two opponents in the election: the first was John Fremont, who became a national hero for his trailblazing exploits in the Far West. Fremont was anti-slavery, which played an important part in him being chosen as the new Republican Party's first presidential nominee. Buchanan's second opponent was former president, Millard Fillmore, of the American, or Know-Nothing, party.

In September, Thomas Garrett wrote to one of the ladies of the Edinburgh Ladies Emancipation Society in Scotland, giving his opinions of the candidates in the forthcoming election. In this letter Garrett uses his strongest language yet. He expresses what must be characterized as utter contempt for Franklin Pierce — whom he calls a "contemptible truckler"— and a total disregard for Millard Fillmore — whom he regards as "but a cipher." Interestingly, what Garrett thought of the others (Buchanan and Fremont) in 1856 is generally what historians think of them today. He also correctly predicts that the contest would be between Fremont and Buchanan and, again, he predicts the coming of the Civil War, this time with greater accuracy:

> I cannot well divest myself of an interest in the approaching Presidential Election, which will be settled in about two months from this time. I believe that Fremont would be [a] more efficient & better President than either Buchanan or Fillmore. I look upon Fillmore as but a cipher, and very much doubt if he will get the electoral vote of any state in the Union. The contest will certainly be between Fremont & Buchanan. Pierce, who now occupies the White House, I look upon as one of the most contemptible trucklers to the Southern interest of any man that ever held a responsible station in this country, & had even-handed Justice been administered to him, he had long been impeached and sent back to New Hampshire.
>
> Fremont is by no means a thorough Anti-Slavery man. He is opposed to the further extension of Slavery, but does not wish to disturb it where it now is, but leave that entirely to the States. He says, if it be confined within its present limits, it will soon die out of itself. The South says if Fremont is placed in the Presidential Chair, the Union must & will be dissolved. I wish I could bring myself to think so. I have but little hope for the abolition of slavery in any other way than by dissolution of the Union.
>
> If Fremont be elected, most likely the present difficulties in Kansas will be settled in favor of freedom, and slavery may be permitted to continue for years to come. But should Buchanan be elected, the South will be more arrogant and overbearing than ever; which will be likely still further to arouse the North to retaliate. When that takes place the South must yield. In case of Civil War the South could do little more than take care of her own slaves; and my opinion is a rupture must take place within the next four years if Buchanan be elected.
>
> (*For the full text of this letter, see Letter No. 3, to Eliza Wigham and Mary Edmundson*)

"Buchanan, won the electoral vote of 9 states. Fremont won the electoral votes of 11, Fillmore won the electoral; votes of 8. However, Buchanan's election was considered a Southern victory."[43] He assumed the office of the president on March 4, 1857, becoming the 15th president of the United States. His presidency, however, was unable to decelerate the worsening controversy over the issue of expansion and slavery, which kept moving the country closer and closer to disunion, especially since he proposed that Kansas be admitted as a slave state, in spite of the fact that most of the residents there were Free-Staters.

Meanwhile, by 1858, John Brown had decided the time had come for an all-out war against slavery. His vision was a slave insurrection. For this, he met with numerous prominent blacks—Frederick Douglass, William Still, Martin Delaney, Jermain Loguen, Henry Highland Garnet, and Harriet Tubman—to assist him in his plan to take the fight directly to the pro-slavery people. His plan was to seize the arsenal at Harpers Ferry, Virginia (now West Virginia), steal the arsenal's weapons, then arm thousands of slaves, who he believed would flock to him upon learning of his raid. Crucial to the success of his plan was Harriet Tubman because of her knowledge of the UGRR and that area of Virginia, as well as the high regard in which she was held by both fugitives and free blacks. So impressed with her when he first saw her, Brown immediately dubbed her "General Tubman" and entrusted her with his plans.

Brown received both financial backing and endorsement from a group of prominent Northerners known as "The Secret Six." They were wealthy New York abolitionist Gerrit Smith; minister, author and editor of the *Atlantic Monthly* Thomas Wentworth Higginson; wealthy Massachusetts merchant George Luther Stearns; author, journalist, editor of the *Boston Commonwealth* Franklin Benjamin Sanborn; physician Samuel Gridley Howe, and the Reverend Theodore Parker, a Unitarian minister.

On June 4, 1859, Sanborn wrote to Higginson: "John Brown is desirous of getting someone to go to Canada and collect recruits ... among the fugitives, with Harriet Tubman, or alone, as the case may be."[44]

Although John Brown was revered for his courage and as a steadfast champion of Negro freedom, his plan for the seizure of Harpers Ferry was considered "inordinately risky, if not foolhardy"[45] by most of the prominent blacks he sought to recruit. Most of them refused to participate. Frederick Douglass thought Brown "had overestimated the propensity of black slaves to rebel ... It is not that blacks did not want freedom..." he told Brown, "it was just that they were generally averse to suicide." Meanwhile, Franklin Sanborn and others reported that Harriet Tubman was in New Bedford, Massachusetts, and was very sick.[46] No doubt disappointed that these two leaders would not be with him, Brown proceeded without them. On the evening of October 16, with an army of 21 men that included five blacks, they raided the government armory and arsenal but, as expected, Brown's plan did not work as he had hoped. Instead, groups of the militia as well as the United States Marines under the command of Colonel Robert E. Lee, converged on Harpers Ferry, trapping Brown and his men in a fire house on October 18. Storming the building, Lee and his men killed ten of Brown's men and captured seven, including Brown."

Brown was tried and found guilty of treason and was sentenced to be hanged. Among his last words were:

> I believe that to have interfered as I have done—as I have always freely admitted I have done—in behalf of His despised poor, was not wrong, but right. Now, it is deemed necessary that I should forfeit my life for the furtherance of the ends of justice, and mingle my blood further with the blood of my children and with the blood of millions in this slave country whose rights are disregarded by wicked, cruel, and unjust enactments—I submit; so let it be done!

John Brown was hanged at Charleston, Virginia, on December 2, 1859. But as a result of his last speech and his fearless demeanor on the gallows, he became a martyr in sections of the North. "During the thirty-day interval between the sentence and the execution," writes Benjamin Quarles, "Brown bore himself with fortitude and serenity ... [But] Brown's inner peace was not shared by his countrymen, particularly those in the North. For his act, however rash and wrong-headed, had dramatized the issue of slavery, forcing neutrals to abandon their fence-sitting posture and giving to the abolitionists a martyr of unprecedented proportions."[48]

"In the Fall of 1860, a Republican senator from Illinois, Abraham Lincoln, ran for president on a platform which denied the extension of slavery to new states and territories. By this time the controversy over slavery had become so intense, tempers were inflamed, and extremists were so uncompromising that the basis for a peaceful adjustment of differences was lost."[49]

On December 20, 1860, South Carolina voted an ordinance of secession from the Union, and its governor proclaimed the act in effect four days later.

In January of 1861, Georgia, Alabama, Mississippi, Louisiana and Florida also seceded from the Union, and together with South Carolina formed the Confederate States of America and chose Mississippi Senator Jefferson Davis as provisional president. They were joined later by Texas, North Carolina, Arkansas, Virginia and Tennessee. However, Delaware and Maryland, which were also southern slaveholding states, did not secede from the Union.

On April 12, 1861, the first gun was fired by the Confederate Army, on Fort Sumter, in Charleston Harbor, North Carolina. On April 20, Colonel Robert E. Lee resigned from the U.S. Army and became commander of the Virginia troops on April 23rd. By June 14, he became full general of the Confederacy.

When President Lincoln made a second call for troops, Governor Richard Yates of Illinois appointed Ulysses S. Grant, an ex–West Point graduate, Colonel of the Twenty-first Regiment of Illinois Volunteer Infantry. Later Grant became commanding officer of the Union Army. The war lasted four year, and during that time there is not much information concerning Thomas Garrett's activity as a Station Master on the UGRR. However, as evidenced by his letters (Wm. Still, Nos. 31 and 33, Wm. Lloyd Garrison, No.5, and Miscellaneous, Nos. 10, 11 and 13), he was very much preoccupied with the war and its outcome. Although by today's standards Thomas Garrett would not be considered a "Hawk," he could by no means be considered a "Dove." He believed that a Civil War was not only inevitable, but the only way the slavery issue could be settled. In this, he broke with the traditional position of most Quakers, as well as with William Lloyd Garrison, which was that emancipation of the slaves should be brought about by peaceful, nonviolent means. New England Quaker Maria Chapman said, "The man who imagines that a civil and servile war would ultimately promote freedom really knows nothing of nature, human or divine, of character, good or evil." But Garrett felt always differently. To him, a Civil War was not only inevitable, but necessary in order to end slavery. Back in October of 1856, in a letter to Eliza Wigham (No.4), he wrote: "I fear that slavery may not be abolished here without civil war." In December of that year, he wrote again, in a more prophetic tone, "I know I may be wrong, but I am sanguine in the belief that 20 years cannot pass bye [sic] before every slave state in the Union will be glad to pass laws for the emancipation of their slaves, and I should not be surprised if it were done in half that time. If they do not do it, the slaves will rise up in mass before 20 years and murder their oppressors—that is my candid opinion." Then he added, "May that dreadful issue be prevented by the slave-holders becoming wiser than ever they yet have been" (Letter to Eliza Wigham, No.5).

In April of 1865, General Lee surrendered the Army of the Confederacy to General Grant at Appomattox, Virginia. The war was over. Thomas Garrett, abolitionists, and Underground Railroad workers throughout the country had seen their dream come true.

On March 30, 1870, the Fifteenth Amendment was ratified, giving Negroes the right to vote. The Negroes in Wilmington celebrated the event by carrying Thomas Garrett through the streets in an open barouche, heralded by a transparency labeled, "Our Moses," and Francis Ellen (Watkins) Harper, a Negro poetess, wrote:

> Beneath the burden of our joy
> Tremble, O wires, from East to West!
> Fashion with words your tongues of fire,
> To tell the nation's high behest.
>
> Outstrip the winds, and leave behind
> The murmur of the restless waves;
> Nor tarry with your glorious news,
> Amid the ocean's coral caves.
>
> Ring out! Ring out! your sweetest chimes,
> Ye bells, that call to praise;
> Let every heart with gladness thrill,
> And songs of joyful triumph raise.
>
> Shake off the dust, O rising race!
> Crowned as a brother and a man;
> Justice to-day asserts her claim,
> And from thy brow fades out the ban.

9. THE TRIAL OF 1848

> With freedom's chrism upon thy head,
> Her precious ensign in thy hand,
> Go place thy once despised name
> Amid the noblest of the land.
>
> O ransomed race! Give God the praise,
> Who led thee through a crimson sea,
> And 'mid the storm of fire and blood,
> Turned out the war-cloud's light to thee.

And in a letter which appeared in the *Liberator* (Miscellaneous Letter No. 12), Thomas Garrett said of this occasion, "I rejoice that I have lived to see this day, when the colored people of this favored land, by law, have equal privileges with the most favored."

10

Thomas Garrett, the Man

What kind of man was Thomas Garrett? He was described by Tilden (who was his contemporary) as "a man with a fine strong physique. He was not tall, but stocky and solid. His broad, heavy, but genial face, as shown in his pictures, gives an impression of repose, kindness and strength. He had a fine sense of humor and looked on the bright side of life. With his broad-brimmed hat, long and well-rounded Quaker waistcoat, telling of good digestion, he must have been a man to inspire respect for his prowess, and in spite of his peaceful principles, to keep impertinence at a distance."[1]

Pictures of Thomas Garrett may be found in some of the books and articles which give sketches of his life or are about the Underground Railroad. There is a bust of Thomas Garrett in *Friends in Wilmington*, and a left profile of him in Robert C. Smedley's book, *History of the Underground Railroad in Chester and the Neighboring Counties of Pennsylvania*. Perhaps the earliest portrait of Garrett can be found in Judith Bentley's *Dear Friend, Thomas Garrett & William Still, Collaborators on the Underground Railroad*. The photograph in this book was made available through the courtesy of the Historical Society of Delaware, and also appears in Wilbur Siebert's book, *The Underground Railroad, from Slavery to Freedom*.

But these descriptions, portraits and photographs give us, at best, only a surface impression of what the man, Thomas Garrett, was really like. They don't tell us what was in his heart and mind that drove him to be as outspoken and defiant as he was, or to take the risks he took, or invest all his time, energy and money to liberate the people he called "God's poor." For this, we must turn to Thomas Garrett's own belief: that it was the mystical experience he had on the road to Philadelphia; an experience in which it is said, "The sun shone in upon his soul revealing to his awakened conscience, the utter enormity of slavery as he had never before seen it. It was borne in upon his mind so vividly as to appall him, and he seemed to feel a voice within telling him that his work in life must be to help and defend this persecuted race."[2]

This experience was more than a mere vision. It affected Thomas Garrett very deeply and personally. During this experience he believed the "Almighty planted feelings of humanity in his breast ... for this oppressed people of color in our midst" (see Appendix II). What followed was inevitable. Garrett interpreted the experience not only as a Divine Revelation in which he saw the evils of slavery; he interpreted the message as his *duty*, a course of action *demanded* of him which he had to obey, regardless of the cost or consequences.

The earliest instance we have of Garrett's reaction to this experience is in February of 1828. In a letter he wrote to his mother he describes the feelings he derived from two Friends who rose to speak at a meeting for worship, each taking a different side of an issue:

> Wilmington, 02-14-28
> Dear Mother,...
> We had, this morning, an excellent Meeting. John Brooks addressed our friends that were sitting with us in a very feeling manner; [he addressed them] with the language Jesus address'd to his disciples in his day, [saying], in whatever city or house ye enter, say peace be to this house, and but should there peace return to them, simply mind, simply to shake the dust off their feet as a testimony against them, which was all the disciples was directed to do.
> After he sat down Sarah Emlen rose, and with this [same] language [said] that Jerusalem was to be searched with lighted candles. And I believe if ever the gospel was preached in its purity it was this day in this place. And that by two Ministers, one taking each side of the question, which has been fraught with deep instruction to my mind.
> We poor, short-sighted, selfish, mortals will sometimes undertake to condemn a disciple and even a Minister because his views are not in every point tally with our own selfish views. Could we but be favor'd to be satisfied with doing that, and that only, which divine wisdom clearly manifests to be our duty [in these days of close trial in our Society] and leave the rest to Him. If ever there was a time when it was necessary for the Members of this Society to dwell [on] love, and keep down a spirit of selfish activity, it is in our day, and I think this active spirit will, in some cases, apply to both sides of the present controversy. Farewell. My love to you and all ...
> Thy attached Son
> Thomas[3]

Through the years we hear Thomas Garrett using the word "duty" over and over, as if he wants those who question him, or doubt him, or do not understand him, to know that his actions were a command dictated by a Divine Source, which he referred to as "the Almighty." "I believe in doing my *duty*," he told an avid religionist who queried him about his beliefs. "A man's *duty* is shown to him, and I believe in doing it."[4] In a letter to his friend and fellow abolitionist, Samuel May, Jr., he first explains that, at the annual meetings of the American Anti-slavery Society, he gives the number of slaves he assisted only when asked to do so as he did not wish to appear egotistical. He then goes on to say, "What I have done was from principle, from a conviction that it was my *duty* to aid all of God's poor in their flight from their cruel Taskmasters...."[5] After his trial in 1848, Garrett makes his strongest statement in this regard. In his address to the court, jury and prosecutors, he first offers an excuse in defense of his helping the Hawkins boys escape. He says: although he knew they were slaves, he thought it would be no breech of law to provide them with transportation, "since the judge had already set them at liberty."[6] Then in the very next breath he declares what were probably his *real* feelings: "and had I known every one of them to be free, I would have done the same thing ... I would have done violence to my convictions of *duty* had I not made use of all the lawful means in my power to liberate those people and assist them to become men and women, rather than leave them in the condition of chattels personal." After the trial, Garrett repeated this statement, verbatim, in a letter to the local paper, *The Blue Hen's Chicken*.[7]

But equally important in Garrett's letter to his mother is his statement, "Could we but be favor'd to be satisfied with doing that, and that only, which divine wisdom clearly manifests to be our duty ... and leave the rest to Him." With that statement Garrett is saying, not only must we do our *duty* (which is shown to us), but we must do that and that *only*, and leave the rest to God. Hence we find that, throughout his life as a station master on the UGRR, Thomas Garrett acted as if nothing in the world mattered but his duty, to assist the runaway slave and help to end slavery. He must do that and nothing else. God would take care of the rest. How deeply Thomas Garrett was affected (possibly obsessed) by that command is evidenced by the fact that, even when two of his children died—within a little more than two weeks of each other—he continued to carry on with his duty of helping runaway slaves, as if that, not the death of his children, were more important. Such was the power of the vision and command that Thomas Garrett received one day on the road to Philadelphia.

On the other hand, there is a quite earthly interpretation to the motivation behind Thomas Garrett's actions. It may be argued that his conviction that slavery was an evil and his lifelong commitment to assist runaway slaves was but a *human* reaction, a deep sense of anger at what he considered a violation of the sanctity of his home. For example, it is one thing to hide runaways, to give them food and clothing, and to provide them with money and transportation. Garrett's family did that from their home in Upper Darby, Pennsylvania. But Thomas Garrett's experience brought the issue of slavery directly and personally to him. The kidnappers had actually entered his home and abducted a free black woman and left his family in distress. Now slavery became a very personal issue. From that moment on he decided that, over and beyond his family's practice of simply providing sanctuary for runaway slaves, he would directly confront and openly oppose the entire system of slavery. And it is significant that he chose as the means to do this the UGRR. For that institution, by it very nature, allowed him to make *personal* contact with the runaway slave; to "snatch" the runaway, as it were, directly away from the slaveholder, just as the kidnappers had done to him and his family. During the course of fulfilling this "duty," Garrett actually held runaways in his home, gave them money, food and clothing before sending them on to freedom. So in becoming a station master on the

UGRR and sheltering runaway slaves in his home, Thomas Garrett was not only fulfilling his duty, but satisfying his anger in a manner that can arguably be labeled as "an eye for an eye." That was the *human* side of Thomas Garrett.

One may choose either of these sources of motivation—the spiritual or the human—to explain Thomas Garrett's lifelong commitment to assist the runaway slave. However, as we read of the reckless manner in which he carried out his duty, it clearly indicates that he felt invulnerable; that no harm could befall him because he was protected by the "Almighty," who commanded him to do what he must. Yet, as we shall see, Thomas Garrett was also a practical man. For when he moved to Wilmington, he placed himself in an ideal location in which to carry out his commitment and at the same time successfully raise a family. Indeed, there are many times when Thomas Garrett has shown himself to be quite human. Yet he has *always* shown himself to be more than that.

• • •

With the exception of a number of individual black UGRR workers and black churches in Wilmington, few people in that city supported Thomas Garrett in his UGRR work. Thomas E. Drake, in *Quakers and Slavery in America*, says they considered his "activity as dangerous to the community and destructive to the Union. [Some] supported him tacitly, but few joined him in the work. Ordinary men were unwilling to assume the serious risks involved."[8]

And serious risks they were, indeed. William Lloyd Garrison was dragged through the streets of Boston by a mob bent on killing him and had to be placed in prison to save his life! Elijah P. Lovejoy, however, was not so fortunate; he was shot to death during an entanglement with a mob which wanted to destroy his printing press, with which he printed his anti-slavery newspaper.

Lewis Tappan, a wealthy merchant from New York, had his house wrecked and his furniture burned in the street for defending the anti-slavery cause, and a sea captain, Jonathan Walker, had his hands branded for helping seven slaves escape to the Bahamas aboard his ship. "Abolitionists were individually reviled and persecuted," says Smedley, "even by churches of all denominations."[9] So the times in which Garrett lived were indeed "risky" for those who supported the anti-slavery cause.

And then there were the slaveholders themselves. As we read about the large numbers of slaves who escaped and made their way to freedom, we ought to bear in mind the words of William Still, a man who personally interviewed more fugitive slaves than any other man of his day. Still says that "One should never feel that the slaveholder was in any way lenient, indifferent or unguarded as to how his property got away." For the men who owned the slaves were fierce men to deal with. The cost of one slave ran anywhere from $500 to $2,000—and more—and the owners of this valuable property did not intend to lose it. The fierce mien of these men were described by Still, who said, "not only slaves cowed before the eye of slave-holders.

Did not even Northern men, superior in education and wealth, fear to say their souls were their own in the same presence?"[10]

But it was when the slaveholders became the *slavehunters* that they were probably at their worst. They armed themselves with bowie knives, revolvers and bloodhounds in pursuit of the runaway slave, and they would stop at nothing. In *Acts of the Anti-slavery Apostles*, Parker Pillsbury quotes the two following incidents from the local newspapers:

> ...A negro who had absconded from his master, and for whom a reward of a hundred dollars was offered, has been apprehended and committed to prison in Savannah. The editor who states the facts adds, with as much coolness as though there were no barbarity in the matter, that he did not surrender until he was considerably maimed by the dogs that had been set on him — desperately fighting them, and badly cutting one of them with a sword.
>
> Two or three days ago a gentleman of this parish, in hunting runaway negroes, came upon a camp of them in the swamp on Cat Island. He succeeded in arresting two of them, but the third made flight. On being shot in the shoulder, he fled to a sluice, where the dogs succeeded in drowning him before assistance could arrive.[11]

These were the men Thomas Garrett had to face, yet Robert C. Smedley wrote that Thomas Garrett was a man who scarcely knew what fear was. "Although irate slave holders often called upon him to learn the whereabouts of their slaves," says Smedley, "he met them placidly, and never denied having helped fugitives on their way. He positively declined to give them any information, and when they flourished pistols or bowie knives to force their demands, he calmly pushed their weapons aside and told them that none but cowards resorted to such means to carry out their ends. Quakers are not afraid of such things."

On one occasion a slaveholder came to his home and said, "I understand you helped one of my slaves escape." Garrett didn't hesitate. "Yes," he said, "I gave him the money and the means to go to freedom." Incensed, the slaveholder warned Garrett that if he ever came south where he lived he would shoot him. "Well," said Garrett, "I think of going that way before long, and when I do I will call upon thee." And he did, and he said, "Here I am friend. Thee can shoot me if thee likes." Well, we know that Thomas Garrett died quietly in his home at the age of 81, not from a gunshot wound. "Such utter fearlessness in a just cause is invulnerable," wrote the Reverend William P. Tilden in a memorial address to Thomas Garrett.

In January of 1860, a resolution was introduced in the Maryland Legislature proposing a reward for Thomas Garrett's arrest on the general ground of slave-stealing. The reward was $10,000. According to Smedley, Garrett wrote to the Maryland Legislature and told them he didn't think $10,000 was enough money for his arrest. If they would make it $20,000, he would come down himself![12] "Thomas Garrett's out-spoken statement of his convictions ... overawed his foes," says Drake, "for he braved this threat without difficulty, just as he had more than once exposed himself in the enemy country of southern Delaware, and even South Carolina. He fairly stormed the citadel by announcing himself and his convictions in a firm if not provocative manner. The disarming candor of his personality seems to have won the respect if not the agreement of his opponents." And it should be pointed out that in 1860 Thomas Garrett was 71 years old!

While traveling through Maryland that year, he wrote to his friends, Joseph and Ruth Dugdale, and to his in-laws, Isaac and Dinah Mendinhall, saying:

> ...I write to say I have not yet been kidnapped by the Marylanders, and hope by this time my friends may breathe freer. I have had sundry letters from friends, some advising me to leave home for a few weeks, and one to go to England for a year or two and take my wife along. I presume you have not been so alarmed about me .... [Miscellaneous Letter No.7]

Another story tells how Garrett, like other UGRR workers, resorted to the following bold and cunning trick: "One summer evening," says Smedley, "when there was a collection of old plain Friends at (Garrett's) house, he was called to the kitchen where he found a greatly terrified poor woman who had run away, and from her statement it was evident pursuers would be there in a few minutes to watch the house. He took her upstairs, dressed her in his wife's clothes, with plain handkerchief, bonnet and veil, and made her take his arm. They walked out of the front door where she recognized her master as she passed. He was eagerly watching the house at the time."

This story seems to be a product of Hollywood. However, it is a rather common story told in UGRR literature about Quakers. J.C. Furnas, in *Goodbye to Uncle Tom,* writes, "Many a fugitive had been made aware that the broad Quaker hat and the queer Quaker coat betokened safety and help. Many another, often male, was smuggled to freedom in the voluminous Quaker gown and deep Quaker bonnet."[13]

Tilden tells of another incident:

> ...a fugitive came to (Garrett) for advice as to the road he should take. He found the man wanted to go by way of Philadelphia, where he had relatives. Knowing that way was carefully watched, Mr. Garrett asked him not to take it. But as the man had set his heart upon it, he sent one of his boys to pilot him as far as Brandywine Bridge. There the lad left him and returned. As the fugitive went on, a constable on the watch — just as Mr. Garrett feared — caught sight of him and, although he knew not for certain whether he was slave or free, he seized him and took him before a magistrate for trial. Someone seeing how things were likely to go, sent word to Mr. Garrett that a black man had been arrested and his assistance might be needed. He at once started off, not knowing who the man was. On arriving at the Squire's office he found a crowd gathered and the door closed. He was a man who, like Emerson, thought that "Difficulties were things to be overcome," so he marched up to the door and gave an authoritative knock. The door was opened. He gave his name, and was admitted. He saw at once it was the man whom his boy had left at Brandywine Bridge. But he didn't know the man's name. It was one of those cases in which he learned that "Ignorance was bliss," but quietly assuming that he knew the man well, he said to him: "Why Bob, what is thee here for?" Bob said he had been taken as a

fugitive. Mr. Garrett scoffed at the idea of his being a slave and said in a commanding tone: "Bob, thee must come with me." And he followed him, those present supposing Mr. Garrett knew him as a free black. As he walked out he said to the Magistrate: "I would advise thee and thy constables to be a little more careful what thee does, or thee will get into trouble." The crowd gave way and the brave, truthful, but sagacious, hero passed out and took the scared fugitive to his home station for a new start on a safer train.

Sarah Bradford tells of an incident in which Garrett had to use his wits again, this time to help Harriet Tubman. Harriet and a party of fugitives she was helping to freedom had gotten stuck in Wilmington, their route being closely guarded. Bradford writes:

> No sooner had [Garrett] received intelligence of the condition of these poor creatures, than he devised a plan to elude the vigilance of the officers in pursuit, and bring Harriet and her party across the bridge. Two wagons filled with bricklayers were engaged, and sent over. This was a common sight there, and caused no remark. They went across the bridge singing and shouting, and it was not an unexpected thing that they should return as they went. After nightfall [and, fortunately the night was very dark] the same wagons re-crossed the bridge, but with an unlooked-for addition to their party. The fugitives were lying close together on the bottom of the wagons; the bricklayers were on the seats, still singing and shouting; and so they passed the guards, who were all unsuspicious of the nature of the load contained in the wagons, or of the amount of property thus escaping their hands.[14]

In several of his letters to Eliza Wigham and to others, Thomas Garrett's closing remarks were that he was a friend of humanity, regardless of religion, nation, or color. The truth of this statement is exemplified in the following incident reported by Drake in *Quakers and Slavery in America:*

> In spite of his intense preoccupation with assisting slaves to escape their bondage, Thomas Garrett's humanitarian feelings also extended to white men who unwisely got into trouble in connection with a practice that was the reverse of the Underground Railroad, namely, the kidnapping of free Negroes for sale in the Southern market. One, Isaac Updike, was convicted of kidnapping in 1846–7, in Wilmington. Thomas Garrett spent a considerable amount of time and money in securing Updike's conviction. In August, 1847, however, Garrett was moved by pity of Updike's condition and that of his needy family to seek a governor's pardon from the remainder of the sentence of lashes, fine, and two years in jail. Pleading that Updike had been shown to be a dupe of a gang of kidnappers, and that he had now received sufficient punishment for his ignorance and folly, Garrett secured thirty eight signatures for a petition for a pardon ... The governor was not persuaded to grant the pardon, unhappily for poor Updike, but the incident shows the breadth of Thomas Garrett's sympathy for unfortunate human beings, no matter what their color.[15]
> [Miscellaneous Letter No.3 is from Garrett to Updike.]

With the reputation of the Quakers to act in a quiet manner as abolitionists, this was probably also expected of Thomas Garrett. But the incidents of Garrett's life indicate that he acted mostly with respect to his *own* feelings first of all. For even as much as he respected and admired William Lloyd Garrison, even though Garrison was a close friend, Thomas Garrett thought and acted independently of Garrison. Garrison was a complete non-resister, believing that one should resist slavery, but only by peaceful means. Thomas Garrett was not completely non-resistant. He believed that a Civil War was inevitable, and probably the only means by which the slavery issue could be resolved. As previously mentioned, Garrison was dragged through Boston's streets by a mob determined to kill him. As people who resort to mob violence are cowards to begin with, this action against Garrison could also have been because of the knowledge that he was a professed non-resister and would therefore commit no violence in return. It is doubtful (at least to this writer) that this would have happened to Thomas Garrett. W. A. Vrooman, in an article in the *Delmarva Star*, February 2, 1936, says that two men were overheard to say that they were going to kill Garrett one night:

> He was warned, but having a meeting to attend that night, he went out as usual. In the street two men leaped upon him, but his brawny hands caught them by the backs of their necks and brought them up standing. He shook them well and looked them over, then said, "I think you look hungry. Come in and we will give you supper." He forced them into his house and his wife prepared a warm supper, while Friend Thomas chaffed them about their adventure, and turned their enmity into friendship.

The reader will agree, perhaps, that when two men come to kill you, you don't turn their enmity into friendship by just plain "chaffing" them!—at least not right away. The men who attacked Garrett were undoubtedly dealers in violence and logically would only have a respect for greater violence. Hence we can probably believe that their immediate "conversion," if you will, was due to the fact that they recognized during their encounter with Thomas Garrett someone who was capable of administering a greater degree of violence than they, and for *this* reason suddenly decided it would be wiser—or at least safer—to have supper than fight.

Those are just a few stories of the manner in which Thomas Garrett showed his defiance of slavery, his contempt of slaveholders and his willingness to confront slavery personally. He was outspoken. Some say he was arrogant. He was bold. He was fearless. Some say he was even reckless in his zeal to bring an end to this "peculiar institution" by rescuing the people he called "God's poor." But his actions also set him apart from his peers. For example, there existed what might be called an "inconsistency" among abolitionists, among those who fought so hard and bravely for the emancipation of the Negro slave, and that is that many of them considered the Negro to be inferior.[16] Many abolitionists made a distinction between the Negro's rights to be free and his status as a human being. Many of those who were willing to risk their lives to help the slaves to find freedom were not willing to risk being socially ostracized by having the Negro as a personal friend. Furnas mentions in *Goodbye to Uncle Tom* that Levi Coffin, the man who claimed to have helped more than 3,000 slaves to freedom, deplored amalgamation!17 Drake, writing in *Quakers and Slavery in America,* says:

> Elisha Tyson, like Anthony Benezet and Elias Hicks, stood out as a notable friend and benefactor of the colored race in a generally hostile world. But their benefactions were mostly of the philanthropic sort. Few Quakers of their day, enthusiasts though they might be, advocated intimate social contact between the races. In spite of all that Friends had said since George Fox's time about Indians and Negroes being "fellow creatures," American Quakers confined their fellowship with red men and black mostly to benevolences. Seeing obvious wrongs to be righted, Friends tried to correct them. But the complex problems of permanent racial adjustment extended far beyond their capacity for solution. A few idealists such as Benezet had hoped that, once free, Negroes might through education achieve a status equal to that of whites. Many Friends tried to improve the lot of colored people; former Quaker masters taught their ex-slaves to read and write, and helped them get established in the world; Quaker ministers expounded the virtues of the Christian life. But Friends only reluctantly opened their Religious Society to colored members, and they wished no more than other whites of their day and generation to associate with different races on terms of social intimacy.18

There is no evidence that Thomas Garrett had this inconsistency regarding the Negro. On the contrary, the evidence is that he was unswerving and uncompromising, not only in his commitment to helping the runaway slave and the abolition of slavery, but in his professed belief in the equality of all men. In Miscellaneous Letter No. 9, for instance, he mentions taking slaves right into his own family. On one occasion, however, he spoke disparagingly of several Irishmen who attacked a group of Negroes with clubs (letters to William Still, Nos. 15 and 16). However, Priscilla Thompson reports that Garrett frequently used Patrick Holland, a native of Galeway, Ireland, who owned a livery stable in Wilmington, to transport runaways. He also accepted donations from some Irish Catholics.19

The position that Thomas Garrett took in helping the runaway slave was one that was held by many others working on the UGRR: he would not personally encourage or entice a slave to run away from his master, but once the slave had taken it upon himself to run away, then Garrett would help him as much as possible (see Letter to William Still, No. 16). This was a practical consideration more than a moral one. For Garrett, as brave as he truly was, was well aware that there were far greater risks involved in encouraging or enticing a slave to run away than there were in helping him after he took the initial step. In the latter case, the white UGRR worker, in particular, if caught, could always say that he simply did not know that the Negroes were slaves, and such a denial would be upheld in court, since, during those times, a Negro's testimony could not convict a white man.

However, helping the runaway slave was Thomas Garrett's business. It was the most important function of his life. We may be sure that he knew it was dangerous for the slave to run away from his master, but many of the incidents of his life, and much of what he expressed in his letters, leaves one with the feeling that he wanted the slave to brave those dangers and run away, nevertheless, just so he *could* help him, for in helping him it gave his *own* life meaning. We can almost hear the deep disappointment in Garrett's voice when he said, in a letter to the *Liberator*, "The war came a little too soon for my business. I wanted to help off three thousand. I had only got up to twenty-seven hundred."[20]

There are three incidents in Thomas Garrett's life that must be given serious consideration before we can truly understand this man and the commitment he made to oppose slavery. The first is, as already mentioned, the mystical, life-altering experience he had on the road to Philadelphia.

The second is the trial of 1848, when he was tried, convicted, and fined for assisting slaves to escape. As the story goes, after the trial, it was the Marshal of the court who once again brought the issue of Garrett's anti-slavery commitment home to his consciousness. He taunted Garrett saying "Well, I hope that you will now mind your own business and not meddle with slaves again."

Let us go back to that moment and put ourselves into Thomas Garrett's mind; to try to see what he was thinking and feeling. The Marshal's taunting certainly must have thrown Garrett in on himself, to cause him to reexamine what he was doing, and to contemplate the consequences if he continued. At this point he may have thought that he could rest on his laurels and say, for example. "Well I already helped over fourteen hundred escape. Perhaps that's enough. I have a wife and children, a home, a business. All of that would be placed in jeopardy if I continue."

If Thomas Garrett decided at that point to give up, one could hardly blame him. Indeed, we would appreciate what he had already done. But it was at that moment that Thomas Garrett clearly demonstrated that the life-altering experience he had on the road to Philadelphia had dictated the course of his life. He rose and faced the court and said:

> I have assisted over 1400 runaways in 25 years on their way to the North. And I now consider the penalty imposed might be as a license for the remainder of my life. But be that as it may, if any of you know of any slave who needs assistance, [you] send him to me, [for] I now pledge myself to double my diligence and never neglect an opportunity to assist a slave to obtain freedom.

In contemplating Garrett's words and decision, it is one thing for us to credit him with helping so many slaves escape, or to admire him for being so outspoken, bold and fearless, but the true measure of this man is not in those things. It is that what he did in behalf of the runaway slave, he did so in spite of the fact that it would cost him everything, the security of his home and his business. All of that would be placed in jeopardy. But he did it anyway. That is why it is the trial of 1848 that must be considered the defining moment of Thomas Garrett's life. It was then, when he was brought to pay perhaps the highest price for his actions, that he made the choice to remain true to the source that dictated his life, whether it be human or divine. That was his trial by fire. After that, nothing would stop him.

In 1853, the third incident occurred. Two of Thomas Garrett's daughters, Sarah and Anna, died within 17 days of each other. Sarah died August 23rd; Anna died September 9th. Yet Thomas Garrett carried on. In only nine months after their deaths (May of 1854) we find Thomas Garrett all the way in Boston, where he was a highly recognized and applauded figure in one of the most publicized slave rescues in American history: the failed attempt by thousands of people to prevent runaway slave, Anthony Burns, from being carried back to slavery (see introduction to letters to Eliza Wigham and Mary Edmundson).

> …federal troops marched Burns to the harbor, where a ship waited to carry him back to Virginia, while tens of thousands of bitter Yankees looked on and bells tolled the death of Liberty in the cradle of the American Revolution.[21]

Five months later we find Garrett writing to William Lloyd Garrison, inviting him to come to Wilmington to address an anti-slavery meeting; "we therefore hope thee will make it suit to be with us and make my house thy home while here." The following month, on November 11th, he wrote again to Garrison informing him that on that day he helped seven more fugitives escape, and that his list of slaves "has now got to 1874" (see letters 2 and 3 to William Lloyd Garrison). Meanwhile, I found no letters by Thomas Garrett in which he mentions the deaths of his two daughters, or of what he felt about them.

11

How Important Was Thomas Garrett?

Whatever motivation we attribute to Thomas Garrett's mission to assist runaway slaves, to that end he was steadfast and consistent. Those two qualities made him dependable and reliable to the runaway slave, who lived in constant fear of being betrayed and captured and returned to slavery. Harriet Tubman, during an interview with New England writer Benjamin Drew, confessed "Every time I saw a white man I thought I was going to be carried away."[1] Runaway slave Ellen Craft became alarmed when she and her runaway husband, William, were placed in the care of a white abolitionist, Barkley Ivens. "I have no confidence in white people," she told her husband. "They are only trying to get us back into slavery."[2]

In Thomas Garrett, however, here was a white man who was on the side of the runaway slave, a man who felt as passionately about their right to freedom as they did and, most of all, who was willing to put his life and all of his possessions on the line for them. Putting ourselves in the mind of the fugitive slave then, we can understand why Thomas Garrett was important to them. As slaves, they endured brutal beatings, forced labor, near starvation, rape and all sorts of inhumane treatment, until they finally mustered the courage to say "No more," and strike out into the unknown for freedom. Hunted like animals by hard-hearted slave hunters and ferocious bloodhounds, they traveled by foot, by horse, by carriage, by boat, on the tops of moving trains, in the backs of wagons. Women ran away, by themselves, some only with babies in their arms, some while pregnant.[3] Boys and girls ran away, some as young as ten.[4] Elderly men and women ran away, some as old as 70. They hid in swamps and caves, in barns and churches, in cellars and attics, in the holds of ships. They shipped themselves to freedom in boxes. They disguised themselves; men dressed as women, women dressed as men. Some who were fair enough pretended to be white and simply walked away to freedom. Others armed themselves with pistols, knives, and hatchets. They walked and ran and, yes, they fought their way out of slavery. And in their flight a few have been known to leave an overseer dead on the road. William Still reports of one runaway who took the whip away from an overseer and whipped him, instead, then ran away.

Thomas Garrett's home in Wilmington, Delaware, then — only five miles from the free state of Pennsylvania — was the last stop to freedom before the passing of the Fugitive Slave Law. But if the runaway slave knew this, so did the slaveholders and slave hunters. So Garrett's house was under constant surveillance by these men. Yet, Garrett was willing to face them down. He not only spoke out against slavery, he confronted slaveholders and slave hunters directly, sometimes in their own territory. So to the runaway slave, Thomas Garrett was the man they had to get to.

Although Garrett's personality earned him both the enmity and respect of slave hunters, kidnappers and slaveholders, as we shall see it also enabled the free black community of Wilmington to support him by acting as station masters, conductors and willing helpers. His voice was also heard in other parts of Delaware, Maryland and Virginia, where conductors and ship captains willingly brought runaways to him, feeling that, in his hands, they could rest assured the runaways were well on their way to freedom. That is probably the prime reason runaway slaves said they felt just as safe when they reached Thomas Garrett's home as they would if they had reached Canada.

But Garrett's singular personality and action also raised the consciousness of those around him who originally did not offer public support of his actions. In a letter to Mary Edmundson, Garrett himself reported that a young man who had served as juryman, after listening to Garrett's public announcement that he would go on to help even more runaways escape, came across the room and taking him by the hand said:

> Old gentleman, I believe every statement that you have made. I came from home prejudiced against you, and now I acknowledge that I have helped to do you injustice.[5]

The effect was also felt by those who, though they may not have supported him publicly, reacted strongly in his favor after he was convicted. For example after his trial, *The Blue Hen's Chicken* printed letters of support for the action he took in behalf of the Hawkins family. One writer voiced strong feelings against the verdict, saying:

> These two men [Garrett and Hunn] are among the most humane and orderly and exemplary of our citizens. When such a result can be brought about there is something rotten either in the laws or the manner of their administration.[6]

Another factor that contributed greatly to Thomas Garrett's importance was simply his location. Just over the Delaware/Pennsylvania line — approximately five miles from Garrett's home — exists Chester County, a hotbed of individual abolitionists as well as anti-slavery communities, black and white. Among them were

Thomas Garrett's in-laws, Isaac and Dinah Mendinhall, whose home in Kennett Square was also a station to succor runaway slaves. William C. Kashatus reports:

> Geographically, Chester County was an ideal sanctuary for fugitive slaves. Located just above the Mason-Dixon Line which divided free and slave states, the region was defined by a series of parallel hills, whose thickly-wooded slopes offered an natural avenue of escape as well as effective concealment for runaways. 29 routes for the Underground Railroad came through both Delaware and Maryland. A northern route entered Lancaster County from Maryland by way of Fulton, then to the north through East Drumore, Eden, Paradise, and Salisbury, then into Chester County by way of Honeybrook and continued through to Phoenixville, then to Norristown and then to Philadelphia. Another major route cut through the center of Chester County, extending from Wilmington into Kennett, East Marlborough, Newlin, Downingtown, Lionville, Kimberton, and Phoenixville. Still another major route headed in an easterly direction, beginning at Wilmington and extending through Kennett, East Bradford, West Chester, Willistown, then to Philadelphia. While these three lines formed the major routes of the Underground Railroad through Chester County, there were many other secondary paths a fugitive could travel.
>
> Once he reached Kennett, just over the Mason-Dixon Line, the particular route a fugitive took depended largely on circumstance. Since Kennett was like the hub of a wagon with spokes leading in all directions, runaways had many choices open to them. Roads led east to Philadelphia and New Jersey; north to West Chester, Downingtown, Phoenixville, Lionville and Kimberton; northwest to Ercildoun and Coatesville; west to Avondale, West Grove, and on into Lancaster County. To the south were the villages of New Garden, Landenberg and Hockessin, Delaware. Similarly, once a fugitive reached Phoenixville, he could cross the Schuylkill River at Port Providence, or at Perkiomen Junction and head for one of many stations at Norristown. Consequently, if there was no space available at one station, the route could easily be altered to accommodate that problem. Alternative stations were often used when a fugitive was being pursued, as well, if only to avoid predictability. In most cases, the destination was Philadelphia, where a sizeable black population offered camouflage to a fugitive.[7]

So the location of Thomas Garrett's home in Wilmington, Delaware, with its close proximity to Chester and the other counties in Southeast Pennsylvania, was ideal for runaway slaves. We'll have more to say about this, shortly.

Another factor, perhaps even more important, was Garrett's close proximity to the Chesapeake and Delaware Canal ("C & D Canal"). As opposed to Chester County, where Garrett sent runaways, the C & D Canal was an important conduit from which Garrett received runaways, especially those who escaped by the boats that plied the Chesapeake Bay — the "Chesapeake Underground."

As early as the 1600s, it was observed that two great bodies of water, the Delaware River and Chesapeake Bay, were separated by only a narrow strip of land. It was proposed that a waterway be built to connect the two. This canal would reduce the water routes between Philadelphia and Baltimore by nearly 300 miles. In his study of the Chesapeake Underground, Vincent O. Leggett writes:

> Due to the landscape's geography and topology, the primary mode of travel and trade in Maryland during the mid–1800s was by water. It should come as no surprise then that Delmarva's Underground Railroad routes comprised streams, creeks and rivers that flowed into the Bay, and onward to the Atlantic Ocean. Hence, the runaway slave network here became known as Chesapeake Station or the Chesapeake Underground.
>
> …Harriet Tubman who was born on the Eastern Shore did indeed travel by water. She once instructed a companion to rent a fishing boat in Cambridge and meet her at Bodkin Point, on the Bay's western shore near Baltimore.
>
> Further evidence of the water's import to the slave network are many accounts of safe houses with tunnels leading to creeks and rivers. Several of these accounts have been documented in Baltimore City, Anne Arundel County and all along the Eastern Shore.
>
> Among the many slaves who would benefit from the Bay and its meandering water trails in escaping from bondage was another famous Marylander, Frederick Douglass. In his autobiography, he recalls watching ships with full white sails traveling on the Chesapeake Bay as a young boy from his Talbot County home.
>
> In his youth, Douglass even predicted the significance the Chesapeake Bay would have in his life as he wrote, this very bay shall yet bear me to freedom.[8]

However it was not until 1802 that the Chesapeake and Delaware Canal Company was incorporated through the combined efforts of the Maryland, Delaware and Pennsylvania legislatures. By 1804 actual construction of the canal began. Its original plan was to connect the Christina River near Wilmington with the Elk River at Welch Point, Maryland. But the project was halted two years later for lack of funds. The canal company was reorganized in 1822, the year Thomas Garrett moved to Wilmington. This time the commonwealth of Pennsylvania, the States of Maryland and Delaware, and the federal government all purchased stock in the company amounting to $625,000. By 1824 with the aid of the U.S. Army Corp of Engineers and two civilian engineers a new canal route was recommended "extending from Newbold's Landing Harbor (now Delaware City, Delaware), westward to the Back Creek branch of the Elk River in Maryland," and by April of that year, construction began. By 1829 the C & D Canal was open for business. Today the C & D Canal is owned by the federal government (purchased in 1919) and through continuous improvements and changes through the centuries is considered "unique as the sole major commercial navigation waterway in the United States built during the early 1800s still in use. It is listed on the National Register of Historic Places and is designated as a National Historic Civil Engineering and Mechanical Engineering landmark."[9] However, in Thomas Garrett's day:

> Teams of mules and horses towed freight and passenger barges, schooners and sloops through the canal. Cargoes included practically every useful item of daily life: lumber, grain, farm products, fish, cotton, coal, iron, and whiskey. Packet lines were eventually established to move freight through the waterway. One such enterprise the Ericsson Line operated between Baltimore and Philadelphia, and continued to carry passengers and freight through the canal into the 1940s.[10]

…as well as runaway slaves.

Finally, Garrett also had the financial means to fulfill his commitment. He was not known to be the best businessman in Wilmington, but he was an honest one. And even when he was fined a large sum of money, even when he suffered business losses, with the aid of friends he was still able to maintain his lifestyle and continue assisting the runaway slave. He did not lose his home or all of his household goods. In a commentary to a letter he wrote to the Edinburgh Ladies Emancipation Society, dated August 28, 1854, Eliza Wigham wrote:

> After some details of his trial and prosecution in 1848 for rescuing a family of slaves, and stating that he had been assisted by some friends to embark in business, he says, "I started again in the iron and hardware business, in 1850, with a cash capital of less than 1000 dollars. I paid my interest, supported my family, and saved 7000 dollars in three & a half years, so that I am not quite so badly off as has been supposed."[11]

Three years later, Garrett reported to Mary Edmundson of that society, "I ought to have acknowledged receipt [of your letter] ere this, but we have been very busy building an addition to my store, moving iron and taking an account of stock."[12]

Throughout his letters to William Still we find Garrett frequently stating that he gave money, clothes and shoes to runaways. He gave money to Severn Johnson, one of his black UGRR helpers in Wilmington. He and Passmore Williamson also gave money to the wife of one of the ship captains, Captain Lambdin, who was arrested for aiding runaways to escape.

All these — the consistency of Thomas Garrett's commitment to oppose slavery by assisting runaways to escape, his willingness to openly speak out against slavery, his willingness to place himself at risk on behalf of the runaway slave, his ideal location, and the financial means to carry out his mission — made Thomas Garrett the most important station master on the UGRR in the entire state of Delaware.

12

Thomas Garrett and Harriet Tubman

When did Thomas Garrett meet Harriet Tubman? A letter to J. Miller McKim, December 29, 1854, is the first recorded instance in which Thomas Garrett speaks of Harriet Tubman. The tone of his letter suggests that he has known her for at least some time. He writes:

> We made arrangements last night, and sent away Harriet Tubman with six men and one woman to Allen Agnew's to be forwarded across the country to the city....[1]

We have no other recorded document when Thomas Garrett first met Harriet Tubman. What we do learn from his letters, however, is that they had a close friendship. Garrett writes of having tea and casual conversation with Harriet Tubman, even at times joking with her and teasing her. He did this during the time of her dangerous UGRR missions—a time when Harriet Tubman was usually not in the mood for joking and teasing. Yet, in his letters, Thomas Garrett often speaks glowingly of Harriet Tubman. She is "a noble woman." "Remarkable, shrewd, courageous," are some of the adjectives he used in describing her character. He also seemed to take great pride in describing her physically. He writes that she is strong and muscular,[2] and he seeks to leave no doubt that she is a true Negress, that none of her "remarkable" qualities and deeds should ever be attributed to her having white blood. In a letter to Eliza Wigham, he writes:

> I feel I cannot close this already too long letter without giving some account of the doings of a noble woman, but a black one, in whose veins flows not one drop of Caucasian blood.[3]

Garrett also expressed concern for Harriet Tubman when he learned she was ill, and especially because he knew she undertook rescue missions of great danger (see letter to William Still, No. 11).

But Thomas Garrett's attraction to Harriet Tubman goes beyond her character and physical characteristics. For example, both had a mystical or life-altering experience in which they received a command telling them that their life's work must be to help the runaway slave. In Garrett's life this happened on the road to Philadelphia, a time in which he said that "feelings of humanity were implanted in his breast to help this poor and despised race."[4] From all of Garrett's statements, this experience, and the command that accompanied it, happened only once in his life. But he perceived it as his duty, and he remained faithful to it for the remainder of his life.

Harriet Tubman, c. 1820–1913, conductor on the Underground Railroad. (From Cayuga Community College, Auburn, New York.)

We have no exact time when Harriet Tubman underwent this experience, but I believe it probably occurred after she received a severe head injury, which left her sick and near death.[5] Her biographer, Sarah Bradford writes that, after this experience, Harriet "began falling into states of somnolency from which it is almost impossible to rouse her."[6] Harriet claimed that she prayed and groaned to the Lord almost constantly for Him to wash away all her sins. She prayed also for her young master, Edward Brodess, until she learned he was going to sell her and her brothers and sisters, then she changed her prayers, asking the Lord to kill him. Shortly after, the young master died and Harriet was remorseful, believing she had killed him. She began having dreams and visions. Bradford writes:

> When these turns of somnolency come upon Harriet, she imagines that her "spirit" leaves her body, and visits other scenes and places, not only in this world, but in the world of spirits. And her ideas of these scenes show, to say the least of it, a vividness of imagination seldom equaled in the soaring of the most cultivated minds.[7]

From that point on Harriet began hearing the voice of God telling her first, that her mission in life was to free her brothers and sisters and her people from slavery[8] and, secondly, when and where she should go to free them, and finally, that she would be guided through its dangers. In contrast to Thomas Garrett, the voice Harriet heard continued largely throughout her days as a conductor on the UGRR. In a letter to Sarah Bradford, Garrett wrote:

> I never met with any person, of any color, who had more confidence in the voice of God, as spoken direct to her soul. She has frequently told me that she talked with God, and He talked with her every day of her life, and she has declared to me that she felt no more fear of being arrested by her former master, or any other person ... then she did in the state of New York, or Canada, for she said she never ventured only where God sent her, and her faith in the Supreme Power truly was great.[9]

Garrett goes on to report an incident in which Harriet had with her "several stout men" that she was guiding to freedom when God told her to stop, leave the road and turn to the left. She obeyed and came to a small stream of tide water. She was told to go through it. It was cold, in the month of March. But having confidence in her Guide, Harriet did as she was told. "The water came up to her armpits. The men refused to follow till they saw her safe on the opposite shore."

"The strange part of the story," wrote Garrett, "was that the masters of these men had put up an advertisement for their arrest the previous day, offering a large reward for their apprehension."[10]

Years later, Harriet told her biographer, Sarah Bradford, that once, when she boarded a boat to Baltimore with a young slave girl she was rescuing, she was detained by a clerk who was suspicious that they were runaways. As the clerk went to verify that they were not:

> Harriet led the young girl to the bow of the boat, where they were alone, and here, having no other help she, as was her custom, addressed herself to the Lord. Kneeling on the seat, and supporting her head on her hands, and fixing her eyes on the waters of the bay, she groaned.
> "Oh Lord! You've been with me in six troubles, don't desert me in the seventh!"

When the clerk returned, he touched Harriet on the shoulder and said, "You can come now and get your tickets." Their troubles were over. "What changed this man from his former suspicious and antagonistic aspect," wrote Bradford, "Harriet never knew. Of course she said it was 'de Lord,' but as to the agency He used, she never troubled herself to inquire. She *expected* deliverance when she prayed, unless the Lord had ordered otherwise, and in that case she was perfectly willing to accept the Divine decree. When surprise was expressed at her courage and daring, or at her unexpected deliverance, she would always reply: 'Don't I tell you...' twan't *me*, 'twas *de Lord.*'"[11]

Both Thomas Garrett and Harriet Tubman embraced the belief that all people are created equal in the eyes of God. Garrett's belief in this comes first from his adherence to the Quaker doctrine of the Inward Light, that "there is that of God in everyone." He expressed this conviction often in his letters as he signed off saying "your friend, and the friend of humanity, without regard to religion, country or color."[12] It was a spiritual conviction he said came from the "feelings of humanity the Almighty implanted in his breast."[13] However, we have to ask what he meant when, in his speech after his trial, he referred with disdain to the inhabitants of Texas as a "mixed breed and degenerate race from all nations" (see Appendix 3). It sounds like a contradiction.

Harriet Tubman, on the other hand, was always consistent. She, like Garrett, embraced a feeling of the relatedness of the entire human race. Sarah Bradford concluded her biography of Harriet with the observation, "Harriet's charity for all the human race is unbounded. It embraces even the slave holder—it sympathizes even with Jeff Davis...." But beyond that broad view, Harriet Tubman also saw the human side of human behavior. She told Sarah Bradford:

Sarah H. Bradford, 1818–1912, Harriet Tubman's biographer.

I think there's many a slave-holder will get to Heaven. They don't know no better. They act up to the light they have. You take that sweet little child [pointing to a lonely baby]—appears more like an angel than anything else—take her down there, let her never know nothing about niggers but they were made to be whipped, and she'll grow up to use the whip on them. No Missus, it's because they don't know no better.[14]

The result of their having a similar mystical experience and a common spiritual perspective, Thomas Garrett and Harriet Tubman both became convinced they must dedicate their life to assist the runaway slave. This conviction also impelled them to take great risks, to place themselves in great danger apparently with the feeling they could do so without personal harm.

So Thomas Garrett and Harriet Tubman were two individuals who had much in common and who were similar in many respects. Thus, when Thomas Garrett met Harriet Tubman, he met a kindred spirit. He recognized in her similar deep-seated beliefs that was the source of their motivation. To be sure, this was at a time when the country was caught up in the belief in Spiritualism, the belief based on the notion that human personalities could communicate with the dead through people called mediums. One of the means mediums used to demonstrate, or "prove," they communicated with the dead was "table rapping." This supposedly occurred when two or more people (usually at a séance) sat at a table, lightly touching it with their fingertips. Spirits of the dead, they claimed, would communicate by causing the table to rock back and forth, or rap on the floor, or even rise up off the floor.

Thomas Garrett, like William Lloyd Garrison, Horace Greeley, Franklin Sanborn, Harriet Beecher Stowe, and even President Lincoln, as well as hundreds of other men and women from all walks of life, was apparently caught up in this belief and attended Spiritualist meetings.[15] There is no evidence that Harriet Tubman ever got caught up in Spiritualist activities or professed a belief in Spiritualism. She stayed focused on her God-appointed mission. In a letter to Eliza Wigham, Garrett wrote:

> I may inform you that Harriet has a good deal of the old fashion Quaker about her. She is a firm believer of spiritual manifestations, but I presume knows nothing about table rappings.[16]

However, Garrett did recognize that Harriet Tubman possessed some sort of extrasensory ability. In his letters to Eliza Wigham and Mary Edmundson of the Edinburgh Ladies Emancipation Society, he frequently expressed a mixture of surprise and admiration at her unearthly ability to know when he had received money they sent specifically for her.

> Some twelve months after, she called on me again, and said that God told her I have some money for her, but not so much as before. I had, a few days previous, received the net proceeds of one pound, ten shillings, from Europe for her. To say the least there was something remarkable in these facts, whether clairvoyance or the divine impression on her mind from the source of all power, I cannot tell; but certain it was that she had a Guide within herself other than the written word, for she never had any education.[17]

Throughout her book about Harriet Tubman, Sarah Bradford seems to have had misgivings about the veracity of Harriet's stories, particularly about her psychic experiences. However, several of the responses she received from the men she asked for testimony about Harriet contain statements reassuring her that Harriet Tubman is a very truthful person. To be sure the country was caught up in the Spiritualism craze. It was a time that was wrought with controversy about the veracity of this belief, when congressmen, lawyers, judges, scientists, philosophers, men and women from all walks of life were either embracing, disclaiming, or investigating the reality of Spiritualism. So on this issue, Sarah Bradford could hardly be blamed for taking a cautious position. Nevertheless, Secretary of State William H. Seward wrote:

> I have known her long, and a nobler, higher spirit, or a truer, seldom dwells in the human form.[18]

Millionaire and philanthropist Gerrit Smith wrote:

> Of the remarkable events of her life I have no personal knowledge, but of the truth of them as she describes them, I have no doubt.
>
> I have often listened to her, in her visits to my family, and I am confident that she is not only truthful, but that she has a rare discernment, and a deep and sublime philanthropy.

New England author, journalist and philanthropist Franklin Benjamin Sanborn wrote:

> ...it is time to notice one singular trait in her character. She is the most shrewd and practical person in the world yet she is a firm believer in omens, dreams and warnings.
>
> I never had reason to doubt the truth of what Harriet had to say in regard to her own career, for I found her singularly truthful ... . Her dreams, misgivings and forewarnings ought not to be omitted in any life of hers, particularly those related to John Brown.

But this is also true of Thomas Garrett. No account of his life should be written that does not recognize and accept that the mystical experience he had on the road to Philadelphia was the source of his motivation, the wellspring of his conviction that he must dedicate his life to freeing the runaway slave. He and Harriet Tubman were very much alike in that respect.

As we know, Harriet Tubman could neither read nor write, so we do not have a written account of what she thought and felt about Thomas Garrett. But we can infer from his letters that she had absolute trust in him. And that word, *trust,* is very important when we speak of Harriet Tubman, particularly during her UGRR days. For example, Harriet Tubman was known by the prominent men and women of the day to be highly intelligent, sagacious, and shrewd, attributes that no doubt contributed to her great success as a conductor on the UGRR. However, what was also known about Harriet Tubman is that she was extremely cautious and observant in dealing with people she didn't know. Sanborn relates the caution with which she received visitors "...until she felt there was no mistake."

> One of her means of security was to carry with her daguerreotypes [likenesses] of her friends, and show them to each new person. If they recognized the likeness, then it was all right.[19]

There is no evidence that Harriet Tubman was so cautious with Thomas Garrett. For example, Harriet was in constant need for money to aid her cause in assisting runaway slaves. She was always asking for money. She frequently went to the secretary of state, William H. Seward, and asked for money. Seward recognized that Harriet was in the habit of giving all her money to the first person she thought was in need. Years later he would tell her, "Harriet, you have worked for others long enough. It is time for you to think of yourself. If you ask for a donation for *yourself,* I will give it to you; but I will not help you to rob yourself for others."[20] Harriet asked New York businessman and abolitionist Oliver Johnson for money. She told him, as she frequently told Garrett, that God sent her to him for money. On one occasion Johnson flatly refused to give her any money, saying, "I guess God was mistaken, this time." Harriet replied, "No sir. The Lord's never mistaken," and laid down on a bench in his office and went to sleep—"probably one of the turns of somnolency to which she has always been subject," said Sarah Bradford. Soon Harriet's

> story was whispered from one to another, and as her name and exploits were well known to many persons, the sympathies of some ... visitors to the office were aroused; at all events she came to full consciousness, at last, to find herself the happy possessor of sixty dollars, the contribution of these strangers.[21]

However, we learn from his letters that when Harriet Tubman went to Thomas Garrett, she didn't have to ask. She simply told him that she *knew* he had money for her. When he asked her how she knew, she, knowing that he would understand, simply said, "Because God *told* me you have money for me." And, of course, he did understand. And, of course, he did have money for her. We do not come across any evidence that Harriet Tubman had that kind of understanding, that kind of trust and confidence, in anyone else during her UGRR days.

But Thomas Garrett and Harriet Tubman were not altogether two peas in a pod. They were different in some respects. For example, during the period when he was assisting runaway slaves, Garrett, as we know, was outspoken, openly defiant of the slave system and critical of slaveholders. Harriet Tubman, on the other hand, was not inclined to reveal what she thought or felt. To be sure, this difference can be attributed to the different positions these two occupied in life. Garrett was white, a well-known businessman and, although he had his enemies, he also had friends, some in high places. As for Harriet, "a reward was offered for her capture," says Sanborn, "and she several times was on the point of being taken, but always escaped by her quick wit, or by 'warnings' from Heaven."[22] And so the nature of the UGRR operation required Harriet to be always involved in covert activities. During that period she had to remain inconspicuous and keep her thoughts and feelings to herself.

Garrett as well as others reported that Harriet was a very modest person. He expressed surprise at how unpretentious, and even unusual, it was that she was so unassuming. In a letter to Eliza Wigham, for example, he gives an account of a rescue by Harriet of a woman and three children, a trip which he characterized as "remarkable" in which Harriet "manifested great shrewdness" to avoid being arrested. He asked her if she was not frightened when she was about to be arrested. She replied, "Not a bit ... she knew she would get off safe." "But the strangest thing about this woman," Garrett wrote, "is [that] she does not know, or appears not to know, that she has done anything worth notice!"[23]

Garrett, on the other hand, intimated that he was modest and often stated that he did not wish to appear egotistical, but in his letters he frequently made known the number of slaves he assisted. He also stated, publicly and in writing, who he was and what business he was about. The best instance of this, of course, is his public statement to the court and jury after his trial in 1848, when he openly challenged those present that, if they "know of any slave who needs assistance, send him to me, as I now publicly pledge myself to double my diligence and never neglect an opportunity to assist a slave to obtain his freedom."

Garrett also wrote a lengthy and detailed account of the events that led to his trial to the newspaper, *The Blue Hens Chicken*. In it he revealed his personal views concerning slavery and left no doubt that he assisted runaway slaves, as well as the length of time that he has done so. He wrote that he was "proud" to be called an "Abolitionist" and enlarged upon the speech he gave after he was convicted: "I should have done violence to my convictions of duty," he said, "had I not made use of all the lawful means in my power to liberate those people rather than leave them in the condition of chattels personal."[24]

So, in the manner in which they presented themselves publicly, there was a great difference between Thomas Garrett and Harriet Tubman. However, it may be argued that their differences complimented each other. Garrett's outspoken manner, coupled with his feeling of invulnerability, seems to have kept kidnappers and slaveholders at bay.

Harriet, on the other hand, though necessarily reticent and secretive, achieved the same results. Runaways whom she guided to freedom felt safe with her. They called her "Moses," believing that she would eventually lead them to freedom. The runaways interviewed by William Wells Brown all believed that Harriet had "supernatural powers." He writes:

> ...the woman herself felt that she had the charm, and this feeling, no doubt, nerved her up, gave her courage, and made all who followed her feel safe in her hands. When the Negro put on the "blue" [joined the Army], Moses was in her glory, and traveled from camp to camp, being always treated in the most respectful manner ... . These black men would have died for this woman, for they believed that she had a charmed life.[25]

Though he was fined a large sum of money, and though he lost much money through imprudent investments of his business partners, Garrett seemed always to get money when he needed it. Harriet, as mentioned, seemed always in need for money.

But the similarities between them were more important than their differences. For it is in Thomas Garrett's letters to William Still that we get the only fully *documented* information about Harriet Tubman's slave rescues. For example, in an article in the *Boston Commonwealth*, Franklin Sanborn describes four different occasions when Harriet rescued slaves:

> In December of 1850, she had visited Baltimore and brought away her sister and two children who had come up from Cambridge in a boat, under charge of her sister's husband, a free black.[26] A few months later, says Sanborn (1851), Harriet brought

away her brother and two other men, and fugitives and brought them safely to Philadelphia. In December of that year she returned for her husband, but learned that he was unfaithful. "Not giving way to rage or grief, she collected a party of party of eleven, among them her brother and his wife."[27] And from Cape May, in the Fall of 1852, she went back once more to Maryland, and brought away nine more fugitives.[28]

Sarah Bradford stated that Harriet made 19 trips into slave territory and brought away some 300 slaves. But Harriet never confirmed that. She said she only remembered making 11 trips and never kept an account of the number of slaves she brought away. Bradford, however, implies that her (Bradford's) account must be believed rather than Harriet's for she (Bradford) received the information from "the reckoning of Harriet Tubman's friends."[29]

In Thomas Garrett's letters to William Still, however, we do not get that important information from the "reckoning of Harriet Tubman's friends," nor do we get the incomplete data that Sanborn gives writing a decade later. Instead we get specific, firsthand information. Garrett reports how many runaways were with Harriet when she brought them to his place. He identifies their gender, reports whether there were children, where they all came from, where they were going, what mode of transportation they were using—that is, whether they were walking, on the "cars" [train], or in a carriage. And his letters were always *dated*, so we know the exact date when those rescues took place. There is no other source that is so specific in giving this vital information about the most important period of Harriet Tubman's life: her activities as an UGRR conductor.

In Thomas Garrett's letters, we also get many personal observations about Harriet Tubman during this period. Sarah Bradford wrote of Harriet Tubman almost ten years later, when Harriet Tubman was recalling her experiences. But, as mentioned, Bradford often intimates that she rarely believed Harriet Tubman. She said she checked up on everything Harriet Tubman said in order to "corroborate" Harriet's stories. She wrote that she didn't even keep all of Harriet Tubman's notes and personal letters.[30] She rarely asked Harriet Tubman what were her thoughts and feelings, even though she reported that Harriet Tubman stayed in her home.[31]

In 1948, Sarah Bradford's great-nephew, Samuel Hopkins Adams, wrote his memoirs of Harriet Tubman for *New Yorker Magazine*, "A Slave in the Family." But this was 35 years after Harriet Tubman was dead—she died in 1913. During her lifetime, however, Franklin Sanborn, Gerit Smith, Oliver Johnson, William Still and William H. Seward all expressed a high opinion of Harriet Tubman based on their personal knowledge and observation of her. But nowhere does anyone speak of Harriet Tubman with so much admiration and fondness as does Thomas Garrett of this simple black woman, this runaway slave, of whom he said he is "proud of her acquaintance," and referred to as the "greatest heroine of the age," and that, if she were white, her name would be "trumpeted over the land."[32] And it is only from Thomas Garrett's letters that we learn why and how Harriet Tubman embarked on what Franklin Sanborn called "her most venturesome journey" to rescue her father and mother from the slave system. And from those letters we learn the vital role that Thomas Garrett played in it.

• • •

It was in June of 1857.

In an examination of only the first 202 cases (of a probable thousand) of runaway slaves recorded in William Still's book, we count 69 slaves running away in 1857 from the following states:

Maryland	50
Virginia	18
Delaware	01

Of that number, 29 came from Dorchester County, 26 from the city of Cambridge, and three from Bucktown. At one point, more than 28 slaves ran away at once, all from the vicinity of Harriet Tubman's former home, Bucktown/Cambridge, Dorchester County, Maryland.[33]

To the question, *why* did Harriet Tubman help her father and mother escape from the slave system, comes the natural assumption, "because they were her father and mother." However, the evidence suggests otherwise ... and possibly a lot more.

The most reliable account of why Harriet Tubman rescued her father and mother comes from the source that was closest to it when it happened — Thomas Garrett. Garrett was there, and he was personally involved. In his letter to Mary Edmundson, of August 11, 1857, he said:

> The old man Ross had to flee. He had been guilty of sheltering in his hut, for one day, those 8 slaves that broke out of Dover jail, early last Spring. A fine colored man who piloted these slaves some 20 miles to his house from Carolina County, was betrayed by one who started with the rest, [then] turned back and informed of the man who piloted them, and told where they went to stop over the first day. The poor man was tried and convicted and sentenced to the Maryland Penitentiary for ten years. They were preparing to have Benjamin arrested when his master secretly advised him to leave. His wife belonged to another plantation and the old man wisely concluding it would be more agreeable to have her along. She left without so much as asking leave, and with such an experienced guide as Harriet, they passed safely on.[34]

The escape of the eight slaves from the Dover jail, then, is the single incident that caused Harriet to embark on her "most venturesome journey" to rescue her father and mother from the slave system.

Thomas Garrett, William Still, and the Delaware State *Recorder* each gave an account of the Dover escape. But these accounts are told from different points of view, with each author adding information according to his perspective. Not only that, in his account, Garrett erred in one of the dates he gave. The result of all this makes for more than a little difficulty in deriving a clear and consistent story. Yet the story is important for, as mentioned, it is the single incident that led Harriet on her "most venturesome journey."

In short, the story is that, in March of 1857, eight runaway slaves, six men and two women, armed with pistols and knives, employed a black man named Thomas Otwell to pilot them to freedom. One of the runaway slaves was Henry Predo, whom William Still described as "physically a giant, about 27 years of age, stout and well-made, quite black, and no fool...."[35] Another was Daniel Hughes, "in features, well-made, dark chestnut color, and intelligent." And a third man was Thomas Elliot, "about twenty three years of age, well-made, wide awake, and of a superb black complexion."[36] Still gives no information about the others.[37] However, Thomas Garrett wrote to Mary Edmundson that "all of the runaway slaves came from the immediate neighborhood of Harriet's old master," then adds the provocative statement: "One of the runaway slaves was named Tubman, the assumed name of Harriet!"[38] To avoid confusion, however, Kate Larson reports that Garrett was referring to runaway Bill Kiah, whose *owner* was named Tubman. "Bill may have used the name Tubman," writes Larson, "but that was the name of his owner."[39] Meanwhile, the "old Master" Garrett speaks of is Anthony Thompson.

As for Thomas Otwell, Garrett said "he lived near Milford some 20 miles lower down the country [Delaware]. He had been employed by the friends of the coloured people, or slaves, for some time as a pilot.... The runaways had paid Otwell 8 pounds to pilot them 30 miles to the next station, within a few miles from Dover." According to Earl Conrad, a Harriet Tubman biographer, Otwell had even made a trip North with Harriet Tubman.[40] So the six men and two women who were presently running away had, in Thomas Otwell, a man who was knowledgeable of the hidden trails and secret stopping places of the Underground Railroad, and he was initially a man who Garrett believed "had always been true to his trust."[41] However, on this occasion, Otwell conspired with a white man named Hollis and betrayed the eight runaways.

On Sunday, March 8th, Hollis went to Sheriff Green in Dover and told him he had eight runaways. He then made arrangements with Green to have the runaways in jail that night, but it wasn't until four o'clock the next morning that Otwell and the eight runaways arrived in Dover. Otwell introduced the runaways to Hollis as his "particular friend." He then turned them over to Hollis, who took them directly to jail and placed them in an upstairs room. "Upon a light being lit," said Garrett, "the runaways saw bars on the window and became suspicious." They stepped out into the entry of the room just as the sheriff was coming up the stairs to lock them in. Realizing they had been betrayed, they staged a sensational escape. As the sheriff ran downstairs to his bedroom (where his wife was asleep) to get his pistols, the runaways followed in hot pursuit. Henry Predo grabbed a hot andiron from the hearth and held the sheriff at bay while the others smashed out the windows, leaped 12 feet to the ground and ran to freedom. Predo then scattered hot coals over the floor of the bedroom—"while the wife cried murder, lustily," said Still.

According to Garrett, two of the men took their course northward, toward his place in Wilmington. The other six took the back track. The Delaware State *Recorder* of March 13 reported that "these six men were tracked to a house in Camden, Delaware, where officers tried to arrest them but could not enter the house without a warrant ("which a local magistrate had no power to give"). They may have found refuge either at the home of Samuel D. Burris, a black UGRR worker or Ezekiel Jenkins, a Quaker who was also active on the UGRR in that area. It was Burris and Jenkins who, in 1845, helped the Hawkins family from Queen Anne's County, Maryland, to escape. This was the event that ultimately led to Garrett being tried and convicted for his involvement (see Chapter 9, The Trial of 1848).

Garrett wrote to his cousin, Samuel Rhoads:

Wilmington, 3rd month, 1857

Dear Cousin, Samuel Rhoads:

I have a letter this day from an agent of the Underground Railroad, near Dover, in this state, saying I must be on the lookout for six brothers and two sisters, they were decoyed and betrayed, he says, by a colored man named Thomas Otwell, who pretended to be their friend, and sent a white scamp ahead to wait for them at Dover until they arrived. They were arrested and put in jail there with Tom's assistance, and some officers. On third day morning [Tuesday] about four o'clock, they broke jail. Six of them were secreted in the neighborhood, and the writer has not known what became of the other two. The six were to start last night for this place. I hear that their owners have persons stationed in several places on the road, watching. I fear they will be taken. If they could lay quiet for ten days or two weeks, they might then get up safe. I shall have two men sent this evening some four or five miles below to keep them away from this town, and send them [if found, to Chester County]. Thee may show this to Still and McKim, and oblige thy cousin,

— Thomas Garrett[42]

On Tuesday night the six were conveyed to a house of a man residing near Willow Grove, Pennsylvania. From there they were forwarded up the country by the Underground Railroad. The other two were seen going out of Dover in a northerly direction.

During their flight, some of the runaways actually caught up with Otwell. "Their first impulse was to kill him," said Garrett, "but Otwell begged so hard and promised so fair if they would only spare his life he would take them to the house he had promised in the first place...." They spared him, and this time Otwell kept his promise. "He ran off as fast as he could, never to be heard of again."

"The runaways were all armed with pistols and knives and it is a wonder that they acted with so much coolness and discretion," said Garrett. "One of the men told me he would have killed Otwell at once had he not thought that, if he did, they would have less chance of escape than if they committed no act of violence, which was no doubt a correct view."[43]

As for Hollis, the *Recorder* reported:

The fault of the escape is attributable entirely to the hoggishness of the man who tolled the Negroes into Dover. Greedy to get the whole reward, he would not permit a small force to share it with him, and [so] he got none.

The following Thursday, one of the two who headed north arrived at Garrett's house, and Garrett provided for him. However, he does reveal that all of the eight runaways came from the immediate neighborhood of Harriet's old master. He then adds that the master of this man (with the "assumed name of Harriet"—that is, Bill Kiah) offered 2,200 pounds for him and "no doubt thinks that he has met with a great loss."

In its next issue (March 20, 1857), the Delaware State *Recorder* reported:

> The escaped slaves noted in our last issue, so far as we have been able to learn, have not yet been arrested.

The following Sunday (March 22), two more of the runaways arrived safely at Garrett's house. Garrett had been on the road several nights watching for them, to keep them from crossing the Wilmington bridges, which were closely guarded. That night, he sent two of his own men with money and directions to meet four of the remaining five, who were several miles from him. They were to take the runaways across the Christina River, across the country, to a place of safety, ten miles from town. The description of the distance suggests that Garrett sent them to the home of his in-laws, Isaac and Dinah Mendinhall.

Several days later Garrett learned that the runaways were all doing well. As for the last man, Garrett had not heard from him since he escaped but felt convinced the man was safe, as he would have heard the news had the man been recaptured.

On the 27th of March, we find Garrett writing an anxious letter to William Still:

> Wilmington, 3rd mo., 27th, 1857
>
> Esteemed Friend, William Still:
>
> I have been very anxious for some time past, to hear what has become of Harriet Tubman. The last I heard of her, she was in the State of New York, on her way to Canada with some friends, last fall. Hast thee seen or heard anything of her lately? It would be a sorrowful fact if such a hero as she should be lost from the Underground Railroad. I have just received a letter from Ireland making inquiry respecting her. If thee gets this in time, and knows anything respecting her, please drop me a line by mail to-morrow, and I will get it next morning, if not sooner. I have heard nothing from the eighth man from Dover, but trust he is safe.
>
> Thomas Garrett

After receiving the above letter, Still informed Garrett that Harriet Tubman was all right. Garrett wrote back:

> I was truly glad to learn that Harriet was still in good health and ready for action, but I think there will be more danger at present than heretofore, there is so much excitement below in consequence of the escape of the eight slaves.[44]

It is most likely that Garrett was trying to contact Harriet Tubman to tell her of her father's plight. In a letter to Mary Edmundson, dated March 29, 1857, Garrett said:

> It was a week of great anxiety, I assure you. I could not think of much else. It cost me nearly half the amount of your liberal donation, but I have no recollection of any money that I ever spent more cheerfully in the cause ... .

Harriet Tubman was on her way. She stopped at the New York office of Oliver Johnson for money. Johnson refused to give her any. Harriet refused to leave his office until she got money. She lay down on a bench in his office and went into one of her trance-like states and, as happened often in her life, when she came out of this state, her prayers—or talk with God—were answered. She received money from a number of people in Johnson's office and began her journey to Thomas Garrett for further assistance. Garrett wrote to Mary Edmundson:

> I have this moment received a letter from Wm. Still [of] Philadelphia informing me that Harriet Tubman had arrived in Phila, and was well, and contemplates making a visit South, this week. This is good news. She is to call on me for money on her way.[45]

Meanwhile, the Delaware State *Recorder* alluded to Garrett in a subtle warning in their April 3rd issue:

> THOSE RUNAWAY NEGROES—We learn from a reliable source that, on Wednesday after the escape of the eight negroes from this town, three of them were seen in a closed carriage, belonging to a well-known and notorious abolitionist of New Castle county, in Wilmington en route for Pennsylvania. It is not improbable this affair may result in mulcting some one in rather heavy damages.

But Benjamin Ross, Harriet Tubman's father, also helped those runaways escape and, as Garrett informed Mary Edmundson, he was going to be arrested as a result.

Exactly how Harriet got the message that her father was in trouble is not known. She may very well have had a "mysterious" and "supernatural intimation," as Sarah Bradford said she had. Or, she may have gotten the message from an "unknown communicant in the Eastern Shore," as her later biographer, Earl Conrad, writes.[46] Whatever the source, Harriet did get the message. And she rescued her father (and in the process, her mother) from the slave system, moving her father, as she told Sarah Bradford, "to be tried by a higher court."[47]

In Summary, almost all of the original information as to when, how and why Harriet Tubman rescued her father and mother from slavery comes from Thomas Garrett's two letters to Mary Edmundson and his letter to Sarah Bradford.

In his August 11, 1857, letter to Mary Edmundson, he states clearly that the date of his direct involvement was June 4th. On that day he gave Harriet Tubman 30 pounds to carry her father and mother to Canada. William Still confirms this when he printed that Harriet Tubman arrived with her parents at his office that same month. So there should be no confusion as to *when* Harriet rescued her parents. What is little short of amazing, however, is that Still never asked Harriet's father and mother *why* they escaped. Or, if he did, he didn't think it was significant enough to print, or perhaps he felt that, at the time, it was better left unsaid.

In his letter to Sarah Bradford, Thomas Garrett supplies us with the only information as to *how* the escape was carried out. All other accounts are taken from this letter. To be sure, most of Harriet Tubman's early biographers retell this story with imagination and invention, but it is the same story originally told by Thomas Garrett, printed in Sarah Bradford's two books about Harriet Tubman.

By far, the most tangible reason why Harriet Tubman went to rescue her parents was given by Thomas Garrett in his March 29, 1857, letter to Mary Edmundson. It was because Harriet's father was about to be arrested for helping the eight slaves who escaped from the jail in Dover, Delaware. If we accept Thomas Garrett's reason (and he was there), then we must conclude (as I have already mentioned) that the escape of the eight slaves from the Dover jail was the sole cause of Harriet Tubman undertaking the dangerous journey to rescue her aged parents from slavery.

Earl Conrad was under the impression that the Dover escape was a separate incident, having nothing to do with Harriet rescuing her father and mother. He writes:

> She [Harriet] was either in St. Catherine's or Auburn, and she knew nothing about the trouble at Dover ... .[48]

To Conrad, the only relationship Harriet had with the "trouble at Dover" was that, Thomas Otwell, the man who betrayed the eight runaways, was able to do so by misusing Harriet's identity. He writes:

> In March of 1857 ... Harriet's name was seized upon by a slave named Thomas Otwell, and her identity and influence used in a scheme for the betrayal of an escaping party of eight Bucktown slaves, two of whom were women. Otwell, who had once made a trip North with Harriet, but had returned, used his knowledge of the Underground and his association with Harriet as a means of luring into his confidence this collection of unsuspecting Negroes, intending to win the reward for their capture. Far from planning to conduct the company to Canada, Otwell connived with the authorities in Dover, Delaware, and so dexterously conceived the route of escape as to have it lead directly into a cell of the Dover jail![49]

But Conrad was obviously without the benefit of Thomas Garrett's letters to Mary Edmundson. For, with these two letters, Conrad would have known that the escape from the Dover jail was not a separate incident, but one in which Harriet's father was directly involved and therefore was related to Harriet undertaking the journey to rescue her parents. We must add that, even though William Still also gives an account of the escape from the Dover jail, he never mentions that Harriet's father was involved, so Conrad could not have known from reading Still's book, either.

We also learn from Garrett's letters that there is good reason to believe that Otwell did not betray the eight runaways by his own volition, as Conrad asserts. According to Garrett,

Otwell had rented a small farm from a white man named Hollis, who had been informed that Otwell was an agent on the Underground Railroad, and Hollis succeeded in corrupting Otwell's morals. He induced Otwell to mislead the eight runaways into the Dover jail where he would have them arrested.

Hollis and Otwell would then collect the reward and divide it between them.[50]

William Still, also believing that Otwell acted by his own volition, felt that the huge reward ($3,000) was too great a temptation for Otwell to resist.[51]

Perhaps so, but Garrett's letters suggest that Hollis blackmailed Otwell, perhaps threatening to turn him over to the authorities if he did not go along with his scheme.

When presented with the available information — Garrett's letters, Still's book, Sarah Bradford's two books, and the Delaware State *Recorder*— one can easily discern where this information differs, contradicts and errs. However, Thomas Garrett was there, and he was involved. True or false, accurate or inaccurate, the information in his letters are firsthand accounts of what took place. And these accounts tell us a couple of important things. The first is that they flatly contradict any notion that Harriet Tubman's father and mother lived in the same house at the time she rescued them. Secondly, they strongly suggest that Harriet Tubman's major concern was with rescuing her father (obviously, because he was the one who was in danger), and that it was her father's idea to take her mother along. And finally, the natural assumption that Harriet Tubman rescued her father and mother from slavery simply because they were her parents does not hold up. On the contrary, it was because her father was in danger of being arrested for helping some of the eight slaves that escaped from the jail in Dover, Delaware.

But the matter of Harriet Tubman helping her father and mother escape seems to be but the tip of an iceberg, and that there's something more to this then meets the eye. For example, what kind of relationship did Anthony Thompson, a slaveholder, have with Ben Ross, a former slave, that he would take steps to protect him from being arrested — especially for helping slaves escape? And he does so by contacting the most active and notorious anti-slavery person in the region — Thomas Garrett!

Garrett, mistakenly believing that Anthony Thompson is Ben Ross's master, writes that Harriet's father's master "secretly advised him to leave" when he learned that the authorities were preparing to have him arrested. This suggests that Anthony Thompson, the master, was concerned for the father's welfare. However, William Still's account is just the opposite. He (also believing that Thompson is Ben Ross's master) reported that Harriet's father said:

> ...his master was a rough man towards his slaves ... that he was a Methodist preacher [who] had been pretending to preach for twenty years; who stinted them for food and clothing and left them with no room to believe that he was anything but a wolf in sheep's clothing.[52]

However, that mean characterization of Anthony Thomson does not ring true. For one, some runaways have felt the need to characterize their owners in the negative as a means of protecting them if their owners were in any way instrumental in letting them go free. Also, Harriet Tubman's parents were *not* slaves at the time she rescued them. Her father had bought her mother's freedom from Eliza Brodess (Thompson's wife) for the sum of $20.00 in 1855.

13

How Many Runaways Did Thomas Garrett Assist?

In the court room after his trial in 1848, Thomas Garrett said he told the Marshal "publicly" that he had assisted over 1,400 runaways in 25 years.[1] This would mean that he started in 1823. In a letter to Samuel May, Jr., dated November 24, 1863, Garrett stated that the length of time he had been aiding slaves to escape was "now covering a space of 38 years,"[2] which would place the year he started as 1825. Years later, in a letter dated April 5, 1870, he writes to Aaron Powell that he moved to Wilmington, Delaware, in 1822. That year he said the Delaware Anti-slavery Society appointed him and William Chandler to investigate the case of two colored girls taken out of the state and sold as slaves. "From that time on," he writes, "I have neglected no opportunity to aid all those oppressed people who called on me for aid...."[3]

So Thomas Garrett gives three different times when he actually started helping runaways escape—1822, 1823 and 1825. Whichever is the actual date, it is from then until his last recorded instance, in 1863 (when the country was right in the middle of the Civil War to end slavery), that Thomas Garrett said he helped 2,700 runaways find their way to freedom. In a letter to *The Liberator* he stated, "The war came a little too soon for my business. I wanted to help off three thousand. I had only got up to 2,700."[4]

But what criteria did Thomas Garrett use to determine that he assisted them? There are any number of variables that one can cite as "aid." For example, did he actually take all the runaways he claimed he assisted into his home, feed and clothe them and give them money and shoes?[5] Or did he see a slave running over there and say, "Go that way and you'll be safe?" Or did one of his helpers come to him with news of a runaway and Garrett advised him to tell the runaway where to go? For example, in letter No. 26 to William Still, Garrett reports that the brig *Alvena* brought four females on board under the charge of a colored conductor. Unable to locate the husband of one of the females (who paid the conductor to bring his wife up), Garrett advised the conductor to take them in the steamboat to the city [Philadelphia], and to the Anti-slavery Office. In the next sentence, Garrett reports:

> I have a man here, to go on to-night, that was nearly naked; shall rig him out pretty comfortably, poor fellow, he has lost his left hand, but he says he can take care of himself.

The question is which of these two incidents did Garrett count as those he assisted? Was it the four females who were brought to him? Or was it the last individual who lost his left hand? Or did he count that he assisted them all?

In the same letter that he wrote to Samuel May, Jr. (above), he stated that, by January 1, 1860, the total number of runaways he assisted was 2,246. He then followed this by detailing the numbers he helped from January 1, 1860, to November 11, 1863, giving a grand total of 2,322 (following table):

1860	33
1861	22
1862	14
1863	7
total	2322

If by November 11, 1863, Thomas Garrett helped 2,322 runaways escape, as he said he did, then in order to have helped the 2,700 he claimed, he would have to have helped an additional 378 runaways by April of 1865, just 17 months later — when the Civil War ended slavery. That amounts to 126 runaways a year, or approximately 22 runaways each month. There is no tangible evidence that he did.

There are three sources of information regarding the number of runaways Thomas Garrett assisted: the first is the totals he frequently gives to friends and collaborators through his letters (such as the one above).[6] However, if Garrett began helping runaways escape in 1822, then in the 41 years from then until 1863 he would have had to have helped an average of 44 runaways each year in order to have helped 2,700 runaways by 1863. If he began helping runaways escape in 1823, then in the 40 years from then until 1863 he would have had to have helped an average of 45 runaways each year in order to have helped 2,700 runaways by 1863. And finally, if he began helping them in 1825, then in the 38 years from then until 1863 he would have had to have helped an average of 59 runaways each year in order to have helped 2,700 runaways by 1863. Regardless of the year he began, there is no tangible evidence that Thomas Garrett helped the required number each year in order to reach the 2,700 he claimed.

The second source of information is the runaways he helped who are found in his letters to William Still and J. Miller McKim, which are in this book. These contain the only documented evidence of the number of runaways Garrett is said to have helped. In these letters Garrett clearly states the number of runaways he's sending to Still. He reports their mode of travel, the routes they will be taking, and whether he gave them food, money, or clothing. And since his letters are always dated, we know the exact date when the event took place. These letters cover six years between 1854 and 1860. However, it is only in 19 of these letters that Garrett mentions the number of runaways he is sending to Still, and in one of them (Letter No. 14, October 31, 1857), Garrett states that he is not sure whether the number of runaways he is assisting is 17 or 27. Whatever the case, the total number of slaves in all of these letters comes to either 106 or 116 (depending on whether Garrett assisted 17 or 27). Whichever number it is, it is a long ways from 2,700.

The third source of information is the number of runaways given by the people to whom Thomas Garrett sent runaways. The majority of these were in Chester County and, as we shall see, a few of them are reported to have received hundreds of runaways from Thomas Garrett. One of them, Dr. Bartholomew Fussell, is reported to have received thousands!

But, without a written record of the individual runaways he helped, we have to take Thomas Garrett's word for it when he says he helped 2,700 escape. But that raises a serious question: Why did Thomas Garrett frequently inform people how many runaways he helped at a time when it was unwise to do so, and then not be able to present the proof that he helped them when there was no harm in doing so? To put it another way, throughout his life as an UGRR agent, all of Thomas Garrett's actions suggests that he *wanted* people to know how many runaways he helped — the most obvious instance, of course, is in his address to the court and jury after his trial. So why then didn't he, like William Still, keep a record of the individual cases as proof that he indeed helped them? Such a question may never be answered, but it had to be raised.

However, giving Thomas Garrett the benefit of the doubt, we ask, "Where did 2,700 runaway slaves come from?" The exact number may never be known, but we do know that many of them came, either alone or from the hands of other UGRR workers in the two counties below Wilmington, as well the other states of the Eastern Shore and mainland, Maryland and Virginia. Richard A. Biondo reports that between 1800 and 1860 there was a steady decrease in the number of slaves in Maryland. BIondo discusses three possible causes: manumission, selling of slaves to other states, and slaves running away. He quotes the following from Barbara Jeanne Fields', *Slavery and Freedom in the Middle Ground*[7]; "The 1850 census reported 279 escapes for the year ending 30th of June, 1850."

Charles Blockson lists a number of UGRR workers, black and white, who operated in Delaware below Wilmington: Daniel Corbet, whose Clearfield Farm in Smyrna had several places of concealment for runaways.[8] In Middletown was Wild Cat Manor and Great Geneva, owned by the family of Quaker John Hunn. "Harriet Tubman was well-acquainted with the [Hunn] family," says Blockson, "for their homes were the first known railroad stops on her route to freedom."[9]

In sparsely populated Star Hill, Delaware, the African American Episcopal

Church was a station on the UGRR and opened its doors to escaping slaves.[10] Blockson also lists Woodburn, the present Governor's Mansion, in Dover, Delaware, as an UGRR station. "During the 19th century the home was owned by Henry Cowgill, a Quaker, whose family was active in helping fugitive slaves to escape."[11]

Harriet Tubman also stayed at the Appoquinimink Friends [Quaker] Meeting House in Odessa, Delaware. "Her route through the state included Camden [home of black UGRR worker, Samuel D. Burris and Quaker abolitionist, Ezekiel Jenkins], Dover, Blackbird, Laurel, Concord, Seaford, Millsborough, Smyrna, Delaware City, Middletown, Georgetown, Lewes, Milford, Frederica and New Castle on her way to Wilmington and Philadelphia."[12]

So there were a number of UGRR stations and agents all along the Eastern Shore who were sheltering and aiding runaway slaves on their way north — through Wilmington — to freedom.

But there was another, perhaps lesser-known route that Harriet Tubman and other rescue workers used: Chesapeake Bay and the C&D Canal.

Blacks on the Chesapeake

As mentioned previously, the Chesapeake and Delaware Canal (C & D Canal) is a 13.6-mile waterway that cuts the Delmarva Peninsula in half between Chesapeake City, in Maryland, and Reedy Point, in Delaware, connecting Chesapeake Bay with the Delaware River at a point approximately ten miles below Wilmington, the home of Thomas Garrett. Peter Dalleo reports that many Negroes worked on the construction of the C & D Canal. He also reports:

> Joe Finney of Kent County, Delaware, was part of an organized network of small craft that operated in small inlets near Little Creek and may have carried away dozens of runaways to freedom. These free black men and women built the groundwork for their late antebellum successors such as Samuel D. Burris, a school teacher near Camden, and William Brinkley who also operated in the southern counties.[13]

However, ship captains were also among the contributors to Thomas Garrett's total of runaways. This should not be surprising since, as Dalleo reports, many free blacks worked in various capacities on board the numerous ships that plied the waters of Chesapeake Bay, running between Philadelphia, Wilmington, Norfolk and Richmond, Virginia, and Baltimore. He writes:

> African Americans in both the city and in southern communities apparently took advantage of maritime opportunities. In Wilmington, jobs held by free blacks included a bargeman, boatman, fishermen, seaman, stevedore, waterman [to which we can add master of a vessel], and an unspecified activity related to oysters. African Americans near places such as the Indian River or Assawoman Bay in Sussex County, employed canoes, bateaux, "saltwater rowboats," and simple hand-nets to catch

migratory fish such as herring and shad, or they dug for oysters and raked for clams.[14]

So we may assume that runaways using the Chesapeake as their escape route would likely find sympathy among the free black sailors and watermen, along the Virginia and Maryland eastern shore of the Chesapeake, as well as on the numerous and various vessels that plied her waters. Charles L. Blockson reports:

> Many slaves found refuge in vessels sailing from the ports of Annapolis and Baltimore, while others were transported in small boats on the Chesapeake Bay into the Susquehanna River and delivered to waiting conductors in Pennsylvania.[15]

In an analysis of the first 202 cases—among the 745—that are in William Still's book, he reported runaways escaped in schooners, steamers and skiffs. Of others, he is not specific. He states that they simply escaped in "boats" or "vessels." Of those 202 cases, I counted 44 runaways who escaped in one of those vessels. Still reports that they came from Petersburg, Richmond, Portsmouth and Norfolk, Virginia, as well as from Baltimore, Maryland. Sheridan Ford, a slave in Portsmouth, Virginia, escaped by steamer from Richmond to Philadelphia, writes Still.[16] In May of 1854, Clarissa Davis escaped from Portsmouth, Virginia, with two of her brothers. They managed to make it to freedom. She did not. So she hid away for 75 days, then, dressed as a man, boarded the steamship, *The City of Richmond,* where she was secreted in a box by a young man who himself had a wife in slavery. She thus made it safely to Philadelphia where, by the advice of the Vigilance Committee, she changed her name to Mary D. Armstead and eventually joined her brothers in New Bedford, Massachusetts.[17]

In November of that same year, Anthony Blow, alias Henry Levinson, also arrived at the office of the Vigilance Committee in Philadelphia. He, too, was secreted aboard *The City of Richmond* by a friend named Minkins who was employed on that steamship. Still reports that Anthony was previously accused of being in "the schooner, *Pearl,* with Captain Drayton's memorable seventy runaways on board, bound for Canada."[18]

Although it was possible to assist a larger number of runaways at one time by boat, it was also a very risky business. The punishment was severe for the ship captains who dared to do so, if caught. A case in point is that of a white captain named Robert Lee, who piloted four runaways, three males and one female, from Portsmouth, Virginia, safely to the Vigilance Committee in a skiff.[19]

"Unfortunately," says Still, "Captain Lee was suspected, ... tried, convicted and torn from his wife and two little children, and sent to the Richmond Penitentiary for twenty five years." Before being sent to the penitentiary, Captain Lee spent ten days in prison in Portsmouth, where five lashes each day were laid heavily on his back. "The further sufferings of poor Lee and his heart-broken wife are too painful for recital," writes Still.

In this city [Philadelphia] the friends of freedom did all in their power to comfort Mrs. Lee, and administered aid to her and her children; but she broke down under her mournful fate, and went to that bourne whence no traveler ever returns .... Captain Lee suffered untold misery in prison until he, also, not a great while before the Union forces took possession Richmond, sank beneath the severity of his treatment and went likewise to the grave.[20]

In 1855, a Captain "B" actually ran a business of assisting runaways to freedom, charging them a fee of $100 each. "His risk was very great," says Still.

"On this account he claimed, as did certain others, that it was no more than fair to charge for his services...."[21] At one time the owners of three runaways, unaware that Captain "B" had taken them to Canada, offered him $2,000 to retrieve them.

He declined the offer.[22] However, in June of 1857, Still received a letter from J. H. Hill informing him that Captain "B" was taken prisoner in Virginia. He was caught with runaway slaves aboard his vessel.[23]

Still reports that the Negro porter, Minkin, frequently hid runaways in a room he built behind the boiler on the ship where he worked as a porter.

Sarah Bradford relates one story where Harriet Tubman used a boat as a means of rescuing a female slave named Tilly. According to Bradford, the location of the boat they were to take was on the Chesapeake.[24]

So Chesapeake Bay, with its willing ship captains and African American sailors and maritime workers, was an ideal area for slaves who, as William Still said, "valued freedom more than slavery." However, the distance down the Chesapeake, around the Delmarva Peninsula, up the Atlantic Ocean side of the Eastern Shore to Wilmington, and from there to Pennsylvania is about several hundred miles. Hence the runaways, if possible, would more than likely seek the shortest and most ideal route: up the Chesapeake, through the Back Creek branch of the Elk River, and through the Chesapeake Canal. Such a journey, if successful, would land them approximately ten miles below Wilmington, the home of Thomas Garrett.

Throughout his letters to William Still, Thomas Garrett mentions runaways brought to him who had traveled by boat.[25] There were two ship captains Thomas Garrett is known to have used: Captain Alfred Fountain and Captain Lambdin. Priscilla Thompson believes both Fountain and Lambdin were residents of Wilmington.[26] Fountain, particularly, was an intimidating force. Still describes him as "no ordinary man ... ."

> Although he had been living a sea-faring life for many years, and the marks of his calling were plainly enough visible in his manners and speech, he was nevertheless unlike the great mass of this class of men, not addicted to intemperance and profanity. On the contrary, he was a man of thought and possesses, in a large measure, those human traits of character which lead men to sympathized with suffering humanity wherever met with.
>
> It must be admitted however, that the first impression gathered from a hasty survey of his rough and rugged appearance, his large head, large mouth, large eyes, and heavy eyebrows, with a natural gift at keeping concealed the inner-workings of his

mind and feelings, were not calculated to inspire the belief, that he was fitted to be entrusted with the lives of unprotected females and helpless children; that he could take pleasure in risking his own life to rescue them from the hell of Slavery; that he could deliberately enter the enemy's domain, and with the faith of a martyr, face the dreaded slave-holder, with his Bowie knives and revolvers— Slave-hunters, and blood-hounds, lynchings and penitentiaries, for humanity's sake. But his deeds proved him to be a true friend of the Slave; whilst his skill, bravery, and success stamped him as one of the most daring and heroic captains ever connected with the Underground Rail Road cause.[27]

Of the 44 cases in the 202 mentioned in which runaways escaped by a boat, the greater portion of them were brought to Thomas Garrett by Captain Fountain.[28] On one occasion Captain Fountain brought 28 runaways to Still at one time! During the war, however, Fountain was finally suspected of harboring runaways. To prevent him from furthering this activity, his boat was impounded and burned at Norfolk, Virginia. He then, in his own intense hatred of slavery, joined the Union Army.[29]

Captain Lambdin, however, did not fare as well. According to Garrett, he was caught hiding runaways on his boat, tried and convicted and given a sentence of ten years in the penitentiary. Garrett and Philadelphia abolitionist, Passmore Williamson, rushed to his aid and gave his wife money.

Another ship captain, Jonathan Walker, had both his hands branded—an "S" burned into each hand for helping seven runaways escape to the Bahamas aboard his ship. He was told that the "S" stood for "Slave Stealer." However, Walker toured the country lecturing about his ordeal and told his audience that both "S's" stood for "Slave Savior."

Dalleo tells the story of a black ship captain who was arrested for not having one white man aboard his ship:

> African American sailors who ventured away from Delaware waters also assumed political risks. In 1848, Jesse Mode, captain of an all black crew out of Wilmington, ventured to Swan Creek in Maryland to pick up a load of logs for a Pennsylvania buyer. Because Maryland law required at least one white man on board a vessel manned by blacks, Mode and his crew endured arrest, imprisonment and a fine. Only the intercession of Thomas Garrett secured their release, and Garrett went to his aid.[30]

Wilmington's Underground Railroad

There were other UGRR workers in Wilmington besides Thomas Garrett who helped runaways escape. Among these were individual blacks and whites. Garrett frequently mentions his black helpers in Wilmington, as well as in the two lower counties of Delaware—Kent and Sussex. They carried messages about his activities to William Still and J. Miller McKim at the Pennsylvania Anti-slavery Society in

Philadelphia. But they also served as station masters and conductors, sheltering and transporting runaways to black and white communities, mainly in Chester County, as well as in Philadelphia. Garrett mentions these men in his letters. To William Still, he wrote:

> Thee may take Harry Craig by the hand as a brother, true to the cause. He is one of our most efficient aids on the railroad, and worthy of full confidence.[31]

Garrett apparently consulted with Harry Craig. He wrote to Still:

> After conferring with Harry Craig, we have concluded to send five or six of them [runaways] to-night in the cars, and the balance, if these go safe, to-morrow night, or in the steam boat on Second day [Monday] morning, directed to the anti-slavery office.[32]

Of Severn Johnson, he wrote:

> This morning I send to thy care four of God's poor. Severn Johnson, a true man, will go with them to-night by rail to thy house.[33]

Severn Johnson also undertook to have the runaways washed and cleaned before carrying them on.[34]

George Wilmer, on the other hand, was still a slave when Garrett used him. Garrett wrote to Still:

> The bearer of this, George Wilmer, is a slave, whose residence is in Maryland. He is a true man and a forwarder of slaves. [He] has passed some twenty-five within four months.[35]

Garrett considered Joseph Hamilton to be another one of his most efficient aids in forwarding slaves: "His house being a regular stopping place." However, Hamilton got into trouble when stolen money was put into his pocket without his knowledge. He was sentenced to be whipped with 20 lashes, stand in the pillory one hour and fined $30.00 and cost. If he did not pay the fine and cost within 30 days, he would receive a seven-year prison sentence out of state. Garrett visited Hamilton in prison and assured him that he would pay the fine.[36]

Comegys Munson was a black mason in Wilmington and active on the UGRR as both a station master and conductor. Garrett wrote to Still, "We have here in this place, at Comegys Munson's, an old colored woman, the mother of twelve children, one half of which has been sold South. She has been so ill-used, that she was compelled to leave husband and children behind, and is desirous of getting to a brother who lives at Buffalo … . Comegys Munson says he can leave his work and will go with her to thy house."[37]

Priscilla Thompson mentions that one of Thomas Garrett's helpers was Patrick Holland, an Irish-born Catholic who lived with Garrett's son, Henry, and owned a livery stable close to the bridge across the Christina River.³⁸ Thompson believes that Garrett used Holland's livery stable to hire horse and carriage to transport runaways. Garrett also received help from some Irish Catholics and that "Patrick Holland was undoubtedly one of those Irish Catholics, and certainly his livery stable was involved in many slave escapes...."³⁹ Isaac Flint, Benjamin Webb and his two sons, William and Edward, were among the white abolitionists in Wilmington who were active UGRR workers with Thomas Garrett.

So Thomas Garrett had a number of UGRR helpers, black and white, in Wilmington. But there was more:

The African American Churches

Of the Underground Railroad in Delaware, Charles Blockson writes:

> Most historians and other writers in the past failed to report the important contribution of the African American churches and their connection with the underground railroad. Their ministers were noteworthy leaders and their churches were used as stations. Their contributions were all the more significant because active abolitionists were few among white congregations in Delaware.⁴⁰

Among the African American ministers who were significant in Underground Railroad work in Wilmington was Peter Spencer. Historian James E. Newton reports that Spencer was born a slave in Kent County, Maryland, in 1782, and was set free when his master died. During the early 1800s, Spencer took up roots in Wilmington where he received a basic education and found some financial success as a mechanic.⁴¹ Spencer built the Mother African Union Protestant Church in 1813 and, "through his impressive personality and moral conviction," says Blockson, "established it as a major stop on the road to freedom. His congregation provided food, clothing and shelter to scores of escaping slaves."⁴² Aside from being a devoted family man, writes Newton, "Spencer was also a father figure and friend to numerous blacks in Wilmington." "Father Spencer," as he became known,

> ...inaugurated the tradition of establishing the last Sunday in August as a time for a general reunion and religious revival—popularly known as "August Quarterly"—the day of jubilation. It originated in 1814 and is Delaware's oldest folk festival. It is also one of 19th-century America's few black religious festivals. Black workers, slave and free, were given time off to attend the festivities. The occasion served as a "homecoming" for many from the neighboring states of Maryland and Pennsylvania. The celebration included preaching, singing, dancing, and offered opportunities to worship, meet friends and relatives, and commemorate the founding and founder of African Union Methodism.⁴³

Newton also reports that Spencer engaged in a host of pro-black activities, including his support of the Underground Railroad in Delaware under the helm of station master Thomas Garrett. It is reputed that Spencer's church was involved in the network to assist runaway slaves. During the "August Quarterly," slaves "used the Mother Church as the starting point for escape to all points North."

Another important African American abolitionist in Wilmington was Abraham Schadd. According to Newton:

> Abraham D. Schadd was probably born in Mill Creek Hundred [Delaware] in 1801. He was a staunch black abolitionist dedicated to ending slavery. Abraham Schadd was the father of 13 children and earned a successful living as a shoemaker, a trade he learned from his father. He acquired property in Wilmington, which reflected of his business skills ... .
>
> Schadd also served as a delegate to the American Anti-Slavery Society (1835, 1836). A clear indication of his commitment and leadership, Schadd was elected president of the National Convention in 1833. As president of that body, he emphasized education, thrift, and hard work to improve the conditions of blacks. In 1816, soon after the American Colonization Society was organized, Abraham Schadd joined with other black leaders such as William Anderson and Peter Spencer to organize forces against the "colonization scheme."

In his biographical sketch of Abraham Schadd, Newton concludes that "his deeds and actions for fellow humans entitles him to be ranked among the top black leaders of the 19th century."[44]

Schadd later relocated to West Chester, Pennsylvania, where he became an active participant on the UGRR. Schadd's oldest daughter, Mary Ann, born in 1823 — the year after Thomas Garrett moved to Wilmington — was educated at a Quaker-based school in West Chester and went on to become a noted educator, lawyer, and journalistcator, lawyer, and journalist. She apparently returned to Wilmington where she became an instructor for black youth in Wilmington.[45] She later taught school in Norristown, Pennsylvania, and then Trenton, New Jersey.[46] In the 1850s, she emigrated to Canada where she founded her own newspaper, *The Provincial Freeman*, making her the first black woman to publish and edit a newspaper in North America.

Historian Benjamin Quarles writes that "in 1857 Wilmington, Delaware, had two schools supported by Negroes, with considerable assistance from Quaker Thomas Garrett, who purchased the land site and hired the building contractor."[47] However, there is no mention of Abraham or Mary Ann Schadd, or Peter Spencer, or the African Union Protestant Church and its activities as an UGRR station, in Thomas Garrett's correspondence.

Chester County

Earlier, when we spoke of Thomas Garrett's importance as a station master, we noted that his location, Wilmington, Delaware, was significant in determining his importance as a station master. This was primarily because of Wilmington's close proximity to the lower counties of Pennsylvania (Delaware, Chester, Lancaster and York). Among these, Chester County was the one used mostly by Garrett. "Although Chester County was not necessarily a safe haven for runaways," says Kashatus, "it was, on the other hand, a hotbed of numerous anti-slavery individuals and communities." Kashatus notes that Chester County also contained many black and white UGRR workers, as well as those of different faiths. He lists 132 UGRR agents in that county. Thirty-one were African American (three women and 28 men), and 101 were white (27 women and 74 men). Of those 132 agents, Kashatus was able to identify the religion of 107 of them. They were:

Quakers = 82
Presbyterians = 9
African Methodist Episcopalian = 8
African Union Methodist Protestant = 5
Episcopalian = 2
Baptist = 1[48]

As previously mentioned, Abraham Schadd and his family relocated from Wilmington, Delaware, to West Chester, Pennsylvania. Kashatus picks it up from there and writes:

> The most noted West Chester Agent ... Was Abraham Schadd, a mulatto shoemaker who was also known to conduct runaways to [Quaker] Samuel Painter's station .... By 1839 [Schadd] and his wife, Harriet had saved enough money to purchase a small farm, which they opened as a station on the northern branch of the Underground Railroad, leading out of Wilmington.[49]

Kashatus also lists Thomas Brown, John Smith and Benjamin Freeman as "aggressive black UGRR conductors in West Chester."[50]

In her two monographs about Kennett Square, *The Trackless Trail*, and *The Trackless Trail Leads On*, Frances Cloud Taylor also notes the contributions of African American UGRR workers who helped Thomas Garrett. For example, "A black man by the name of Jackson," writes Taylor, "often brought women and children to the Kennett Square home of the Quakers, John and Hannah Cox, from Thomas Garrett. Jackson also kept the Coxes informed about pursuing slave hunters."[51] Taylor also notes "James Walker, a freed Negro who lived on South Union Street in the Borough of Kennett Square, who often helped Thomas Garrett in his anti-slavery activities."[52]

Kashatus lists the Quakers, Moses and Mary Pennock and their son, Samuel, and Mahlon and Mary Brosius and their sons, Edwin and Daniel, to whom Garrett sent runaways. Frances Cloud Taylor reports that Garrett sent runaways to the homes of Isaac and Thamazine Meredith Pennock, Eusebius Barnard, Allen Agnew, and John and Lydia Agnew, all in Chester County.

Dr. R.C. Smedley, in his seminal work, *History of the Underground Railroad in Chester and the Neighboring Counties of Pennsylvania*, reports of numerous agents in

Chester County who received runaways from Thomas Garrett: Probably the first stop was at the home of his in-laws, Isaac and Dinah Mendinhall. He writes:

> The home of Isaac and Dinah Mendinhall, in Kennett township, near Longwood, ten miles from Wilmington, was always open to receive the liberty-seeking slave. Their station being nearest the Delaware line was eagerly sought by fugitives as soon as they entered the Free State. They were generally sent by Thomas Garrett, of Wilmington, who, starting them on the road, directed them to "go on and on until they came to a stone-gate post, and then turn in." Sometimes he sent a note by them saying, "I send you three," [or four or five, as the case might be?] "bales of black wool," which was to assure them that these colored persons were not impostors. No record was kept of the number they aided but during a period of thirty-four years it amounted to several hundred.[53]

Of Micajah and William A. Speakman, Smedley writes:

> Of the hundreds of fugitives who passed through the hands of Micajah and William A. Speakman in Wallace township, Chester county, as in the instance of many other agents, no record was kept nor any effort made to learn of them concerning their bondage and escape ... . Slaves came to their place from Maryland and Virginia, through the hands of Thomas Garrett, Lindley Coates, Daniel Gibbons, Thomas Whitson, Gravner Marsh and others ... .[54]

Of Dr. Bartholomew Fussell, he writes:

> Dr. Fussell was an intimate friend of Thomas Garrett, of Wilmington, and laboring in connection with him and many others at available points, *about two thousand fugitives passed through his hands on their way to freedom.*[55] [italics added]

They were no doubt helped by an old Negro named "Davy." Davy sold fruit, fish and other commodities that he purchased in Delaware and sold in Kennett Square. He "became a very important person between Thomas Garrett and Dr. Fussell," writes Smedley. Davy's frequent journeys between the two locations made him well-known by everyone, and therefore he aroused no suspicion, "not only when he was accompanied by friends of his own color, either by day or night. There can be no doubt that many loads other than fish or peaches, came in the dark from Thomas Garrett's to the house of Dr. Fussell, and was forwarded by him in safety."[56]

Another Negro agent was Joseph G. Walker, who, also at the age of 76, was one of Thomas Garrett's principal assistants in the removal of fugitives out of Wilmington to safe routes northward.

> During one fall he took away one hundred and thirty slaves and on one occasion he went with seven. From three o'clock in the afternoon until six o'clock next morning he walked over sixty miles; he did complain a little of this, however, and said he would not do it again in the same time. His father was a West Indian and his mother was English or Scotch; hence his inherited powers of locomotion and endurance.[57]

Smedley also reports that Eusebius and Sarah Barnard of Pocopsin, Chester County, received runaways from Garrett,[58] as did Graceanna Lewis and her sisters,[59] and Chandler and Hannah Darlington,[60] and Benjamin and Hannah Kent.

Charles Blockson reports that, along with Lewis Peart, Elijah Pennypacker of Phoenixville, Chester County, "hid hundreds of slaves in the Valley Forge vicinity, in Montgomery County, while they were on their way to freedom in Canada."[61] Since Thomas Garrett is known to have sent runaways to Pennypacker (see Letter to William Still, No. 8), the question is, how many did he send to him, a few, or hundreds?

However, as in Wilmington and in other parts of the country, it was the African American churches that played perhaps the most significant role in the UGRR. "Among the earliest and most active black churches in Chester County was Hosanna in Upper Oxford Township, organized in 1829."[62] According to Kashatus, the church began as "a small, red-brick meeting house ... built on land donated by Edward Walls, a tree black farmer. Hosanna would later become dedicated as a Union Methodist Protestant Church...."

> Walls and his two brothers, William and George, were one of twelve property-owning free black families who settled the small community of Hinsonville, one of many small black settlements which sprang up along the southeastern border of Pennsylvania in the 1840s as sanctuaries for fugitives from Virginia, Maryland and Delaware.
> According to local tradition, Samuel Glasgow, Thomas Amos and the Walls brothers were among the active black agents on the Underground Railroad, during the 1840s, and often used Hosanna as a station, hiding fugitives in a tunnel concealed beneath the pulpit. They were especially busy on Saturday evenings when anti-slavery meetings were held at the church. Hosanna was a transfer point for runaways going west to Christiana, a free black community in neighboring Lancaster County .... Among the white station masters who assisted them were Edward Webb, a Presbyterian minister, and Alice and Charles Hambleton, a Quaker couple who lived in nearby Penn's Grove.[63]

The Bethel AME was another black church in West Chester that was involved in UGRR activity.

In summary, there is no tangible evidence to support Thomas Garrett's claim that he helped 2,700 runaways escape. His personal totals are subjective and unverifiable. The documented accounts of those he helped (i.e., sent to William Still) are far too insufficient in number to validate his claim. And the reports of the UGRR agents in Chester and the neighboring counties of Pennsylvania are, at best, secondary sources of information. We may not doubt their veracity, but we cannot substantiate them either. For example, R. C. Smedley reports that the number of runaways Garrett sent to Dr. Bartholomew Fussell in Chester County, was "two thousand." He also reports that Joseph G. Walker was one of Thomas Garrett's principal assistants in the removal of fugitives out of Wilmington and that, during one fall, he took away 130 slaves, and on one occasion he went with seven. These and other UGRR agents, reports Smedley, received "hundreds" of runaways from Garrett. Taken at face value, those figures do support Garrett's claim that he helped 2,700 runaways escape. However, there is no evidence to substantiate those figures. Who were those runaways? When did Garrett send them? When did Fussell and the other agents receive them? We do not have that specific information. The most we can say then is that Thomas Garrett probably did indeed help a large number of runaways escape. However, into that large number we must, in all fairness, include the vital assistance given to him by the black and white individuals in Wilmington — Severn Johnson, Harry Craig, Joseph Hamilton, Comegys Munson, Davy Moore, Patrick Holland, Isaac Flint, Benjamin Webb and his two sons, and many others. We must include the major role played by the black churches in Wilmington and in Chester and Delaware County. We must include the contributions made to him by the other station masters and conductors, black and white, of many faiths, who operated all along the Eastern Shore, from Cape Charles, Virginia, to New Castle, Delaware. We must especially include the ship captains, Fountain and Lambdin, as well as the unnamed black maritime workers, oystermen and watermen of the Chesapeake and the C&D Canal. All of these individuals and establishments most surely made significant contributions to the total number of runways Thomas Garrett said he assisted, and some of them paid dearly with their lives in doing so.

But in the final analysis we may also say that, apparently to the runaway slaves, it really made no difference whether the number Garrett said he helped was actually 2,700. Those who came to Thomas Garrett for assistance *received* it, whether they were runaway slaves or free blacks. When they were in need, he gave them food, clothes, money, shoes, a place to hide, protection. When they were in trouble, he personally went to their aid. He provided money and land to educate black children. He pledged that he would never resist an opportunity to assist a runaway to freedom, and many of them found their freedom because of him, and they obviously didn't care of the numbers he claimed, as long as they or their people were among them. That, no doubt, is why they claimed they felt just as safe when they reached Thomas Garrett's house as if they were in Canada. And after the signing of the 15th Amendment, giving Negroes the right to vote, the Negroes in Wilmington carried him through the streets in an open barouche with a sign labeled "*Our* Moses" [italics added]. And that is very significant when one considers that the appellation, "Moses," was given to a Negro woman — Harriet Tubman, the most outstanding conductor on the UGRR. So then what were those Negroes saying, or what were they feeling, when they referred to Thomas Garrett as their Moses? We may get some idea of this from their actions when he died. And no one can tell us of this better then the Reverend William P. Tilden.

14

The End of the Line

On Wednesday, January 25, 1871, Thomas Garrett died. "At last his strong frame began to fail him," said William P. Tilden, in his Memorial Address. "He suffered much at times but calmly waited for the hour of release. To a beloved and trusted servant in the family, he said one morning, 'Come in, come in; I am still here, waiting, waiting. I have lived to see my Divine Master's will accomplished. My mission is ended. I am ready to go.'" Brave, but humble, he was not priding himself on what he had done, but rejoicing that his Divine Master's will was accomplished.

"A little later he said to a friend: 'All is peace within, but no rest,' alluding to his physical suffering. Shortly after, he crossed the River, and the peace was crowned with rest."

"The funeral was simple and plain in its arrangements, after the manner of the Society of Friends, of which he was a birthright member.

"There was only one thing to distinguish it from other funerals, and that was the outpouring of the people of every creed, color and condition. For an hour or two before the time for the procession to leave the house, there was a constant stream of people passing into it, to take a last look at the familiar and beloved face. I am told that many were impressed with the peaceful and glorified look. The lines of age had vanished, and the manly prime came back with a restful smile. He seemed like a conqueror taking his rest after the great battle of life had been fought and won.

"Arrangements had been made that his colored friends should bear his body to the grave. It was their earnest desire to give this expression of their honor and love, and he was glad to have it so. The arrangement was made before he died. It seems most fitting [that] after giving his life so largely to the rescue of fugitives from slavery, that the free representatives of an emancipated people should bear his body to the field of peace. But how should they do it? One of the men who still survives the story, told me that they first thought of using the hearse and pulling it by hand. But that seemed too distant and cold. They would come closer to him. They would bear him on their shoulders.

"So the body was laid on a bier, and eight strong men were selected from their number to take the bier, four at a time, on their shoulders. And so he was borne: slowly and tenderly, through the crowded streets, the family and friends; and a long procession on foot, following.

"The Friends Meeting House was already nearly filled, [and] after the bier [was] rested in front of the speaker's seats, the crowd pressed in, filling every niche. It is said that 1,500 people pressed within the doors, while a greater number remained outside. The vast audience was silent. The serene face, touched with the peace of Heaven, was before them in the place where for many years he had come to sit in silent thought and worship. How many a good deed he had planned in those silent seasons, no one can tell. It is said that some of the most touching scenes in *Uncle Tom's Cabin* came to Mrs. Stowe at the communion service. Here, in this plain Meeting House, where the bread of life was broken invisibly, and the cup of self-sacrifice poured with no witness but God and the soul, it is reasonable to suppose that our great-hearted hero saw visions and dreamed dreams of help for the panting slave that, afterward, were put into act in the strength of the Lord.

"When there was silence in the vast assembly, the venerable Lucretia Mott rose, and paid such a tribute to his noble life and heroic labors, as only that Quaker saint could. Aaron M. Powell of New York, William Howard Day, an eloquent colored man, Rev. Alfred Cookman of the Grace M.E. Church, and T. Clarkson Taylor, paid tender and unqualified tributes to his heroism and nobleness.

"William Lloyd Garrison, in a letter to Henry Garrett, wrote:

> If it were not for the inclemency of the weather, and the delicate state of my health, I would hasten to be at the funeral, long as the distance is, not indeed as a mourner, for in view of his ripe old age and singularly beneficent life, there is no cause for sorrow, but to express the estimation in which I held him, as one of the best men who ever walked on earth, and one of the most beloved among my numerous friends and co-workers in the cause of an oppressed and down-trodden race, now happily rejoicing in their heaven-wrought deliverance ... .
>
> His career was full of a dramatic interest from beginning to end, and crowded with experiences and vicissitudes, most eventful. What he promised, he fulfilled; what he attempted, he seldom or never failed to accomplish; what he believed, he dared to proclaim upon the housetop; what he ardently desired and incessantly longed for, was the reign of universal peace and righteousness. He was among the manliest of men and the gentlest of spirits. There was no form of suffering that did not touch his heart; but his abounding sympathy was especially drawn out toward the poor, imbruted, slaves of the plantations, and such of their number who sought their freedom by flight. The thousands who passed safely through his hands to Canada and the North will never forget his fatherly solicitude for their welfare, or the danger he unflinchingly encountered in their behalf.

"His body rests under the green sod — green even in mid-winter, in the peaceful graveyard attached to the Friends' Meeting House. Only a humble stone, six inches high, such as the Friends allow, with only his name and the date of his birth and death,

Harriet Tubman/Thomas Garrett Memorial Plaque in Peter Spencer Plaza, Wilmington, Delaware. (Photograph by the author, James McGowan.)

Thomas Garrett's gravestone.

marks the spot. The visitor must push aside the grass to find it. But a beautiful, vigorous, oak tree, planted soon after his burial, directly over, has already become a tree thirty or forty feet high, in whose wide spread and rapidly growing branches the Spring birds sing their happy songs and are invited, the sweet quiet around, to build their nests and rear their young. Better than any marble shaft, chiseled all over with eulogy, is this monument of Nature's own to the memory of one so simply and unselfishly consecrated to the welfare of his fellow-man.[1]

"Wilmington cannot afford to forget such a man; the state of Delaware cannot afford to forget him. His is indissolubly linked with her history. He was born with the Nation. He grew up an implicit believer of the Declaration of Independence, and the Golden Rule, giving, as the years rolled on, the fullness of his strength, the ripeness of his manhood to our second crowning Revolution, the Revolution that gave freedom to four millions of human beings held as chattels under the Stars and Stripes, and made it possible for 'Liberty and Union' to remain 'One and inseparable now and forever.'

"Such men will be sure of being held in ever-increasing honor, as the world rises to a clearer and clearer perception of the beauty and glory of self-sacrificing love for man."[2]

The Garrett home at 227 Shipley Street no longer exists. The narrow, slanted street where it once stood is no longer a highway of refuge for fugitive slaves, no longer a battleground between freedom and bondage, no longer the command post where one man, moved to action by the feelings the Almighty planted in his breast, inspired others to join him to ultimately win the fight to liberate those people he called "God's poor." Today, on the corner of Shipley and West Streets, only a short distance from where once stood the Garrett home, is the Delaware Technical and Community College. On that same corner, on Friday, August 20, 1993, at 10:30 A.M., the State of Delaware, Division of Historical and Cultural Affairs, and the Harriet Tubman Historical Society presented the unveiling of a Thomas Garrett Historical Marker. At 11:00 A.M., a program and reception followed at the Wilmington Friends' Meeting House on 4th and West Streets, Dr. James Newton was the keynote speaker. Later that day, in the Quaker tradition, a silent vigil was held at the plain and simple gravestone marking the final resting place, the end of the line, for Wilmington's great Station Master.

15

Letters to William Still & J. Miller McKim

Undoubtedly, the most important testimony as to what Thomas Garrett did, why he did it, and what he thought and felt about what he did lies in his letters. During his lifetime he was not interviewed, and he left no records of his activities. However, he did write to the local newspaper, *The Blue Hen's Chicken*, largely about his trial and his views concerning slavery. He also wrote to Harriet Tubman's first biographer, Sarah Bradford, giving her his views of Harriet Tubman. Hence we are fortunate that Thomas Garrett was in the habit of writing letters. Not only are they the best source of information that we have about him, they are the most reliable. Most of the accounts of his life are inaccurate and secondhand. For example, William Still's book, *The Underground Railroad*, contains a sketch of Garrett's life, but most of the information in Still's book is material reprinted from the local newspaper, *The Wilmington Daily Commercial*, which inaccurately states the year Garrett moved to Wilmington, as well as being wrong about his first wife's first name. *Friends in Wilmington* also fails to mention Garrett's three daughters in the genealogy (see page 148 of that book).

I will assume that some readers will wish to examine the original Garrett letters. Although this can be a pleasant and rewarding experience, it can sometimes be a frustrating one, particularly if, like myself, one approaches it without a knowledge of some of the peculiarities in the handwriting of earlier periods. For this reason I would like to alert the traveler into this territory to some of the difficulties that I encountered, with the hopes that it will make his or her journey a little easier.

The following is a sample of Thomas Garrett's handwriting. He wrote with the flourishing script found in much of the writing of the 19th century (and before). On a few of his letters, his handwriting could very well be called beautiful. However, this sample is not the best representative. It was chosen because it contains most of his writing peculiarities.

A sample of Thomas Garrett's handwriting.

I ask the reader to note the way the first letter "s" is formed in the word "passed" (on the fifth line from the top), and the same letter in the word "Happiness" (fifteenth line). This way of writing the small letter "s"—so that it looks like an "f"—is found in all of Garrett's words in which there is a double "ss." I also found this particular letter formation in the letters of Garrett's friends and contemporaries (Lucretia Mott and Parker Pillsbury, for example), as well as in actual *printed* material. Until I became familiar with this, of course, it was a problem to interpret. After spending many hours (often frustrating ones) deciphering these words, I came across a little book entitled, *The Handwriting of American Records for a Period of 300 Years*, by E. Kay Kirkham, which reveals these peculiarities. I regret that I did not come across this book earlier. To the reader interested in examining the original Garrett letters, I recommend this book.

Another peculiarity in Garrett's writing is in the small letter "d." When this letter is a terminal letter (such as in the word "and"), it is finished with what Kirkham describes as a "right-left-flourish" (note the letter "d" in the word "and," on the second line). In many of Garrett's letters, this flourish is so exaggerated that it swings back and almost embodies the entire word; and sometimes, if the word happens to have an "l" in it, the flourish would cause the "l" to be mistaken for a "t." An example of this is in the word "would," on the ninth line. According to Kirkham, this way of writing the small letter "d" can be traced back to the 1600s.

In reading the original Garrett letters, one will note that, in the fashion of his day, Garrett also capitalized quite freely, seemingly without fixed rules. It appears that when he wanted to place emphasis on a word, he would occasionally underline that word, but most of the time he would capitalize the word. An example is the word "Happiness" on line 15. He also capitalized names of places and events that he thought were important. For example, when speaking of his own house (in a letter to William Lloyd Garrison—Letter No.2), he capitalized "House," and "Home." In another instance, to Samuel May, Jr., he capitalized the word "Gladly," in expressing his enthusiasm to open his house to his friends. The word "Slaves" is capitalized both times it is used (lines 4 and 9), as well as the word "Seven" (line 5). It may be argued that such was Garrett's way of making the small letter "s." However, if the reader will compare the *size* of the letter "s" in the words "Slaves" and "Seven" with that of the words "so" (line 10), "sincere" (line 14) and "sincerely" (line 16), he will note that the difference in size is in favor of the letter "s" in "Slaves" and "Seven" being capitals. And there are many other instances of this to be found in Garrett's writing. At other times in his writing, in referring to these very same things, Garrett would use small letters.

This looseness was also used by Garrett in his punctuation. He made excessive use of commas, sometimes to a point where it becomes difficult to grasp a single thought. Then again, at other instances, he would run on for many sentences without a comma, almost without a period. Sometimes his periods looked like commas, and at such times it becomes difficult to determine where one sentence ends and the other begins. Garrett would also begin a sentence with a small letter. He very seldom paragraphed, and was in the habit of using word contractions, such as "Esteem'd," "rec'd," and others.

In transcribing Thomas Garrett's letters, then, it was necessary to do some editing. But I have tried to leave as much as possible of the original intact. I retained most of the original misspellings, sentence structure, abbreviations and contractions. I did add some punctuation—though very little. Of course, many times punctuation had to be added, simply because the original letters from which they were copied were so old and faded that such small things as commas and periods had practically faded out of sight. I do believe that the small liberties I have taken in adding punctuation have not changed any of the original thoughts and meanings.

Where illegibility existed, I chose the word that I thought was originally intended. These, too, were only a few, and I have set them off in brackets with a question mark following the word. On occasion the word will appear so self-evident that perhaps the reader will question why I took the trouble. The reason is, in spite of how self-evident is the word chosen, in the actual handwriting the word is illegible. If the reader feels differently towards the words I have chosen, I welcome his or her opinions and suggestions, and perhaps an addendum may be published which will include these comments.

Letters to William Still and J. Miller McKim

William Still was the last of 18 children of a slave family. His father bought his own freedom and moved from his native Maryland to New Jersey. His mother escaped later and joined the family—forced to leave two children in bondage during her escape. She changed the family name from "Steel" to Still, and her own given name from Sidney to Charity.

In 1844 William Still left the family in New Jersey and moved to Philadelphia. It is said he arrived with only five dollars in his pocket, and no friends, and that he taught himself to read and write.[1]

While in Philadelphia, Still met J. Miller McKim, a former Presbyterian minister and a graduate of Princeton Theological Seminary. "A radical change of opinion on theological questions led (McKim) to sever his connections with the Presbyterian Church,"[2] and in 1840 he was made publishing agent of the Pennsylvania Anti-Slavery Society and later the Corresponding Secretary. He also became editor of *The Pennsylvania Freeman,* the first abolitionist newspaper in Pennsylvania, and had the privilege of accompanying Mrs. John Brown to Harpers Ferry, Virginia, for John Brown's execution and to bring away his body.

Not long after he arrived in Philadelphia, Still also became a member of the Pennsylvania Anti-Slavery Society, and later, this self-taught man was appointed secretary. Through the work of the Society as a whole, the combined efforts of Still and McKim enabled large numbers of runaway slaves to escape to freedom. However, William Still was more closely connected with the runaways than was McKim. Still was appointed chairman of a four-man "Acting Committee" of the Society. As chairman, it was his duty to keep a record of every case claiming the committee's interposition. This duty brought William Still into personal contact with more runaway slaves than perhaps any other person on the eastern route of the UGRR. Not only did he meet and assist those slaves who found their way to his office on their own, but also countless others who were sent to him by Elijah Pennypacker in Phoenixville and Thomas Garrett in Delaware. One writer says that "William Still was awakened hundreds of times in the middle of the night to give refuge to escaping slaves. He kept his big house stocked with food and clothing for the runaways bound for freedom."[3]

Still's descriptions of the runaways came from his personal observations, and his narratives of their backgrounds and escapes were recorded directly from their own lips. These were later published in his book, *The Underground Railroad.*

One of the most outstanding figures on the UGRR was Harriet Tubman, and she naturally appears as a major figure in some of these letters. She was born on a plantation in Dorchester County, Maryland. The year is estimated to be around 1822; the exact day is unknown.

In her youth Harriet Tubman was subjected to the severe hardships and cruelties that were the daily lot of the slaves. Nevertheless, she emerged a woman of great moral courage. While still a young woman, she escaped (alone) to freedom by the UGRR, and then went back again, many times, to inspire and lead many others to escape. Not one person she helped to freedom was ever captured. She became a legend in her own time and was known as "the Moses of her people."

During the Civil War, Harriet Tubman became a scout, a spy, and a nurse for the Union Forces. Although she was a plain, uneducated woman, she was held in the highest esteem by some of the most prominent people of her day. She died in Auburn, New York, on March 10, 1913.

This outstanding conductor on the UGRR was probably the most frequent visitor to the Garrett house at 227 Shipley Street. The close and warm friendship Harriet Tubman had with Thomas Garrett is evidenced throughout Garrett's letters. He spoke, glowingly, of her dangerous excursions into the South, and of her bold and daring feats in bringing her "passengers" to freedom. He often expressed concern and fear for her safety and well-being (See Letters to William Still, Nos. 1, 11, and 32, and Letters to Eliza Wigham and Mary Edmundson, Nos. 2 through 7).

• • •

The following section contains 33 letters. Twenty-three of these are taken from the 1872 edition of William Still's book, *The Underground Railroad*. Letters 19, 20, 21, and 25 through 31 are from other sources, which are given. The letters in this, and all the sections, are arranged chronologically and are also numbered for added convenience.

LETTER NO. 1

Wilmington, 12th mo. 29th, 1854

ESTEEMED FRIEND, J. Miller McKim:

We made arrangements last night, and sent away Harriet Tubman, with six men and one woman to Allen Agnew's, to be forwarded across the country to the city. Harriet, and one of the men had worn their shoes off their feet, and I gave them two dollars to help fit them out, and directed a carriage to be hired at my expense, to take them out, but do not yet know the expense. I now have two more from the lowest county in Maryland, on the Peninsula upwards of one hundred miles. I will try to get one of our trusty colored men take them tomorrow.

— Thomas Garrett

LETTER NO. 2

[Author's Comment:

The following letter is part of the tragic tale of Captain Lambdin (also referred to as "Lambson"— see Letter No. 3), a young schooner captain who was arrested and jailed in Norfolk, Virginia, for helping 21 slaves escape aboard his ship. For more details of the story see page 388 of Still's book, Garrett's letter to Eliza Wigham (No. 2), his letter to J. Miller McKim (No. 20), and his letters to William Still (Nos. 3 and 7).]

Wilmington, 11th mo. 21st, 1855

ESTEEMED FRIEND, Wm. Still:

    Thine of this date, inquiring for the twenty-one, and how they have been disposed of, has just been received. I can only answer by saying, when I parted with them yesterday afternoon, I gave the wife of the person in whose house they were, money to pay her expenses to thy place. I gave her husband money to pay a pilot to start yesterday with the ten men, divided in two gangs; also I had to leave soon after noon yesterday to attend a brother ill with an attack of apoplexy, and today I have been very much engaged. The place they stayed here is a considerable distance off. I will make inquiry to-morrow morning, and in case any other disposition has been made of them than the above I will write thee. I should think they have stopped today, in consequence of the rain, and most likely will arrive safe to-morrow. In haste, thy friend.

— Thos. Garrett

LETTER NO. 3

Wilmington, 12th mo. 19th, 1855

DEAR FRIEND, William Still:

    The bearer of this is one of the twenty-one that I thought had all gone North; he left home on Christmas day, one year since, wandered about the forests of North Carolina for about ten months, and then came here with those forwarded to New Bedford, where he is anxious to go. I have furnished him with a pretty good pair of boots, and gave him money to pay his passage to Philadelphia. He has been at work in the country near here for some three weeks, till taken sick; he is, by no means, well, but thinks he had better try to get further North, which I hope his friends in Philadelphia will aid him to do. I handed this morning Captain Lambson's wife twenty dollars to help fee a lawyer to defend him. She leaves this morning, with her child for Norfolk, to be at the trial before the Commissioner on the 24th instant. Passmore Williamson agreed to raise fifty dollars for him. As none came to hand, and a good chance to send it by his wife, I thought best to advance that much.

Thy friend,
— Thos. Garrett

LETTER NO. 4

Wilmington, 12th mo. 26th, 1855

ESTEEMED FRIEND, Wm. Still:

    The bearer of this, George Wilmer is a slave, whose residence is in Maryland.

He is a true man, and a forwarder of slaves. (He) has passed some twenty-five within four months. He is desirous of finding some of his relations, Wm. Mann and Thomas Carmichael, they passed here about a month since. If thee can give him any information where they can be found thee will much oblige him, and run no risk of their safety in so doing. I remain, as ever, thy sincere friend,

—Thos. Garrett

LETTER NO. 5

Wilmington, 3rd mo. 23rd, 1856

DEAR FRIEND, William Still:

Since I wrote thee this morning informing thee of the safe arrival of the Eight from Norfolk, Harry Craige has informed me, that he has a man from Delaware that he proposes to take along, who arrived since noon. He will take the man, woman and two children from here with him, and the four men will get in at Marcus Hook. Thee may take Harry by the hand as a brother, true to the cause; he is one of our most efficient aids on the Rail Road, and worthy of full confidence. May they all be favored to get on safe. The woman and three children are no common stock. I assure thee finer specimens of humanity are seldom met with. I hope herself and children may be enabled to find her husband, who has been absent some years, and the rest of their days be happy together. I am, as ever thy friend,

—Thos. Garrett

LETTER NO. 6

Wilmington, 3rd mo. 23rd, 1856

DEAR FRIEND, William Still:

Captain Fountain has arrived all safe, with the human cargo thee was inquiring for, a few days since. I had men waiting till 12 o'clock till the Captain arrived at his berth, ready to receive them; last night they then learned, that he had landed them at the rocks, near the old Swedes church, in the care of our efficient Pilot, who is in the employ of my friend, John Hillis, and he has them now in charge. As soon as my breakfast is over, I will see Hillis and determine what is best to be done in their case. My own opinion is we had best send them to Hook and there put them in the cars to-night and send a pilot to take them to thy house. As Marcus Hook is in Pennsylvania, the agent of the cars runs no risk of the fine of five hundred dollars our State imposes for assisting one of God's poor out of the State by steamboat or cars.

As ever thy friend,
—Thos. Garrett

LETTER NO. 7

[Author's Comment:

In the last paragraph of this letter, Garrett refers to the tragic case of Captain

Lambdin, a ship captain who was arrested for hiding runaway slaves aboard his ship. See also Letters Nos. 2, 3, 20, and Letter to Eliza Wigham, No.2. For more details of this case, see William Still's book, page 388.]

Wilmington, 5th mo. 11th, 1856

ESTEEMED FRIENDS, McKim and Still:

I propose sending to-morrow morning by the steamboat a woman and child, whose husband, I think, went some nine months previous to New Bedford. She was furnished with a free passage by the same line her husband came in. She has been away from the person claiming to be her master some five months; we, therefore, think there cannot be much risk at present. Those four I wrote thee about arrived safe up in the neighborhood of Longwood, and Harriet Tubman followed after in the stage yesterday. I shall expect five more from the same neighborhood next trip.

Captain Lambdin is desirous of having sent him a book, or books, with the strongest arguments of the noted men of the South against the institution of slavery, as he wishes to prepare to defend himself, as he has little confidence in his attorney. Cannot you send me something that will be of benefit to him, or send it direct to him? Would not Goodsell's book be of use? His friends here think there is no chance for him but to go to the penitentiary. They now refuse to let anyone but his attorney see him.

As ever, I your friend,
—Thos. Garrett

Letter No. 8

Wilmington, 7th mo. 19th 1856

RESPECTED FRIEND, William Still:

I now have the pleasure of consigning to thy care four able-bodied human *beings* from North Carolina, and five from Virginia, one of which is a girl twelve or thirteen years of age, the rest all men. After thee has seen and conversed with them, thee can determine what is best to be done with them. I am assured they are such as can take good care of themselves. Elijah Pennypacker, some time since, informed me he could find employment in his neighborhood for two or three good hands. I should think that those from Carolina would be about as safe in that neighborhood as any place this side of Canada. Wishing our friends a safe trip, I remain thy sincere friend,

—Thos. Garrett

[P.S.] After conferring with Harry Craig we have concluded to send five or six of them to-night in the cars, and the balance, if those go safe, to-morrow night, or in the steamboat on Second day [Monday] morning, directed to the Anti-Slavery office.

LETTER NO. 9

Wilmington, 11th, mo. 4th, 1856

ESTEEMED FRIENDS, J. Miller McKim and William Still:

Captain F., has arrived here this day with four able-bodied men. One is an engineer, and has been engaged in sawing lumber, a second, a good house carpenter, a third a blacksmith, and the fourth a farm hand. They are now five hundred miles from their home in Carolina, and would be glad to get situations, without *going* far from here. I will keep them till to-morrow. Please inform me whether thee knows of a suitable place *in* the country where the mechanics can find employment at their trades for the winter; let me hear to-morrow, and oblige your friend.

— Thomas Garrett

LETTER NO. 10

[Author's Comment:

The following letter is part of a daring escape by eight slaves (six men and two women) from a jail in Dover, Delaware. William Still gives an account of this escape in his book on page 72, and Garrett describes the part he played in it in some detail in a letter to Mary Edmundson — Letter No.6. Garrett refers to the men as "brothers" and the women as "sisters." Still does not.]

Wilmington, 3rd mo. 13th, 1857

DEAR COUSIN, Samuel Rhoads

I have a letter this day from an agent of the Underground Rail Road, near Dover, in this state, saying I must be on the lookout for six brothers and two sisters, they were decoyed and betrayed, he says by a colored man named Thomas Otwell, who pretended to be their friend, and sent a *white scamp* ahead to wait for them at Dover till they arrived; they were arrested and put in jail there, with Tom's assistance, and some officers. On third day morning [Tuesday] about four o'clock, they broke jail, six of them are secreted in the neighborhood, and the writer has not known what became of the other two. The six were to start last night for this place. I hear that their owners have persons stationed in several places on the road watching. I fear they will be taken. If they could lay quiet for ten days or two weeks, they might then get up safe. I shall have two men sent this evening some four or five miles below to keep them away from this town, and send them (if found, to Chester County). Thee may show this to Still and McKim, and oblige thy cousin,

— Thomas Garrett

LETTER NO. 11

Wilmington, 3rd mo. 27th, 1857

ESTEEMED FRIEND, William Still

I have been very anxious for some time past, to hear what has become of Harriet Tubman. The last I heard of her, she was in the State of New York, on her way to Canada with some friends, last fall. Has thee seen or heard anything of her lately? It would be a sorrowful fact, if such a hero as she, should be lost from the Underground Rail Road. I have just received a letter from Ireland, making inquiry respecting her. If thee gets this in time, and knows anything respecting her, please drop me a line by mail to-morrow, and I will get it next morning if not sooner, and oblige thy friend.

I have heard nothing from the eighth man from Dover, but trust he is safe.

— Thomas Garrett

[Note]
After receiving the above letter, William Still informed Garrett that Harriet Tubman was "all right." He then printed the following reply from Garrett, in which Garrett expresses his satisfaction over the good news about Harriet, and at the same time expresses his sympathy for a runaway slave who had fallen victim to cold weather and, being severely frostbitten, died of lockjaw.

I was truly glad to learn that Harriet Tubman was still in good health and ready for action, but I think there will be more danger at present than heretofore, there is so much excitement below in consequence of the escape of those eight slaves. I was truly sorry to hear of the fate of that poor fellow who had periled so much for liberty. I was in hopes from what thee told me, that he would recover with the loss perhaps of some of his toes.

— Thomas Garrett

LETTER NO. 12

Wilmington, 6th mo. 9th, 1857

ESTEEMED FRIEND, William Still:

We have here in this place, at Comegys Munson's an old colored woman, the mother of twelve children, one half of which has been sold South. She has been so ill-used, that she was compelled to leave husband and children behind, and is desirous of getting to a brother who lives at Buffalo. She was nearly naked. She called at my house on 7th day night [Saturday], but being from home, did not see her till last evening. I have procured her two undergarments, one new; two skirts, one new; a good frock with cape; one of my wife's bonnets and stockings, and gave her five dollars in gold, which, if properly used, will put her well on her way. I also gave her a letter to thee. Since I gave them to her she has concluded to stay where she is till 7th day night, when Comegys Munson says he can leave his work and will go with her to thy house. I write this so that thee may be prepared for them; they ought to arrive between 11 and 12 o'clock. Perhaps thee may find some fugitive that will be willing to accompany her. With desire for thy welfare and the cause of the oppressed, I remain thy friend.

— Thos. Garrett

Letter No. 13

[Author's Comment:

The Captain "F-n-t" Garrett mentions in this letter is most likely the same Captain Fountain he mentions in Letter No. 6, and the Captain "F" he mentions in Letters Nos. 9 and 18.]

Wilmington, 9th mo. 6th, 1857

RESPECTED FRIEND Wm. Still:

This evening I send to thy care four of God's poor. Severn Johnson, a true man, will go with them to-night by rail to thy house. I have given Johnson five dollars, which will pay all expenses, and leave each twenty-five cents. We are indebted to Captain F-n-t for those. May success attend them in their efforts to maintain themselves. Please send word by Johnson whether or no, those seven arrived safe I wrote thee of ten days since. My wife and self were at Longwood today, had a pleasant ride and good meeting. We are as ever thy friend.

—Thos. Garrett

Letter No. 14

Wilmington, 10th mo. 31st, 1857

ESTEEMED FRIEND, William Still :

I write to inform thee that we have either 17 or 27, I am not certain which, of that large gang of God's poor, and I hope they are safe. The man who has them in charge informed me there were 27 safe and one boy lost during last night, about 14 years of age, without shoes; we have felt some anxiety about him, for fear he may be taken up and betray the rest. I have since been informed there are but 17 so that I cannot at present tell which is correct. I have several looking out for the lad; they will be kept from Phila. for the present. My principle object in writing thee at this time is to inform thee of what one of our constables told me this morning; he told me that a colored man in Phila. who professed to be a great friend of the colored was a traitor; that he had been written to by an Abolitionist in Baltimore, to keep a look out for those slaves that left Cambridge this night week, told him they would be likely to pass through Wilmington on 6th day or 7th day [Friday or Saturday] night, and the colored man in Phila. had written to the master of part of them telling him the above, and the master arrived here yesterday in consequence of the information, and told one of our constables the above; the man told the name of the Baltimore writer, which he had forgotten, but declined telling him the name of the colored mart in Phila. I hope you will be able to find out who he is, and should I be able to learn the name of the Baltimore friend, I will put him on his guard, respecting his Phila. correspondents. As ever thy friend, and the friend of Humanity, without regard to color or clime.

—Thos. Garrett

Letter No. 15

Wilmington, 11th mo. 5th, 1857

ESTEEMED FRIEND, William Still:

I have just written a note for bearer to William Murphy Chester, who will direct him on to thy care; he left his home about a week since. In here in the lower part of this State, he met with a friend to pilot him some twenty-five miles last night. We learn that one party of those last week were attacked with clubs by several Irishmen, and that one of them was shot in the forehead, the ball entering to the skull bone, and passing under the skin partly around the head. My informant says he is likely to recover, but it will leave an ugly mark it is thought, as long as he lives. We have not been able to learn, whether the party was on the look out for them, or whether they were rowdies out on a Hallow-eve frolic; but be it which it may, I presume they will be more cautious hereafter, how they trifle with such. Desiring thee prosperity and happiness, I remain thy friend,

— Thomas Garrett

Letter No. 16

Wilmington, 11th mo. 14th, 1857

ESTEEMED FRIEND, Wm. Still:

Thy favor of a few days since came to hand, giving quite a satisfactory account of the large company. I find in the melee near this town, one of the Irishmen got his arm broken in two places. The one shot in the forehead is badly marked, but not dangerously injured. I learned to-day, that the carriage in that company, owing to fast driving with such a heavy load, is badly broken, and the poor horse was badly injured; it has not been able to do anything since. Please say to my friend, Rebecca Hart, that I have heretofore kept clear of persuading, or even advising slaves to leave their masters till they had fully made up their minds to leave, knowing as I do there is greater risk in so doing, and if betrayed once would be a serious injury to the cause hereafter. I had spoken to one colored man to try to see him, but he was not willing to risk it. If he has any desire to get away, he can, during one night, before they miss him, get out of the reach of danger. Booth has moved into New Castle, and left the two boys on the farm. If Rebecca Hart will write to me and give me the name of the boy, and the name of his mother, I will make another effort. The man I spoke to lives in New Castle, and thinks the mother of the boy alluded to lives between here and New Castle. The young men's association here wants Wendell Phillips to deliver a lecture on the lost arts, and some of the rest of us wish him to deliver a lecture on Slavery. Where will a letter reach him soonest, as I wish to write him on the subject. I thought he could perhaps deliver two lectures, two nights in succession. If thee can give the above information, thee will much oblige.

— Garrett & Son

LETTER NO. 17

Wilmington, 11th mo. 25th, 1857

ESTEEMED FRIEND, Wm. STILL:

I now send Johnson one of our colored men, up with the three men I wrote thee about. Johnson has undertook to have them well washed and cleaned during the day. And I have provided them with some second-hand clothes, to make them comfortable, a new pair of shoes and stockings, and shall pay Johnson for taking care of them. I mention this so that thee may know. Thee need not advance him any funds. In the present case I shall furnish them with money to pay their fare to Philadelphia, and Johnson home again. Hoping they will go on safe, I remain thy friend.

—Thos. Garrett

LETTER NO. 18

Wilmington, 11th mo. 25th, 1857

RESPECTED FRIEND, William Still:

I write to inform thee, that Captain Fountain has arrived this evening from the South with men, one of which is nearly naked, and very lousy. He has been in the swamps of Carolina for eighteen months past. One of the others has been sometime out. I would send them on to-night, but will have to provide two of them with some clothes before they can be sent by railroad. I have forgotten the number of thy house. As most likely all are more or less lousy, having been compelled to sleep together, I thought best to write thee so that thee may get a suitable place to take them to, and meet them at Broad and Prime [Pine?] streets on the arrival of the cars, about 11 o'clock to- morrow evening. Johnson who will accompany them is a man in whom we can confide. Please send me the number of thy house when thee writes.

—Thomas Garrett

LETTER NO. 19
Cornell University Libraries

5th mo. 1st, 1858

ESTEEM'D FRIENDS, McKim & Still:

Last evening I was call'd on ... by a colour'd man, a slave from below in this state. He said his wife, two children, and two other women had left a week previous, and had passes to travel. They were to stop at Princeton till he arrived and then go on to Jersey City. I gave him his supper, paid for nights lodging, and gave him in silver 1.75/100 Dolls to carry him to Princeton. I made arrangement last evening with the Chambers maid of the Boat to have him safely taken to your office. This morning a colour'd man says he took (him) nearly to the boat and told him to go on board, and go below. I was at the Boat 15 minutes before the Boat left but could not find him, neither could the Chambers-maid or Cook. Please let me know whether such a person got to your office. He had, he said, the (Eusipilus ?) in his face, and had a piece of court plaster on each cheek, it may be he was an imposture, but I do not think he was, as he certainly was acquainted in the neighborhood he said he came from. Please let me hear from you and oblige

— Thos. Garrett

LETTER NO. 20
Cornell University Libraries

Wilmington, 5th mo. 1st, 1858

ESTEEM'D FRIEND, J. Miller McKim,

Near two years since, I sent to thee several letters from Captain Lambdin who was convicted at Norfolk of aiding slaves to escape, and sentenced to the Virginia Penitiary for 7 years. He was very anxious to have what he had written publish'd, but I believe thee thought best not to publish it in the *Standard*,[iv] his wife was here today, she has just returned from a visit to her husband, and he is very anxious to have those papers, believing they may be of use to him. If thee can find them please send them by the bearer and oblige thy friend

— Thos Garrett

LETTER NO. 21
Cornell University Libraries

Wilmington, 8th mo. 16th, 1858

ESTEEM'D FRIEND, J. Miller McKim,

I herein inclose Five Dollars handed me this morning from my brother in law, Joseph Mendinhall. He handed it to me, and says I cannot spare but five Dollars for the Abolition Cause and left. He lives in the country, and at first thought it was given to me to ¥tttle Colour'd people, but on re-flection, I recollect that some weeks since he told me had got a letter from James Mott requesting aid for the general Cause. Please place it to his credit on your books and oblige Joseph Mendinhall

— Thos. Garrett

LETTER NO. 22

Wilmington, 8th mo. 21st, 1858

ESTEEMED Friend, William Still:

This is my 69th birthday, and I do not know any better way to celebrate it in a way to accord with my feelings, then to send to thee two fugitives, man and wife; the man has been here a week waiting for his wife, who is expected in time to leave at 9 this evening in the cars for thy house with a pilot, who knows where thee lives, but I cannot help but feel some anxiety about the woman, as there is great commotion just now in the neighborhood where she resides. There were four slaves betrayed near the Maryland line by a colored man named Jesse Perry a few nights since. One of them made a confidant of him, and he agreed to pilot them on their way, and had several white men secreted to take them as soon as they got in his house; he is the scoundrel that was to have charge of the 7 I wrote you about two weeks since; their master was to take or send them there, and he wanted me to send for them. I have since been confirmed it was a trap set to catch one of our colored men and me likewise, but it was no go. I suspected him from the first, but afterwards was fully con-firmed in my suspicions. We have found the two Rust boys, John and Elsey Bradley, who the villain of a Rust took out of jail and sold to a trader of the name of Morris, who sold them to a trader who took them to Richmond, Virginia, where they were sold at public sale two days before we found them, for $2600, but fortunately the man had not paid for them; our Attorney had them by habeas corpus before a judge, who detained them till we can prove their identity and freedom; they are to have a hearing on 2nd day [Monday] next, when we hope to have a person on there to probe them.

In haste, thine,
— Thos. Garrett

LETTER NO. 23

Wilmington, 8th mo. 25th, 1858

ESTEEMED FRIEND, William Still:

Thine was received yesterday. Those two I wrote about to be with thee last 7th day evening (Saturday), I presume thee has seen before this. A. Allen had charge of them; he had kept them out of sight at the depot here till the cars should be ready to start, in charge of a friend, while he kept a lookout and got a ticket. When the Delaware cars arrived, who should step out but the master of both man and woman, (as they had belonged to different persons); they knew him, and he knew them. He left in a different direction from where they were secreted, and got round to them and hurried them off to a place of safety, as he was afraid to take them home for fear they would search the house. On first day morning [Sunday] the boat ran to Chester to take our colored people to the camp at Media; he had them disguised, and got them in the crowd and went with them; when he got to Media, he placed them in care of a colored man, who promised to hand them over to thee on 2nd day last [Monday]; we expect 3 more the next 7th day [Saturday] night, but how we shall dispose of them we have not yet determined; it will depend on circumstances. Judge Layton has been on with a friend to Richmond, Virginia, and fully identified the two Bradley boys that were kidnapped by Clem Rust. He has the assurance of the judge there that they will be tried and their case decided by Delaware laws, by which they must be declared free and returned here. We hope to be able to bring such proof against both Rust and the man he sold them to, who took them out of the State; to teach them a lesson they will remember.

Thy friend,
— Thos. Garrett

Letter No. 24

Wilmington, 11th mo. 21st, 1858

DEAR FRIENDS, McKim and Still:

I write to inform you that on the 16th of this month, we passed on four able-bodied men to Pennsylvania, and they were followed last night by a woman and her six children, from three or four years of age, up to sixteen years; I believe the whole belonged to the same estate, and they were to have been sold at public sale, I was informed yesterday, but preferred seeking their own master; we had some trouble in getting those last safe along, as they could not travel far on foot, and could not safely cross any of the bridges on the canal, either on foot or in carriage. A man left here two days since, with carriage, to meet them this side of the canal, but owing to spies they did not reach him till 10 o'clock last night; this morning he returned, having seen them about one or two o'clock this morning in a second carriage, on the border of Chester County, where I think they are all safe, if they can be kept from Philadelphia. If you see them they can tell their own tales, as I have seen one of them. May he who feeds the ravens, care for them.

Yours,
— Thos. Garrett

Letter No. 25

Historical Society of Pennsylvania

Wilmington, 11th mo. 29th, 1858

ESTEEM'D FRIEND, William Still,

Yesterday week, a colour'd woman and 7 children was taken to my brother Edwards in Upper Darby, I heard she was anxious to get to her brother at Mount Holly, New Jersey, or rather I heard she was anxious to get to him at Woodberry, which is correct I cannot tell, but I think it most likely you have seen her, and can tell where they are. A colour'd man has just come up from Dover on the Carrs, and says the woman's Master came up in the same Carrs. The man says the Master heard she had gone to her brother at Mount Holly, he had a colour'd man taken up at Dover on suspicion of having aided them. It's very important that they should be got out of the way as, should she be taken, she may be the means of having several other colour'd persons convicted that assisted her. Do use the necessary means to get them out of the way, and to get her Brother away, as he will be likely to be taken, as I hear that he also is a slave. I have not time to write more at present,

Thy Friend,
T.G.

Letter No. 26

Wilmington, 8th mo. 25th, 1859

ESTEEMED FRIEND, Wm. Still:

The brig Alvena, of Lewistown, is in the Delaware opposite here, with four females on board, the colored man, who has them in charge, was employed by the husband of one of them to bring his wife up. When he arrived here, he found the man had left. As the vessel is bound to Red Bank, I have advised him to take them there in the vessel, and to-morrow take them in the steamboat to the city, and to the Anti-slavery office. I have a man here, to go on to-night that was nearly naked; shall rig him out pretty comfortably, poor fellow, he has lost his left hand, but he says he can take care of himself. In haste, thy friend,

— Thos. Garrett

LETTER NO. 27

Boston Public Library

[Author's Comment:

After Harriet Beecher Stowe's *Uncle Tom's Cabin* appeared in 1852, another book appeared (in 1857) which had the same effect of infuriating the South. This was *The Impending Crisis of the South*, written by a poor white North Carolinian named Hinton Rowan Helper. Helper "attributed the backwardness of [the South] and the poverty of the poor whites directly to the cupidity of the slave system and the greed of a small minority of slave-holders. He quoted government statistics to prove his economic points: how cotton culture had exhausted the land, limited diversified crops and starved the masses. 'There is no legislation except for the benefit of slavery, the slave-holders,' he said, and of the treatment of the poor whites by wealthy slavers."[5]

Although Helper's book was banned in the slave states, we find in the following letter that Thomas Garrett was still willing to act in defiance of that system and purchase several copies. This and Letter No. 28 are related.]

Wilmington, 3rd mo. 28th, 1860

RESPECTED Friend, J. Miller McKim:

A friend of mine living in Hartford County, Maryland, has left three dollars with me today to procure as many copies of Helper's *Impending Crisis* as it will purchase and deliver to me free from expense further than the money sent, Taggert Steam Boat, if sent to the Boat, I have no doubt will bring them (12½ cents) to me. He informs me that himself and a friend has purchased and distributed 15 in the neighborhood, and have been sued and bound over to attend Court at Bel Air. I think next month, but says he thinks they have not got proof sufficient to convict them. He thinks what they have distributed has done much good, and several of his neighbors is anxious to have them. I therefore enclose thee 3 Dollars. When they get here I will box them and he will send a friend for them. He says the Post Master will not deliver the *Crisis*, the *Tribune*, or anything of the kind. He has to send 6 miles into Penna for the *Tribune*.

Thy friend,

— Thos Garrett

LETTER NO. 28
Cornell University Libraries

Wilmington, 4th mo. 2nd, 1860

ESTEEM'D FRIEND, J. Miller McKim:

Thine of the 29th came to hand on the 30th of last month, and the package of books came to hand this morning. Thee says that thee did not find the 3 Dollars enclosed. I certainly intended to have sent it, and full believed I had sent it till the receipt of thine. I now enclose three Dollars, certain this time. Should it not be found all right, please let me know, I have within a few days been solicited by a man from Greensborough, Maryland, to employ him as an agent to [run?] off slaves. It look'd rather suspicious, and I did not trouble myself to answer his letter. I would not trust a man in that district. So I will let him wait for an answer.

Thy friend,
— Thos. Garrett

LETTER NO. 29
Cornell University Libraries

Wilmington, 5th mo. 28th, 1860

ESTEEM'D FRIEND, J. Miller McKim:

I this morning send by my son Eli a receipt for the 5 pound Sterling from the Ladies Emancipation Society at Edinburgh. Thee will please pay the amount to him. Isaac Mendinhall was here on 5th day last [Thursday] and told me he had the previous day receiv'd a letter from J. A. Dugdale, saying that himself and wife expected to get home on 5th day next, the 31st. I see by the last Standard that is made today that Joseph & Ruth [Dugdale] are now at home, which is not the case. As ever thy friend and well wisher.

— Thos. Garrett

LETTER NO. 30
Boston Public Library

Wilmington, 6th mo. 2nd, 1860

ESTEEM'D FRIEND, J. Miller McKim:

Thine of yesterday, enclosing thy check on the City Bank for 24, 21/100 Dollars, amount sent for me from Edinburgh, is at hand, for which please accept my thanks.

I have been daily watching the report of the trial of Henry Burk with considerable interest, and sincerely desire that it result as the friends of humanity hope for.

While I was at New York attending the Anniversary Meetings, a Colour'd man named Joseph Hamilton, was tried at New Castle for receiving money from a girl that stole it from her employer. The money was taken from the girl by his wife and put in his coat pocket, and there found the same day. Joseph declares he had never seen the money, or knew anything about it, till his wife told the Constable she had put the money in his coat pocket. The Court assigned him no Attorney to defend him, he was too poor to employ one, and of course he was convicted. He was sentenced to be whipped with 20 lashes, stand in the Pillory one hour, and fined 30 Dolls and costs, about 20 to 25 Dollars, and if not paid the fine and cost of the expiration of one month, the term of imprisonment to be sold to pay the same for seven years in or out of the state, which means for life, for few that are sold out of the state for 7 years ever get back again. Joseph has been one of our most efficient aids in forwarding slaves, his house being a regular stopping place. I went to see him in jail, and to him to make himself easy about being sold, as on the 11th [the time his imprisonment expires], I would be on hand [to] pay the fine and cost myself if I could get no help. Please not name him as agent to any one that will make it public, as it may hereafter operate against him, thy friend,

— Thos. Garrett

LETTER NO. 31
Historical Society of Pennsylvania

Wilmington, 7th mo. 10th, 1860

ESTEEM'D FRIEND, William Still:

Thine of the 7th reach'd me yesterday morning. I have made inquiry for Alfred Fountain and the Bailey's. The rebels burn'd Fountain's vessel at Norfolk, last year, and he is now a volunteer in McClellan's Army. One of the Baileys is a prisoner in Richmond. Another sold his vessel last fall, and I cannot learn what became of the other. There is but one vessel that sails from here that I know of, he is a clever fellow, and I am not certain what his feelings are towards the colour'd people, more especially Contrabands. His name is Captain Applin (of the) Sloop Alfred. He is in Philadelphia today, and I will try to see him on his return, (to find out) who wants (to) purchase the coal in Phila. and to whom would it be consigned in Washington. I would like to be able to answer all those questions if I found a Captain willing to undertake it. I hear just now that Baileys has been taken out of prison in Richmond, and is now in the rebel army there, if you do not get suited, I will see Captain Applin and ascertain what he will do, thy friend,

— Thos. Garrett

LETTER NO. 32

Wilmington, 12th mo. 1st, 1860

RESPECTED FRIEND, William Still:

I write to let thee know that Harriet Tubman is again in these parts. She arrived last evening from one of her trips of mercy to God's poor, bringing two men with her as far as New Castle. I agreed to pay a man last evening to pilot them on their way to Chester county; the wife of one of the men, with two or three children, was left some thirty miles below, and I gave Harriet ten dollars to hire a man with carriage to take them to Chester county. She said a man had offered for that sum, to bring them on. I shall be very uneasy about them, till I hear they are safe. There is now much more risk on the road, till they arrive here, than there has been for several months past, as we find that some poor worthless wretches are constantly on the look out on two roads, that they cannot well avoid more especially with carriage. Yet, as it is Harriet who seems to have a special angel to guard her on her journey of mercy, I have hope.

Thy friend,
— Thomas Garrett

LETTER NO. 33

Wilmington, 1st mo. 23rd, 1864

RESPECTED FRIEND, William Still:

The bearer of this, Winlock Clark, has lately been unrightously sold for seven years, and is desirous of enlisting and becoming one of Uncle Sam's boys; I have advised him to call on thee so that no land sharks shall get any bounty for enlisting him; he has a wife and several children, and whatever bounty the government or the state allows him, will be of use to his family. Please write me when he is snugly fixed in his regimentals, so that I may send word to his wife. By doing so, thee will much oblige thy friend, and the friend of humanity,

— Thomas Garrett

N.B. Am I naughty, being a professed non-resistant, to advise this poor fellow to serve Father Abraham?

16

Letters to William Lloyd Garrison

Little can be said of William Lloyd Garrison that has not already been said: "Fiery and adamant," "stormy and turbulent," "militant and radical," he was by far the most outstanding abolitionist of his day and was greatly admired by Thomas Garrett, who said that he had "frequently to refer to Garrison as one of the greatest philanthropists of the age — a man who had thought and reflected much on the evils and cruelty of Slavery; and one who dared to express what he thought, and act accordingly..." (see Miscellaneous Letters, No. 4).

Yet, in spite of his seemingly violent nature, the means by which Garrison carried out his total commitment to the abolition of slavery was that of complete nonviolence. In describing this paradoxical man, one writer observed that "Garrison came to advocate nonviolence in considerable part through his association with Quakers. Yet to some Quakers, Garrison seemed violent in spirit at the same time that he advocated nonviolence. He seemed both abusive in his language to opponents and insistent on forgiving them. He seemed at once fanatical in his courting of martyrdom and gentle in his love of children and the oppressed of the world."[1]

Garrison was born on December 12, 1804, in Newburyport, Massachusetts, the son of a New England sea captain, who left his family when William was only three years old. William was the youngest of five children, and he learned shoemaking at the age of eleven. In 1818 he became indentured to Ephraim W. Allen, editor of the Newburyport *Herald*. This launched him on a newspaper career through which he became the leading voice of the abolitionists.

When his apprenticeship came to a close, he started his own paper, *The Free Press,* which failed, due to lack of support. In 1827 he was engaged to edit the *National Philanthropist,* the first American newspaper devoted to the prohibition of alcohol. "On a change of proprietors in 1828, he was induced to join a friend in Bennington, Vermont, in publishing the *Journal of the Times,* which advocated the election of John Quincy Adams for president, besides being devoted to peace, temperance, anti-slavery, and other reforms."[2] He became an admirer of the New Jersey Quaker, Benjamin Lundy, and in 1829 joined Lundy as co-editor of Lundy's paper, *The Genius of Universal Emancipation,* but the partnership was short-lived. They parted due to sharp differences in editorial policy and an unfortunate legal encounter by Garrison with the owner of a slave-carrying vessel.

Finally, in Boston, on January 1, 1831, Garrison again started his own paper, *The Liberator.* His inaugural editorial has often been quoted by his admirers and biographers, for in it, Garrison summed up his whole life:

> I am aware, that many object to the severity of my language; but is there not cause for severity? I will be as harsh as truth, and as uncompromising as justice. On this subject, I do not wish to think, or speak, or write with moderation. No! No! Tell a man whose house is on fire, to give a moderate alarm; tell him to moderately rescue his wife from the hands of the ravisher; tell the mother to gradually extricate her babe from the fire into which it has fallen-but urge me not to use moderation in a cause like the present. I am in earnest — I will not equivocate — I will not excuse — I will not retreat a single inch — And I will be heard!

LETTER NO. 1

Boston Public Library

[Author's Comment:

The George Thompson mentioned in this letter (also in Letters Nos. 4, 6 and 7 of this section) is the British abolitionist who was a personal friend of both Garrett and William Lloyd Garrison. In 1835, Garrison was speaking at a meeting of the Female Anti-Slavery Society of Boston. Thompson was also present. A mob raided the meeting with intentions of lynching. Both Garrison and Thompson were dragged through the streets and narrowly escaped with their lives. Thompson also published the life story of Moses Gandy, an illiterate slave who bought his own freedom.[3]

The "Crafts" Garrett refers to are William and Ellen Craft, described as "the most famous married couple ever to use the UGRR."[4] Their escape from the Georgia cottonbelt and eventual safety in Britain made them a sensation among abolitionists. Ellen Craft was a house servant, light enough in complexion to pass for white, while her much darker husband, William, was a skilled cabinet maker. They effected their escape with a bold disguise. Ellen was dressed in men's clothing and posed as a white Southern gentleman-traveler. William posed as his body-servant. They traveled to freedom under the pretense that they were hastening to Philadelphia for special medical treatment for the young master (Ellen). Along the way they continuously called upon their sharp wits to overcome many obstacles. To conceal Ellen's lack of beard, her jaws were wrapped in toothache-like bandages. She carried her right arm in a sling to conceal her inability to sign hotel registers. To avoid conversation, and to conceal Ellen's high voice, she played deaf. They successfully reached Philadelphia, where the UGRR in that city passed them on to Boston. But their safety in Boston was soon threatened by the passage of the Fugitive Slave Bill in 1850, after which slave hunters came seeking them to take them back. The slave hunters were thwarted in their attempt, however. The Vigilance Committee sent Reverend Theodore Parker, a militant abolitionist, to tell them to leave town or be forced to suffer dire consequences. They left on the afternoon train, and from the tone of Garrett's letter, Garrison apparently had something to do with this, also.

The attempt to recapture the Crafts caused their friends to become alarmed, and so they were sent to England. After the Civil War the Crafts returned to Georgia, where they settled down as free people.[5]]

Wilmington, 12th mo. 5th, 1850

ESTEEM'D FRIEND, Wm. Lloyd Garrison:

Enclosed please find a letter for our mutual friend George Thompson. I feel very anxious to see him once more, and am so situated in business that I cannot well leave home for more than one or two days at a time. After having lost by imprudent partners, and unprincipled slave holders, all that had accumulated for Forty Years, about 40,000 Dollars, I commenced business anew last new year's day on borrow'd capital entirely, and it becomes me as an honest man, to attend closely to business, till I feel confident that in an emergency I shall have enough saved to pay my friends that have loaned me money to commence with.

William Lloyd Garrison, 1805–1879, fellow abolitionist and friend of Thomas Garrett's and publisher of abolitionist newspaper, *The Liberator*.

I have watched with great interest the course you have pursued in respects to the Crafts, and think it was managed in such a manner that Slave Holders will hardly think [it] worth while to risk the expense and mortification of sending agents from the South to Boston to look up their runaway slaves. The slave population who have escaped to the free states have been very much alarm'd by the passage of this infamous bill, but I very much doubt whether on the whole there will be more arrested under the new law, than the law as it stood for years past. There are so many more who feel an interest in affording them shelter, and protection. May this feeling increase till not a soul can be found in the free states mean enough to assist the master in reclaiming them.

There has lately been several free persons arrested as runaway slaves in the neighborhood, but we have so far succeeded in getting all released pretty soon after they were imprison'd — any white man here may arrest a colour'd man on suspicion of his being a slave [and] put him in jail. If he is proved a slave, the man taking [him] up gets a reward, if free, the County pays the expenses, and the poor Black has no remedy or compensation for loss [sic] time.

Please hand the enclosed to our friend Thompson when opportunity offers, and oblige thy friend.

— Thos. Garrett

LETTER NO. 2

Boston Public Library

[Author's Comment:

Isaac Flint, mentioned in this letter, was a station master with Thomas Garrett in Wilmington, Delaware.]

Wilmington, 10th mo. 9th, 1854

ESTEEM'D FRIEND, William Lloyd [sic] Garrison: Isaac Flint, and myself, are very desirous for thee to Address an Anti-slavery Meeting in this City, as may suit thy convenience on the way to, or from the West Chester Meeting. I believe thou hast never had a meeting of the kind in our City, and I really believe that many here, are now prepared to hear the truth Gladly, that but a short time since acknowledged their sympathies to be with the oppressor. Several here that have never attended an Anti-slavery meeting, have expressed a desire to hear thee. We therefore hope thee will make it suit to be with us, and make my House thy Home while here. We can provide thee a way from here direct to West Chester, or from there here, as may best suit.

This has been an eventful year for the successful escape of slaves from the Peninsular, over 30 has passed on t'wards Canada since the first of the year, two fine young men the past week.

Please let me hear from thee soon, so that I may make arrangement for the meeting here in case thee can make it suit to be with us.

Very respectfully thy friend,
— Thos. Garrett

LETTER NO. 3

Boston Public Library

[Author's Comment:

Lucy Stone, mentioned in this letter, was an outspoken abolitionist, advocate of temperance, and a strong supporter of women's rights. It is reported that she was the object of male contempt and opposition wherever she spoke. Nevertheless, she was considered a hard and tireless worker for all of these various causes.

Wilmington, 11th mo. 11th, 1854

MUCH ESTEEM'D FRIEND, William Lloyd Garrison:

Thee will perhaps recollect, that I gave thee when at my House some four weeks since 1. 25/100 Dolls for six months subscription of the Liberator, to be sent to this office for F. I. Hay. He call'd today to see me about it, (and) says he has call'd at the post office for it every week since, but there was none for him, please enquire whether it has been for-warded. If they are on hand please commence with the back numbers, so far as to have the proceedings of the women's rights meetings in Phila., as he is anxious to see the account of their proceedings.

Lucy Stone had three Lectures here after the West Chester Meeting. Her meetings increased in numbers and respectability to the last. She realized about 50 Dolls over expenses by the three lectures, and we were much gratified by having her in our family during her visit here. She is a sweet spirited pure woman. I took her to see Sarah Ann Scofield, the female machinist, mention'd at the Women's Rights Meeting in Phila., and I think they were both pleased with the interview.

My list of slaves has now got to 1874, having passed seven this day week, and the one day previous, and the best of it is, for our little State, they were all natives of Delaware. Would to God that all of the remaining slaves would run off before this time next year, so that we might take rank with the nominally Free States, for I have hopes that, bad as they have been, and still are, there is some evidence of improvement — with sincere desires for thy health and Happiness.

I remain thy sincerely attach'd Friend,
Thos. Garrett

LETTER NO. 4
Boston Public Library

Wilmington, 1st mo. 10th, 1856

MY DEAR FRIEND, William Lloyd Garrison: I write to request thee to forward me a copy of the Liberator of last week. I generally get it on 7th day (Saturday), and have look'd for it every mail since. I now think it either was not mailed, or has been overlooked in one of the post offices.

My wife desires me to enquire of thee, whether either thyself, or our friend George Thompson, left a linen over coat when you were last at our house. She found it hung up in the room where you slept. Till lately she thought it belonged to me, as I had two, but some one of our friends must have left it. If the coat does (not) belong *to* thee, please enquire of our friend Thompson if it belongs to him, and oblige thy friend,

— Thos. Garrett

LETTER NO. 5
Boston Public Library

[Author's Comment:

This letter was written in Garrett's worst handwriting, probably due to his illness at the time he wrote it. Yet the spirit he shows throughout is remarkable for a man of his age!]

Wilmington, 1st mo. 5th, 1863

Dear Friend Garrison,

I see in the Liberator thee proposes to advance the price of it 50 cents per annum in consequence of the advances in paper, &c. All right, the Liberator must be sustained; it cannot be dispensed with while a slave clanks his chains in this land of boasted liberty.

The beginning of the end of the slave's deliverance has commenced by the [Proclamation?] of Abraham Lincoln, of freedom of the slaves in the rebel States, with a few exceptions named; which exceptions, in my humble opinion, were wrong. They will lead *to more* difficulty, both with master and slave, than if it all had been declared free, without the reservation. I believe it would have been much better for the whole country if a general proclamation of emancipation had been declared by the President to take effect at once, paying reasonable compensation to all loyal slave holders in the border States (provided any such could have been found), believing as I do that, had such a proclamation been made it would have done more toward stopping the effusion of blood than any other plan that will be adopted, and in the end cost the Government less to pay for such slaves than to prolong the war — not that I believe it right to pay the master for the slaves, but as a matter of expediency.

Every sentiment of my nature is oppose to war; but non-resistant as I profess to be I have not been able to see how the North could have avoided war. Slavery must die; till then, the country can have no peace.

I enclose five dollars for my subscription for the present year, and hold myself as a subscriber for that sum annually, for the *Liberator,* as long as I live, or slavery remains to curse our soil. I am not willing to give up either the *Standard* or *Liberator.* I would prefer doubling my subscription to either, than that they should stop or be embarrassed!

With sincere regard I remain, thy friend, and the friend of suffering humanity the world over,

— Thos. Garrett

PS: I have been suffering very much for two weeks with an attack of Bilious, and severe cold combined, but with the faithful application of steam and the free use of water, without any medicine, I am now improving. I have kept out of doors part of each day, and today am at my desk at the store again; My wife is quite well this winter and has proved an excellent and faithful nurse to me. As ever, thy friend

— Thos. Garrett

LETTER NO. 6

Boston Public Library

[Author's Comment:

Isaac and Dinah Mendinhall mentioned in this letter were relatives of Garrett's wife, Rachel. Aaron Mendinhall was the oldest son of Isaac and Dinah.

Oliver Johnson mentioned in this letter, was a New York business man, a non-resistant, and a convert to Quakerism. He was also the editor of the abolitionist newspapers *The Ohio Anti-slavery Bugle* and *The Pennsylvania Freeman*.]

Wilmington, 2mo. 24th, 1864

Dear Friend, W. L. Garrison, I yesterday accompanied by my wife attended the burial of Ellie, wife of Aaron Mendinhall, and Daughter in law of Isaac & Dinah Mendinhall. She was buried at Longwood, the corpse was followed to the grave by a large concourse of sympathizing Friends, amongst which was our loved friends, Oliver and Mary Ann Johnson. Oliver gave a very interesting and truthful discourse, and was follow'd by Jane Price, who seemed to sympathize with the communication deliver'd by Oliver.

I see by the Liberator some weeks since that thy wife was quite poorly. I hope by this time she has quite recover'd her health. I should have been very happy to have been with you at the reception meeting of our friend Thompson, but my wife's health is so frail, that I seldom leave her for even 24 hours.

I feel very anxious that thee and G. Thompson should call and spend at least one night with me on your way to or from Washington, as Wendell Phillips inform'd me last week, when giving a lecture in our Institute last week, that thee expected to accompany Thompson to Washington some time next month. I have written a few lines enclosed with this to our friend Thompson, hand it to him and oblige thy friend,

— Thos. Garrett

LETTER NO. 7

Boston Public Library

[Author's Comment:

Gerrit Smith mentioned in this letter was a militant abolitionist who supported and aided John Brown. He was one of a group of anti-slavery figures elected to Congress in 1848. He also took part in the famous "Jerry Rescue," in Syracuse, New York, in 1851.]

Wilmington, 6 mo. 30th, 1865

My dear Friend, Garrison,

The bearer, George Ford, has been a member of my own and son's family for some ten years, since has been a good Union lad all that time, and conducted himself with propriety. He being now about the age of twenty-one years, and out of health, a sea voyage has been recommended to him. He proposes leaving for Boston tomorrow by sea, in a Steamer. He expressed a wish to call on thee, (he being identified by birth) with that class for which thee and I have labor'd for very many years. His mother was a slave for life. I purchased her time, and set her free the same day. She lived with me several years after, and proved trustworthy and honest. He has been employ'd in our store for 8 or 9 years, and is now learning with my son the Dentist profession, and will attend the Lectures in Phila. next winter, if health permits. As he may wish to see the sights of your city during his stay, any information thee may give him, I shall consider a favor as though conferred on myself.

Please say to my friend, George Thompson, I would thank him to send me by the bearer one box of his superior matches, so that I may try them, and if found superior to what I have, will endeavor to introduce them here, or get someone else to do it.

I presume thee has read Gerrit Smith's last Lectures at the Cooper Institute. Most of his views I can adopt, but I do not agree with him when he states that, neither Congress, or the President, can rightfully require the Slave States to alter their laws and give the colour'd population the elective Franchise.

As ever, thy attached friend,
— Thos. Garrett

17

Letters to Eliza Wigham and Mary Edmundson

Eliza Wigham and Mary Edmundson were sisters who lived in Scotland. They were fifth generation Quakers. The family is reported to have been connected with the north of England and is said to have been "among the promoters of a great memorial to the young Queen, Victoria, when she came to the throne in 1837."

Of the two sisters, Eliza, the youngest (born February 23, 1820), became well known, not only for her tireless labor in behalf of the abolition of slavery (in both the British West Indies and in the United States) but also as one who was deeply religious. She was described as having a "saintly disposition." At the end of a long and active life in the service of suffering humanity, her name became a synonym for goodness and righteousness, throughout England, Ireland and Scotland.

Eliza was a personal friend of such abolitionists as Frederick Douglass, William Lloyd Garrison, Wendell Phillips and George Thompson. She was also intimate with Levi Coffin, the Quaker from Cincinnati who became known as "the reputed President of the Underground Railroad," and she wrote of these men and others (including Thomas Garrett) in her book, *The Anti-Slavery Cause in America, and Its Martyrs*. There is no information whether Mary became as eminent as Eliza, or that she published any writings. She married Joshua Edmundson, from Dublin, in 1840, and all available information indicates that she lived with him in Dublin for the remainder of her days. Eliza, on the other hand, never married, and spent all but the very last year of her life in Edinburgh. She died on November 3, 1899, at her sister's home in Dublin.

Both sisters were members of the Edinburgh Ladies Emancipation Society, and it was through this organization that they raised and donated money to Thomas Garrett (and presumably other American abolitionists) to assist him in his work of aiding the fugitive slaves.

17. LETTERS TO ELIZA WIGHAM AND MARY EDMUNDSON

The letters in this section were donated to the Haverford College Library Quaker Collection by Mrs. Alfred Cope Garrett. Excerpts from these letters were printed in *Delaware History,* March 1950 (Vol. IV, No.1) as "Thomas Garrett's Letters to Two Ladies in Britain," and annotated by William W. Comfort, president emeritus of Haverford College, and president of the Friends Historical Association.

Comfort's presentation of these letters have some shortcomings. In transcribing the original letters, Comfort makes what must be considered a serious error. He quotes Garrett as saying, "the South will never yield" when in truth, Garrett said, "the South *must* yield," the statements having entirely different, and significant, meanings (see page 41 of *Delaware History,* Vol. IV, No.1).

Another shortcoming of Comfort's presentation of these letters is that he all but ignores Thomas Garrett's most famous visitor, Harriet Tubman. Although Garrett speaks at length about Harriet Tubman in all but one of these letters, Comfort saw fit to give only Harriet Tubman passing reference. The letters are presented here in their entirety, following an extract from an American newspaper of June 6th [1854]. This extract, and letters 1, 2 and 3, were published in the annual report of the Edinburgh Ladies Emancipation Society of 1854. It tells briefly of Thomas Garrett's appearance in Boston at the failed rescue attempt of the runaway slave, Anthony Burns.

Burns was a runaway slave who was arrested and placed under guard in the Federal Jury Room of the Boston Court House at the request of his former master.

> ...the news spread quickly, although an attempt was made to keep it secret. The next morning, three distinguished lawyers were in court to defend him ... .
>
> The following evening Faneuil Hall was filled to overflowing with citizens gathered to protest Burns' arrest, and to denounce the posse sworn in as special constables to guard him, nearly a third of whom were known thugs with prison records. On the platform of Faneuil Hall that night, after Wendell Phillips and Theodore Parker had spoken, a man cried, "When we go from this Cradle of Liberty, let us go *to* the tomb of Liberty-the courthouse!" The crowd broke for the Court Square, where the Reverend Thomas Wentworth Higginson and Lewis Hayden (a Negro abolitionist) were already leading a group of abolitionists in battering down the door of the courthouse to rescue Burns. But within, constables and deputies were ready with pistols and clubs. The Reverend Higginson was wounded, and in the scuffle one of the deputies was killed. Military reinforcements arrived. The abolitionists were routed and many of them were arrested.
>
> Despairing of freeing Burns by force or by legal means, over the weekend the friends of freedom raised 1,200 dollars and negotiated to purchase his freedom. But the U.S. Attorney refused to permit this transaction, insisting that in keeping with the Fugitive Slave Law, the refugee must be returned to Virginia.
>
> When Burns came to trial on Monday police and soldiers surrounded the courthouse, guarded every door and window, and lined the staircase leading to the courtroom. From Washington, President Pierce wired to spare no expense in having the military protect the court "to insure execution of the law." On Friday, when Burns was sentenced to return to slavery, twenty-two military units, including the entire Fifth Regiment of Artillery, were assembled in Boston to see that Burns did not escape, and a cannon was set up in front of the courthouse. Besides the police of

Boston, 1,500 dragoons, marines and lancers, with Burns in their midst, marched to the dockside through the streets lined by a crowd of 50,000 persons hissing and crying, "Shame!" At one point, the populace tried to break through a police cordon and rescue Burns. Several were injured. As the revenue cutter, *Morris,* sailed for Virginia that day with Burns aboard, the Reverend Daniel Foster ordered the crowd on the dock to kneel in prayer.

Although the slave's market value was only $1,200, it had cost the government more than $40,000 to return Anthony Burns to his master. "We rejoice, wrote the Richmond Enquirer," but a few more such victories, and the South is undone."[1]

Extract From Annual Report of Edinburgh Ladies Emancipation Society, 1854:

> We quote from an American paper of June 16th. "Whilst the crowd were anxiously awaiting the appearance of the mournful cortege which was about to convey Burns to the hateful torment of Slavery, a venerable man in Quaker's garb made his appearance with a carpet bag in his hand, edging his way in the direction of one of the wharves. One or two persons recognized him & proposed 3 cheers, which were given with a will: that man was Thomas Garrett of Delaware, whom the Fugitive Slave Law had stripped of all his property. His farm was sold about two years since in order to raise money an (execution?) levied for a fine of 5000 dollars under the Fugitive Slave Law. Mr. Garrett finds himself a poor man in his old age, but he has that which is better than riches, viz. a conscience void of offence toward God & man & the happy consciousness of having enabled 1853 slaves to change their condition of chattels to that of free men. Who would not rather be Thomas Garrett carrying his own carpet bag than Franklin Pierce at the head of the nation!"

LETTER NO. 1

Haverford College Library Quaker Collection

[Author's Comment:

The remark preceding this letter was made by one of the ladies of the Society. In all likelihood it was Eliza Wigham, who was Secretary of the Society.]

As many inquiries have been made respecting the present condition of Thomas Garrett, we have much pleasure in giving the following extracts from a private letter dated 8th mo. 28th, 1854:

> After some details of his trial & prosecution in 1848 for rescuing a family of slaves and stating that he been assisted by some friends to embark in business, he says I started again in the iron and hardware business in 1850, with a cash capital of 1000 dollars. I paid my interest, supported my family, and saved 7000 dollars in three & a half years, so that I am not so badly off as has been supposed.
>
> It was not the Sheriff, but the Marshal, who in Court said he hoped I would now mind my own business, & not meddle with slaves again! I told him publicly in the Courthouse that I had assisted over 1400 in 25 years on their way to the North, & I now consider the penalty imposed might be as a license for the remainder of my life; but be that as it may, if any of you know of any slave who needs assistance send him

to me, as I now publicly pledge myself to double my diligence, & never neglect an opportunity to assist a slave to obtain freedom.

This has been an eventful year in the forwarding line. More slaves have passed this station on the Underground Railway during the last 8 months than in the previous. I passed on, last evening, two fine healthy young men, & one during the past week; making, since I kept a "Station," 1853, almost 1854, by which thou wilt perceive that I am not disheartened in the service.

I was in Boston when poor Burns was carried off into slavery; what I saw there then was not calculated to check my zeal in the cause. Thy old friend & the friend of suffering humanity all the world over.

— Thomas Garrett

LETTER NO. 2

Haverford College Library Quaker Collection

[Author's Comment:

The "intelligent young captain" of whom Garrett speaks in this letter is Captain Lambdin, whose tragic case is also told by William Still in his book (p. 388). To get the full story, of course, one must read both Still's book and Garrett's account. In conjunction with these, also read Garrett's letters to Still, Nos. 3 and 7.

In relating Captain Lambdin's case to the Edinburgh Ladies Emancipation Society, Garrett withheld the Captain's name for fear that if this information leaked out it would be severely damaging to the Captain's defense, and would also incriminate others.

In the second part of this letter, Garrett speaks of a "noble black woman" of whose acquaintance he is proud. He tells the Edinburgh Ladies Emancipation Society of this woman's bravery in going into slave territory and bringing her brothers, sisters and friends away to freedom, but he withholds the woman's identity, apparently for the same reasons that he withheld Captain Lambdin's identity. However, a coincidence occurs which creates a bit of confusion: the Edinburgh Ladies Emancipation Society received a copy of the Trenton (New Jersey) *Gazette,* which carried the story of a "Slave Heroine," whose deeds of bravery are similar to those of Garrett's "noble black woman." The *Gazette* story created some interest in the friends of the Society, for after reading the story, one of them wanted to send five pounds to help the "Slave Heroine." Thinking that the two women were the same person, or, if not, were at least worthy of the same benevolent gift, the Edinburgh Ladies Emancipation Society sent a letter of inquiry to Garrett. Garrett's first response (Letter No. 3) does not really clear up the confusion. He reveals that the noble black woman he spoke of was none other than the great Harriet Tubman, but he does not state that she was *not* the "Slave Heroine" spoken of in the *Gazette*. At this time Garrett was apparently not aware of the story in the *Gazette,* and consequently believed that the "Slave Heroine" the Society referred to was Harriet Tubman, and thus he accepted the gift of five pounds for Harriet. Not until Letter No. 4 does Garrett clear up the confusion. He writes: "The piece cutout of the Trenton New Jersey Gazette giving a history of the slave heroine who returned to a slave state & rescued 7 of her children & grandchildren, is not the person I have given you a history of. I happened to be in Philadelphia when that woman was there with her children. She also was a noble woman."]

December 16, 1855

Dear Friend, E. W.

Thy valued letter enclosed to our mutual friend, J. McKim, for me, enclosing a second 5lb note to assist slaves from our boasted Republican, America, to Queen Victoria's domain, came safely to hand, & I desire thee to present my thanks to the Ladies Emancipation Society of Edinburgh, for their valuable remembrances for the aid and benefit of those oppressed & noble men and women for whose benefit you entrusted it to my care. Very nearly all of your valuable gifts has been expended, [along] with [money] received from a friend in England; besides these, I have received no material aid from any source except four dollars, which was handed to me by two friends to aid in one particular case, when I had 21 men & women to provide for in one gang.

No less than 60 of God's poor have passed here within the last three months, every one of whom were passed safely over what was formerly termed the Underground Railroad, but now, in many instances, I consider it safe to forward them in open day on their way North, most of these surely have gone to Canada. I need not tell you that in a general way they are the most valuable, intelligent, & enterprising slaves that effect their escape.

I had written a letter ten days since, to send to you, giving you an account of several gangs of those already enumerated, but some of my friends advised me not to send it for fear that myself & some others might be implicated by your Society publishing my letters in some of the European papers, [and] by that means it should get transferred to some of the papers on this side of the Atlantic. I have no fears on my own account, as I felt willing to trust your discretion; but knowing I had the [organ?] or fear very fully developed, & its [opposite?] quite large, I yielded the point, but rather think I shall not gain much this time by my extra caution, as during the past week.

The Anti-slavery Meeting at _____ Street Hall in Philadelphia [The name of the street was omitted by Garrett], where McKim in addressing the meeting in respect to finances, remarked that the meeting could have no idea of the demands made on the funds of the Society to assist slaves on their way to Canada. A friend from Ohio checked J. McKim by telling him that they knew comparatively little about the Underground Railroad here in Pennsylvania, that in Ohio the whole state was converted into Underground Railroads leading to Canada, where they went in gangs of 6, 8 & 10, & in one instance he had known 20 pass on the road in one day. Here E.M. Davis[ii] arose & told him that here, or in Delaware, Thomas Garrett, pointing to me, had helped on 21 in one gang a few days since, and upwards of 1950 in thirty years—he replied, "I will knock under and sit down." Now I had no objection for *all mankind* to know that I would assist all in my power to freedom, but I fear it may prove to have been impertinent to name the number of 21 that had passed within three weeks, for this reason, three had come from Carolina & 18 from Norfolk in the same vessel, & the Norfolk people had a suspicion they had come this way, but had suspected two vessels that had left for New England on the day they were missed, but felt confident that the eighteen were on board one or both of them. Now I beg you will never publish one word about the twenty-one named above, or where they came from.

A very intelligent young captain from the port, who had at different times brought slaves from the South, had taken five on board at Norfolk. Some time after, the vessel left port in a hurricane. His vessel became disabled, & to *save himself* & *crew,* he had to put back, His vessel was wrecked but a few miles from Norfolk; having no alternatives, the wreckers being on the beach, he went to a magistrate, & gave himself up, & to save himself, stated that the slaves were on board without his knowledge or permission; himself and mate were at once imprisoned, charged with attempting to carry slaves to the North. They are to have their trial on the 24th of this month before the commissioner there. If not set at liberty, they will have to be in prison till the 6th mo. next. If [they are] convicted, & the full penalty of Virginia Law meted out, they will have to serve or remain in prison 10 years in each case, or 50 years in all.

The Captain has a young wife here, with one child, 15 months old, a sweet little creature. I went to the wife, yesterday. I encouraged her to go on, so as to be there at the trial, & to take *her babe along.* I have pledged to raise 50 dollars towards furnishing lawyers to plead his cause, and hope he may be favored to get off, as by law in Virginia, a slave's testimony cannot convict a white person, so if he did agree to bring them on here, the testimony of the slave will not be deemed valid. So it is, the Slave-holders, to accomplish the most vile of acts with their slaves, pass laws so that their evidence cannot be taken to convict them, & in cases like the present, if the law be *fairly* carried out, it will *prevent* the conviction of those, who in truth were guilty of no crime (except the deviation from truth, which is, in *all* cases, reprehensible).

I feel as if I could not close this already *too long* letter, without giving some account of the doings of a noble woman, but a *black* one, in whose veins flows not one drop of Caucasian blood. She is strong & muscular, now about 55 years of age, born a slave, and raised [as] what is termed a *field hand.* She escaped from slavery some 8 years since. Her master lived nearly 100 miles below this. She has made 4 successful trips to the neighborhood she left, & brought away 17 of her brothers, sisters & friends, & had mostly made the journeys down on foot, *alone,* & with her companions mostly walked back, traveling the whole distance at night, and secreting themselves during the day. She has three times gone to Canada with those she brought, and spent every dollar she could earn, or *get in the cause.* She, in one instance, was in the immediate neighborhood of her Master for three months, before she could get off safely with her friends, & but one family — & they colored — where she stopped, knew her. She twice in that time met her master in open day, in the fields, but he did not know her. Having always worked in the open air fields, her color had changed so much, that her own brother & sister did not know her.

Last week, after a trip of two weeks, she brought up one man. She took tea with me, and left again with a determination during the Christmas holidays to bring away her sister—now the last [one] left in slavery—and her [sister's] three children [as well as] a sister in-law & her three children (the husband of the latter has been a year in Canada), and one male friend. She says if she gets them away safely, she will be content and give up such hazardous journeys, but she will either accomplish it, or be arrested & spend the remainder of her days in Slavery. For should she be arrested for assisting a slave, even if she had been *free-born,* she would be sold a slave for life.

Were a *white person,* man or woman, to peril life & health, & spend everything he or she had earned in such a noble & disinterested cause, the name would be trumpeted over the land; but be sure you *do not trumpet* her noble deeds in the Newspapers. I can assure you I am proud of her acquaintance.

Our country is now in a sadly distracted state. Our politicians stand aghast We are on the eve of Civil War. The residents in Kansas [who] are in favor of freedom have been compelled to take up arms. Governor Shannon & the border ruffians of Missouri are in turns arriving *to put them down,* & I fear, as slavery has ever carried the day in this *boasted* Republican Government, they will force Slavery into Kansas, contrary to the wish of the majority of the actual settlers. Again Congress has been two weeks in Session, & has not been able to select a Speaker in the House of Representatives. The vote for freedom has mostly been from 100 to 105, that of the North (75, 75, 75), hardly varying a vote for the two weeks. There are, in addition, 40 or 50 scattering votes, but I fear, as heretofore, the North will yield, & go, as it has heretofore done, for the Compromise, that is to fix on *another name,* but the man who bears it be as ultra Southern as the one they are now voting for. But I must close; & must request thee to thank those ladies who have contributed such efficient aid for the fugitives, & shall ever hold their memory in grateful remembrances. With sincere desires for your welfare, & that of the cause you advocate.

I am ever thy sincere Friend,
—T. Garrett.

A Slave Heroine

The Trenton N.J. *Gazette* records the passage through that town of a party of fugitive slaves, under the following remarkable circumstances: Two years ago, a Slave woman, advanced in years, the mother of six children, who had all been sold from her when old enough to be useful, overheard her master bargaining for the sale of her grandson, a boy fifteen years old, to a trader. This being the last of her family, she resolved not to permit it, & the same night fled with the boy. They traveled by night Northward, guided by the polestar, &, after long wandering, reached Canada. There she hired herself out for wages, and two months ago, with the result of her own and her boy's labor, returned to the South, where concealing herself in the woods, she revealed her presence *only* to her friends, & thus collected several of her children

& grandchildren they started Northward, traveling only by night, & concealing themselves during the day. Before reaching Philadelphia they were so worn with hunger & hardship as to be obliged to seek aid. Friends were found, & the whole party were fed and clothed and for-warded to Canada. This woman is nearly 50 years of age, yet alone she has done all this!

LETTER NO. 3
Haverford College Library Quaker Collection

Wilmington, 9, 12, 1856

My dear Friend,

Thy kind note of 6th mo. 26th came to hand by the kindness of our friend, Sarah Pugh, & I can truly assure thee that it gave me great pleasure to receive a note from thee. Since the receipt of them, I had not known of the colored heroine thou inquired for till the 8th of the month, when she very unexpectedly came to my store. She says she went to Canada some four months since, to pilot two fugitives, & was taken ill there, & is now just able to travel again. She is to leave this day for Baltimore, to bring away two slave children. When she returns, if successful, she will set out for her sister & two children [that is, her *sister's* two children], on the coast of Maryland, near where her legal master now lives. She is quite feeble, her voice much impaired from a cold taken last winter, which I fear has permanently settled on her lungs.

While sick in Canada, the colored man with whom she had made her house in Philadelphia, died; she had left in his care her clothes & ten dollars. His widow had broken up housekeeping and returned to Harrisburg, 120 miles distant. She yet hopes to get all her [assets?] sometime. She told me, if she should be successful in getting the two from Baltimore, & the sister & two children from the eastern shore, she would be satisfied to remain at home till her health should be restored. The name this noble woman is now known by is Harriet Tubman, & she requests me to inform thee that if the friend still feels disposed to send the five pound sterling to aid her in her trustworthy calling, it may be sent to the care of Wm. Still, a clerk in the Anti-Slavery Office, Philadelphia, where our friend J. Miller McKim is employed. She will continue to report herself in the office whenever she is in the city.

The Anti-Slavery Cause is progressing with rapid strides. I think in this country the friends of the slave have more cause than ever to hope that the days of Slavery are numbered. The North is becoming alarmed at the arrogance of 350,000 Slave-owners undertaking to rule 20,000,000 of freemen. I never knew the country so aroused politically as at the present time. I cannot *vote* myself, or take part further than cannot be avoided in such a tyrannical government, being a firm believer in *disunion* being the only certain & effectual remedy for abolishing slavery. Should *that* take place, the slaves will soon be free; at least that is my opinion.

I cannot well divest myself of an interest in the approaching Presidential Election, which will be settled in about two months from this time. I believe that Fremont would be more efficient & better President than either Buchanan or Fillmore. I look upon Fillmore as but a cipher, and very much doubt if he will get the electoral vote of any state in the Union. The contest will certainly be between Fremont & Buchanan. Pierce, who now occupies the White House, I look upon as one of the most contemptible trucklers to the Southern interest of any man that ever held a responsible station in this country, & had even-handed Justice been administered to him, he had long been impeached and sent back to New Hampshire.

Fremont is by no means a thorough Anti-Slavery man. He is opposed to the further extension of Slavery, but does not wish to disturb it where it now is, but leave that entirely to the States. He says, if it be confined within its present limits, it will soon die out of itself. The South say if Fremont is placed in the Presidential Chair, the Union must & will be dissolved. I wish I could bring myself to think so. I have but little hope for the abolition of slavery in any other way than by dissolution of the Union.

If Fremont be elected, most likely the present difficulties in Kansas will be settled in favor of freedom, and slavery may be permitted to continue for years to come. But should Buchanan be elected, the South will be more arrogant and overbearing than ever; which will be likely still further to arouse the North to retaliate. When that takes place the *South must yield.* In case of Civil War the South could do little more than take care of her own slaves; and my opinion is a rupture must take place within the next four years if Buchanan be elected.

The ten pounds which your Society sent to me was appreciated, I can assure you, much more than its value in dollars. It was a satisfaction to know that my labors for the slaves was appreciated by friends of humanity at a distance. I can assure you that I have been richly repaid for my labors in the cause of humanity by that Spirit that is ever near to bless those who are willing to live up to the light furnished by an all-seeing God. The number of God's poor who are escaping from the prison-house of slavery does not diminish. I passed on two who had spent more than half their lives (should they live to four-score years) in Slavery, this week, & four, ten days since.

My list now counts 2011 slaves that I have been enabled to assist on their Northern journey. I received many letters written by those poor creatures, expressing their gratitude for favors rendered. I have passed a pretty active life till the present time, now 67 years of age, and do not recall to mind anything I have ever done which has given me so much real satisfaction as what I have done to benefit the colored race, bond and free. For 20 odd years I spent much time in establishing and attending the colored schools here, as the colored children were not admitted to schools with white children. We have now two large schools almost entirely supported by the Society of Friends, both Hicksite & Orthodox, & four private schools for colored children, all taught by colored teachers. Our own town contains about 20,000 inhabitants, 3000 of whom are colored.

Please remember me affectionately to all members of your Society, & send me when time and inclination permit, and I shall feel obliged.

      Thy Friend,
     — Thomas Garrett

LETTER NO. 4

Haverford College Library Quaker Collection

[Author's Comment:

In the first part of this letter, Garrett tells of an incident between him and Harriet Tubman in which he jokingly tells Harriet he has no money for her, and relates her response. He elaborates further on this story in Letter No. 5 and tells the same story to Sarah Bradford in Miscellaneous Letter No. 10. The reader might want to compare this story with one told by Tilden in his "Memorial Address." Tilden's story is very similar, except that the woman in his story is Sojourner Truth, a black woman and ex-slave who became famous for crusading against slavery. Garrett never mentions that he ever personally met Sojourner Truth. However, it is on record that Sojourner Truth did speak at the Longwood Progressive Meeting of Friends in 1853, and Garrett regularly attended that meeting. Indeed, Priscilla Thompson says Garrett was one of the founders of that Meeting (p. 18). So it is likely that Garrett did meet Sojourner Truth. However, in this letter Garrett is speaking of Harriet Tubman, not Sojourner Truth.]

Wilmington, 10–24–56

My dear friend, E. Wigham,

Thy esteemed favor of 9th Month 11th was handed to me by J.M. McKim on the 18th of this month, also five pounds designated for that noble woman, Harriet Tubman, forwarded by thee. As I had not heard (from) her for several weeks past, I left a letter at the Anti-Slavery office with Wm. Still, informing her of the handsome donation I had just received for her.

On sixth day [Friday] last, less than a week after I received thy letter and money, Harriet came into my office and addressed me thus—"Mr. Garrett I am here again, out of money, and with no shoes to my feet, and God has sent me to you for what I need"—I said-Harriet, art thou sure thou art not deceived? I cannot find money enough to supply all God's poor. I had five here last week and had to pay 8 dollars to clothe and for-ward them. She said, "Well, you have got enough for me to pay for a pair of shoes, and to pay for my own and a friend's passage to Philadelphia." Then she said, "I must have 20 dollars more: to enable me to go down to Maryland for a woman and three children."

She said she had paid her last copper that morning to a coloured man that had brought her, and a delicate female — a house servant — some 30 odd miles in his carriage. I then told her that the Good Spirit had put it into the heart of a kind friend in England to send, especially for her, five pounds, so that she would have enough for all her present wants without calling on her Philadelphia friends for aid. She said, "I thank you very much. I was sure I could get money from you, but I did not expect so much."

The history of this trip was remarkable, and manifested great shrewdness. This girl was a slave in Baltimore, and was engaged to be married to a slave 8 years since.

For some reason his master determined to sell him to go South. A friend very kindly informed him of (this) fact. He went to see the object of his affections, bid her farewell, and left. He arrived safe in the interior of New York, and after being absent more than 7 years, furnished Harriet with some money, and she went to Baltimore in pursuit. After considerable search she found the woman and brought her away. She had gone to Philadelphia with the captain of a steam-boat, trading through the Delaware, and Chesapeake canal, and had taken the precaution to get from him a certificate of her being a resident of Philadelphia, and free. She knew she could not bring a strange woman from Baltimore to Philadelphia, either by railroad or steamboat, without giving bonds in 500 dollars, and therefore took passage for herself and companion to [Seaford], on the eastern shore of Maryland, in the steamboat; and showing the Captain her pass-port from Philadelphia to Baltimore, and he, knowing the captain of the boat that took her to Baltimore, was on to give her a certificate, also.

When the boat arrived at Seaford, she boldly went to the Hotel and called for supper and lodging. Next morning, when they were about to leave, a dealer in such stock attempted to arrest them, but on showing the captain's certificate, the landlord interfered, the woman went to the railroad and paid their passage to Camden, some 50 miles below here, and then came up in private conveyance.

I asked her is she was not frightened [when] arrested. "*Not* a bit," she said. She knew she would get off safe. And now I hope by this time she has taken the girl to her long lost lover. But the strangest thing about this woman is, she does not know, or appears not to know, that she has done anything worth notice! May her Guardian continue to preserve her many perilous adventures.

The piece cut out of the Trenton New Jersey *Gazette*, giving a history of the slave heroine who returned to a slave state and rescued 7 of her children and grandchildren is not the person I have given you a history of. I happened to be in Philadelphia when that woman was there with her children. She was also a noble woman.

Harriet's health [has] much improved since I last saw her. She now looks as though she might be able to perform good service in the cause for years to come.

Our whole country is agitated at present about Politics, whether Buchanan or Fremont will be elected President. No one can certainly tell, but I think most likely Buchanan will be. But no matter which is elected, the slavery agitation must continue till slavery is abolished. The South is becoming bold and insolent towards the North, and towards the advocates of freedom. If the North once becomes fairly aroused, they have the power to dictate terms. But I fear that slavery may not be abolished here without Civil War. Slaves still continue to follow the North Star when favorable opportunity offers. My list now numbers 2028. Nothing gives us more pleasure than to have an opportunity to assist them on their way.

I hope your anti-slavery efforts will be continued, as I can assure, you that the slave-holders and their apologists on this side of the water are anxiously watching what is going on with you. I am no politician, and therefore need not say any more on that subject, as you can learn from the papers all that is going on here. You will no doubt conclude that there never was a more contemptible or unjust government on earth than ours at the present time, not only in respect to Kansas and Nebraska, but also to Central America. Walker[3] in his marauding expeditions, is discouraged by the man called Frank Pierce and all his under-strappers, more especially, Southerners. If a rupture take place between the North and the South, then, and not until then, will the South discover their weakness, for the majority of the whites at the South are poor, and do not hold slaves, and in reality are opposed to slavery, but dare not express their honest convictions on the subject, for the penalty would surely be expulsion from their houses, or imprisonment, till they would agree to Southern views respecting slavery. There is now no freedom of speech or of the press in any southern state, except little Delaware, and here only in Wilmington. There is about as much anti-slavery feeling here as in Boston, and quite as freely expressed. I can have published in one paper at least anything I wish on the subject of slavery, as I always put my name to what I write.

When time and opportunity offers, a line from thee or any other of our anti-slavery friends in Europe will be gladly received by your friend, and the friend of Humanity, without regard to religion, country, or colour.

— Thomas Garrett

LETTER NO. 5

Haverford College Library Quaker Collection

[Author's Comment:

In this letter Garrett speaks of a number of outstanding abolitionists he knew personally. The first of these are James and Lucretia Mott. Lucretia Mott, particularly, achieved an outstanding reputation as an abolitionist. She was born on Nantucket Island, Massachusetts, of Quaker parents (Thomas and Anna Coffin). She has been described as small in stature, frail, tiny, demure, and with an extremely nervous temperament. Yet, in spite of her small physical proportions, she was heralded as a woman of great strength of character, swiftness of mind, and with an indomitable determination ... but always gentle. Lucretia and James Mott met at a Quaker boarding school in Poughkeepsie, New York, and were married in 1812. Later, they moved to Philadelphia, where Lucretia became involved in the activities of the Twelfth Street Friends Meeting. There she became an outstanding speaker against slavery and soon won the friendship of many prominent abolitionists, among them, William Lloyd Garrison. Like Garrison, Lucretia Mott held what was considered a "radical" position on the abolition of slavery, believing that there should be no compromise, but *total* abolishment of the slave system and absolute equality for the slave. In 1833 Lucretia and James Mott were among the numerous outstanding abolitionists who joined the newly formed American Anti-Slavery Society (founded in Philadelphia that year). Out of that organization came the Female Anti-Slavery Society, which Lucretia personally organized and served at different times as secretary, vice president, and president.

In 1840 Lucretia Mott was sent to the World's Anti-Slavery Convention in London, where she was refused a seat because she was a woman. Her persistence prevailed, however, and she made a speech at a breakfast meeting to the astonishment of many of the delegates, as well as the London newspapers, which dubbed her "the Lioness of the Convention." In 1848 she attended the first Women's Rights Convention, at Seneca Falls, New York. Here she first became associated with Elizabeth C. Stanton.

In 1857 James and Lucretia Mott moved from the city of Philadelphia proper, to Cheltenham Township. Their house on Old York Road — which was called "Roadside"— became a station on the UGRR. Because of her tireless devotion to the abolition of slavery, Lucretia Mott became known as "the black man's goddess." She was paid eloquent tribute by Frederick Douglass, one of the greatest runaway slaves and freedom fighters, who said of her that she was "foremost among those noble American women ... in the clearness of vision, breadth of understanding, catholicity of spirit, weight of character, and widespread influence," and that "When the true history of the anti-slavery cause shall be written, she shall occupy a large place in its pages."

Lucretia Mott died on November 11, 1880. "Of all the tributes bestowed upon that noble little Quaker lady," says one writer, "none is more meaningful than the naming of the village of LaMott (Pennsylvania), a community where men and woman, black and white, live together proudly and peacefully, a living example of the equality she sought for all people."[4]

Oliver Johnson, mentioned in this letter, was the editor of the abolitionist newspapers, the Ohio *Antislavery Bugle* and the Pennsylvania *Freeman*. He had been brought up a Calvinist on a farm in Vermont, but later converted to Quakerism. He was a nonresistant in his approach to the abolition of slavery, believing that, if need be, one should be willing to suffer any injury in the cause of abolishing slavery, but inflict none.

Parker Pillsbury, mentioned in this letter, was a Congregational Minister and abolitionist from New Hampshire who, like Lucretia Mott and William Lloyd Garrison (and Thomas Garrett) was considered a "radical" in his position toward the abolishment of slavery. He, Garrison and Johnson were also among those abolitionists who practiced *non-cooperation* with the government; that is, by refusing to vote or pay taxes, or serve on jury duty, and discourage enlistment in the armed forces until the government abolished slavery. After the Civil War, Pillsbury wrote his memoirs, entitled *Acts of Anti-slavery Apostles*. He also wrote *Brotherhood of Thieves*.

The Francis Jackson of whom Garrett speaks in this letter (although he spells the name incorrectly) was a wealthy Boston merchant, abolitionist, and partial nonresistant.

Samuel May, Jr. (not to be confused with his cousin, Samuel J. May, who was also an abolitionist, as well as pastor of a Unitarian Church), was an agent of the Massachusetts Antislavery Society and a nonresistant. He was the author of *The Fugitive Slave Law*, which was published in New York in 1861.

Charles K. Whipple was the treasurer of the Non-Resistance Society and also wrote for the *Liberator*.

Frances Ellen Watkins, mentioned in this letter, was an outstanding poetess and lecturer. She was born in Baltimore of free parents and received her education in a school for free Negroes, taught by her uncle who himself was an abolitionist. In August of 1854 the Boston Anti-slavery Society invited her to give her first lecture. The place was New Bedford, Massachusetts, and the subject was "Education and the Elevation of the Colored Race." This lecture established Frances Watkins as a truly outstanding and inspired speaker. Not only does Thomas Garrett express this (in the following letter), contemporary historian Benjamin Quarles also reports that she was "slender and graceful, with a soft and musical voice," and that she could "take hold on the human heart." In October 1857, says Quarles, "the Pennsylvania Anti- Slavery Society hired her as a lecturer and agent for Eastern Pennsylvania and New Jersey, and received glowing reports of her lectures until the termination of her appointment in May, 1858. A reporter at Mount Holly called her the best speaker he had ever heard. A listener at Norristown, Pennsylvania, was just a shade less enthusiastic, rating her as 'the most eloquent woman he has ever heard except Lucy Stone.'"[5]]

Wilmington, 12th mo. 27th, 1856

Esteemed Friend, Eliza Wigham,

Thy much valued letter of [the] 20th of 11th [month] last, came to hand a few days since, and I received the five pound sterling your Society so kindly sent me, while attending the Anti-Slavery Fair in Philadelphia, from our mutual friend, J. M. McKim, for which token of regard please return thanks to your Society. Their kind remembrance I highly prize, I can assure thee.

I had just commenced this letter when two colored men called to say they had three fugitives at their house, all able-bodied men, not more than 15 miles from their master's, and wishing me to give them directions how to evade their pursuers. I employed a pilot to convey them to the house of a friend in Chester Co. Thence they could pursue their journey with comparative safety, the whole neighborhood there being abolitionists. These make my register 2044.

If I recollect rightly, in my last letter I wrote thee that I had handed Harriet Tubman the five pound sterling you sent for her, but I then felt some hesitation about giving you some facts connected with it, which I think might be of interest to your Society, and more particularly, to the donor. In the first place I may inform you that Harriet has a good deal of the old fashion Quaker about her. She is a firm believer in spiritual manifestations, but I presume knows nothings bout table rappings, but she has confidence [that] God will preserve her from harm in all her perilous journeys, as she says she never goes on her missions of mercy without his consent, or approbation. At the same time [that] I gave her money thee sent her, she came into our store and asked for me. She was directed to the back counting house, where I was writing. I said to her, "Harriet, I am glad to see thee. Thee looks much better than when I last saw thee." Her reply was, "Yes, I thank you. I am now well, and God has sent me to you for money."

I said, "Harriet, how is this? I expected thee would want a new pair of shoes, as usual, when thee has been on a journey. These I can give thee, but thee know I have a great many calls for money from the coloured people, and thee cannot expect much money from me."

Her reply was, "You can give me what I need, now. God never fools me." I said, "Well, Harriet, how much does thee want now?" She said it would take 3½ shillings to get shoes for herself and the friend she had with her, to pay their expenses to Philadelphia, and she must have 20 shillings more to enable her to go for her sister and children, making 23½ in all.

I said to her, "Harriet, has thee been to Philadelphia, lately?

"No, not for several weeks."

"Has anyone told thee I had money for thee?"

"No, nobody but God."

I then gave her 24 shillings 31 cents, the proceeds of the five pounds thee sent her, and gave her an account of where it came from, and how thee came to get it to forward to her. After which she said, "Thank God."

I thought seriously of giving thee these facts in my last letter, but do not think I did so, fully. On mentioning the circumstances last week to William Lloyd Garrison and Jas. and Lucretia Mott, they encouraged me to write you and give [you] the facts, as near as I can now recollect in her own words, which I have endeavored to do.

And now for a history of her last mission of love and daring in order to rescue her sister and her children from Slavery:

She went for them at the time proposed, and had one or more interviews with her sister. But after waiting some ten days, [Harriet] found she could not get her [sister] and all three of the children, as two [of them] were placed at some distance from the mother. The mother was in the hopes they would be permitted to visit her during the holidays, which generally last from Christmas to New Year's day, and Harriet agreed to be in the neighborhood at that time, ready to bring all away together, as her sister would not leave without having all her children with her. When (Harriet) found such was the case, she left with 5 slaves—4 men and 1 woman—and reached here safely on foot, 90 miles through the enemy's country, having traveled six nights. Three days before they arrived, the masters of three of them arrived here, and had hand bills printed up and put up about the town (which were torn down by the colored people as fast as they were put up). They also had them distributed at the railway depots, and (in) principle towns all the way to where they left, offering 1500 shillings reward for one, 800 for another, and 300 for the third—the other man or woman I have never seen any reward offered for.

Four days after leaving here, I received a letter from our friend, Oliver Johnson, of New York, saying Harriet with her 5 friends had left that morning for Canada by railroad. Since that time I have not heard from her, and I very much fear she is sick, or something has happened to her, as she expected, when she left, to have been here 10 days since, on her way to her sisters. I feel almost confident she has not passed, as I have not heard of her in Philadelphia at the Anti-slavery Office since she left for Canada.

Oh how pleasant it is to know that those poor, oppressed, down-trodden, human beings can have a house in Canada under what our proud Republican Democrats call a Monarchial government — where they can rest under their own vine and fig tree, and none can make them afraid. How happy Queen Victoria must be when such truths loom up before her. I should rejoice with thee as would most of the inhabitants of New Castle County, if our Legislature could be induced to pass laws abolishing slavery in this State, immediately. If that could not be done, I would rejoice if they would go so far as to pass a law that no child born after this date could be held till more than 21 years of age, even in that case, real estate would increase more in value in 5 years than all the slaves would sell for, as by our laws (except for crime) slaves cannot be sold out of the state — they will not bring here more than two-thirds their market value in Maryland.

Since I commenced this letter, I have received one from our excellent friend, Parker Pillsbury, by which I find his health is improving, and he says his friends are not willing to spare him to come and spend the winter with us as we had expected, but in case he breaks down, he says he will come at once. As I cannot possibly give you anything more interesting, I will give you some extracts from his 1 letter. I have just received a circular from W. L. Garrison, Frances Jackson, and Sam May Jr., inviting me to attend the 25th anniversary of Immediate Emancipation, to be held at Boston on the 2nd of next month. My mission in the cause is of a more humble nature. I would gladly be with them, and no doubt would enjoy myself much, but at the close of the year, my business requires my presence, and more than at any other season of the year, my services are required for the assistance of the fleeing bondsman. So I must remain at home for the present.

I will now give you some extracts from our friend P's letter —

> Health with me is now a great object, but just at present I am able to labour so much that friends would a little rather have me at my post-and you need not be told that it is always the place of my choice. Were it not for this, many noble friends, with their generous offers and kind invitations, would almost (miss?) me, and I do strive to merit some of this beautiful and friendly consideration. But my way to do it is to be ever, as far as possible, at my post of duty and devotion to the great work of our mission. Should I break down a little, I would fly to your hospitable home and great heart, like a (born?) dove to her window. I am now very busy, and a part of my work is to assist at the Boston Bazaar, which opened yesterday. One old doorkeeper is ill, and Mr. May, Mr. C.K. Whipple, and myself, share the disagreeable duty among us. The receipts, yesterday, were 1568 dollars, the largest sum ever received in one day since the Fair was established. I hardly now have an auxiliary in the New England Guild. You refer to letters for me in the boxes from Great Britain. They all come to the number of one dozen, twelve epistles from twelve apostles, everyone of whom is as bold as Peter and as loving as John and as true to Him whom John and Peter called, "Lord." Oh the dear ones. I wish you knew them as I do. My family are in pretty good health, not the best. My daughters attend school. They would send

remembrances if they were here (as they ought to be). It is always pleasant to hear from you. I will keep you ever in view. My kindest regards to your household. Most truly yours,

P.P.

So it seems we are likely to miss the company of our friends this winter. His wife is a quiet, unassuming, but sweet, intelligent, woman. It is quite a trial to think we are not likely at present to have their society, but we abound with blessings and must not murmur.

We were favored a few weeks since with the company of Frances E. Watkins, a coloured lady, raised in Baltimore. Her mother died when she was 4 years of age, and she never knew her father. She was bound out to service, and went very little to school until she was 18. After that time she managed to get some education, and went to Little York, Pennsylvania, and kept school. For two years past she has been lecturing, mostly in the state of Maine. She is one of the most efficient, talented, pleaders for her color and race I ever heard speak. She delivered two lectures here that were amongst the most thrilling and interesting I ever listened to. You can find in the *Liberator* of last week a notice of her lectures by the Editor of one of our city papers.

I must now close, as I have written already enough to tire you, and more, I fear, than will interest you. But you must excuse an old man for dwelling on a subject that has been near to his best life from youth to the present time. I am of a sanguine temperament — I know I am, and may be wrong, but I am sanguine in the belief that 20 years cannot pass by before every slave state in the Union will be glad to pass laws for the emancipation of their slaves, and I should not be surprised if it were not done in half that time. If they do not do it, the slaves will rise up in mass before 20 years and murder their oppressors. That is my candid opinion. May that dreadful issue be prevented by the slave-holders becoming wiser than ever they yet have been.

With sincere desires for the happiness and welfare of all my kind friends beyond the wide waters of the ocean. I am your attached friend and the friend of humanity, without regard to nation or color.

— Thos. Garrett

LETTER NO. 6

Haverford College Library Quaker Collection

[Author's Comment:

This letter contains Garrett's account of the famous escape from the Dover, Delaware, jail, by eight runaway slaves, and the part he played in aiding the fugitives. See Chapter 12, Thomas Garrett and Harriet Tubman, for the complete story.]

Wilmington, Delaware, 3rd mo. 29th, 1857

My dear friend, Mary Edmundson,

Thy very acceptable letter, or note, reached me on the 24th instant. I feel very much flattered by the handsome donation your society has made to the cause of humanity in this land of boasted freedom, but in truth, a land of whips and chains. No one but those who have been for themselves, or heard from the lips of those who have been sufferers, can tell how much human nature can endure, and live.

Some 18 months since, I passed on a man of noble form in company with several others, who had met with a friend to pilot him thus far from the old Dominion, a distance of 300 miles, and delivered him to my care. He had left a beloved wife and three sweet children behind, all daughters, from 7 to 12 years of age. Soon after he had made his escape, the mother left with her three children and remained secreted in a cave for four long months, during the winter of 1855–6. In the Spring they were brought to me in a vessel, a fairer form of countenance I hardly ever saw in a woman or children. They were really white and very intelligent. I inquired her history. She told me her husband was about to be sold, six months previous, and made his escape, since which she had never heard of him, and thought most likely she never would. After making inquiry for his real name, and all about him, I told her I knew where her husband was, and would send her and the children to him in a few hours. He was in the state of Massachusetts, some 400 miles distant. I would have paid for months of labour to have witnessed the joy of the whole family — it was First Day (Sunday), but to gratify me, she let the youngest daughter sing and dance, and I thought she had one of the most sweetest, most musical, voices I ever listened to. I enjoyed their happiness as much as I ever enjoyed a Quaker meeting with the best of preachers. In 36 hours she was with her husband.

I will now give you an account of the miraculous escape of 8 slaves from Dover, the capital of this state, about 50 miles below here, on 3rd Day morning (Tuesday), the ninth of the present month:

They were decoyed into Dover jail about 4 o'clock in the morning by a coloured man named Otwell, who lived near Milford, some 20 miles lower down the country. He had been employed by the friends of the coloured people, or slaves, for some time as a pilot and these slaves had paid him 8 pounds to pilot them near 30 miles to the next station, within a few miles from Dover, and I believe he had always previously been true to his trust. Within the last year he had rented a small farm from a white man *outside,* named Hollis, who had been informed that Otwell had been employed as an agent in the Underground Railroad, and had so far succeeded in corrupting his morals as to induce him to pilot the slaves into Dover jail, where they would divide the reward between them.

Hollis had gone on the previous day to prepare the Sheriff for their reception. The Sheriff waited up until two o'clock, and then went to bed, leaving Hollis to watch.

It was near four o'clock when they arrived. Otwell introduced them to Hollis as his particular friend, and a great friend of the slaves, and told them to go with him and he would take care of them. Hollis took them directly to the jail, upstairs, into a room where the windows were barred with iron across them, which could be seen by the light of the moon. One of the men noticed this, and said he did not like the looks of the place, and stepped out into the entry, taking the rest with him. The

Sheriff, as soon (as he was) dressed, ran upstairs expecting to find them all in the room where he would have nothing to do but turn the key and have them all safe. In finding them in the entry he ran downstairs to where his wife and children were in bed, for his pistols, but they followed so close he could not reach the pistol before they were in the room. One of the men picked up a hot andiron from the hearth, throwing the fire over the room, even to the bed, and with the red hot andiron kept the Sheriff off until the rest broke out the window-sash and all — and then jumped out, a distance of 12 feet to the soft mud.

When all the rest were safe, the man gave the Sheriff a push, and jumped out after them. Two of the men took their course this way, four men and two women took the back track. Not knowing which way to run, fortunately, as it proved for them, they soon overtook the *scamp, Otwell,* who had betrayed them. Their first impulse was to kill him, but he begged so hard, and promised so fair, if they would only spare his life he would take them to the house of the friend he had promised in the first place instance to take them to, which he did, and then ran off as fast as he could, and we have never heard of him since.

The men were all armed with pistols and knives, and it is a wonder that they acted with so much coolness and discretion. One of the men told me he would have killed him at once had he not thought, if he did do it, he would have less chance to escape than if they committed no act of violence, which no doubt was a correct view.

The next morning, after their escape, the person who had charge of the six wrote to me and sent a special message up by the railroad, giving me a full account of what had occurred, and wishing my advice how to proceed. I at once wrote to an intimate friend near him to communicate to him my views, as I could not safely write to a coloured man while there was so much excitement there. He at once got my letter and all worked well.

On Fifth day night [Thursday], one of the two that separated from the rest came to my home. He was provided for. The next First Day night [Sunday], two more of the men arrived safe. I had been on the road several nights watching for them, to keep them from crossing the bridges, which were closely watched.

The same day, a coloured man that had the other four in charge several days, and had piloted them safely over 20 miles and left them with a friend who was to bring them up here next night, a distance of 22 miles, came up on the cars. I, that night, sent two men to meet them several miles from here with directions to cross the Christiana river in a boat, and take them across the country to place of safety, ten miles from town. Those I have never seen, but learned they got along nicely. I heard of them several days after, all doing well. One of the men I have never heard of since he left jail, but feel convinced he is safe, as I should have heard from him had he been taken.

It was a week of great anxiety, I can assure you. I could not think of much else. It cost me in money nearly half the amount of your liberal donation, but I have no recollection of any money that I ever spent more cheerfully in the cause. These coloured men came up as pilots, distances of 22 to 58 miles, and I gave each of them a trifle to help pay expenses home on the cars.

Thou mentions [that] a small part of the money sent is intended especially for Harriet Tubman. Poor Harriet, I fear something has happened to her. She left here last 11th month with 3 or 4 slaves for Canada. She got a friend in New York to write me. She got along that far, safely, and would leave next morning for Canada, and expected to be here again in two weeks—since which I have never been able to learn anything respecting her, but should I ever have an opportunity, I shall most assuredly give her the money sent to her.

Those eight slaves mentioned in this (letter) came from the immediate neighborhood of [Harriet's] old master; one of these men I saw (the first that arrived) his name is Tubman, (also), the assumed name of Harriet. The man told me that his master has been offered 2200 pounds for him. No doubt he thinks he has met with a great loss.

Three of the masters of three of those slaves arrived in Dover on 2nd Day [Monday] before the slaves arrived. [They] had their advertisement printed and put up in the afternoon, but I have not been informed whether or not they lodged in town that night. Taken altogether, it has astonished the whole neighborhood how they managed to get clear.

I was just commencing a letter to thy sister, Eliza Wigham, from whom I had received several favors, and at once concluded to write to thee instead of her and request thee to send it to her so that the Ladies Emancipation Society of Edinburgh may have it, if they desire it. I would also like my friend, Rich Webb, to see it. I lately received a kind note from him, and will enclose a note with this for him if I can find him.

Some years ago I considered myself rich, and spent several hundred dollars a year in the cause of suffering humanity. When near sixty years of age, I lost nearly all, but still had enough to pay my debts, and at that age, commenced the world anew, and am now pretty fairly on my feet once more.

I am in the mercantile iron and hardware business, have a very efficient aid in my youngest son, who sympathizes with me. The last two years I received aid from England and Scotland to meet all my outlays within about 20 dollars. The money is acceptable, but that is not to compare with the pleasure produced by knowing that my labors for those oppressed creatures meet with approbation and sympathy from the good and the true, not overly in this land, but on your side of the water.

Last year I received about 70 dollars from England, through Samuel Rhoads of Philadelphia, but I never knew to whom I was indebted for it.

First day morning, 29th: I have this moment received a letter from Wm. Still [of] Philadelphia informing me that Harriet Tubman has arrived in Phila, and was well, and contemplates making a visit South, this week. This is good news. She is to call on me for the money on her way. When in the city she makes her home at Wm. Stills house, and two weeks ago, he had not heard from her for months.

Still writes me that last second day they met with the first death in that city of a passenger by the Underground Railroad, a very Interesting subject. He had traveled for more than two weeks. During the last cold spell, the first of this month—nine days—he laid *out* every night and day without fire. His feet became badly frozen. His toes became mortified and came off, and he died after great suffering with lockjaw. And yet with all his suffering, when death stared him in the face, he rejoiced he had escaped from slavery! Truly a sad picture to contemplate. Neither Mrs. Stowe's Uncle Tom, nor the Autobiography of a Female Slave paints the horrors of slavery in too high colors. You will see at once that part of this will not do to publish, but thru it, I welcome all who feel an interest in human freedom—from thy sincere friend,

—Thomas Garrett

Many thanks to all kind friends for their sympathy and liberality. It is very pleasant to have the sympathy of friends.

LETTER NO. 7
Haverford College Library Quaker Collection

Wilmington, 8th mo. 11th, 1857

Esteemed Friend, Mary Edmundson,

Thy much esteemed favor of 7th mo. 1st reached me by due course of mail, and I ought to have acknowledged its receipt ere this, but we have been very busy building an addition to my store, moving iron, and taking an account of stock.

Last week I received from our mutual friend, McKim, the five pound sterling thee enclosed to him for me to aid the fugitives. I have truly cause to be thankful to thee and other kind friends on your side of the ocean for the aid thus received, not that I shall aid one friend more on their flight from the whips and chains of their taskmasters, but the means thus afforded enables me now to furnish some whom I know to be worthy with funds to carry them safely to the dominions of England's Queen.

I lately say that the 4th day of the 6th mo. furnished Harriet Tubman's father and mother, Benjamin and Catherine Ross with 30 pounds to carry them to Canada. Thee may see their names in the arrivals of fugitives in Canada in last weeks *Antislavery Standard*. Harriet Tubman accompanied them. The old man Ross had to flee. He had been guilty of sheltering in his hut, for one day, those 8 slaves that broke out of Dover jail, early last Spring. A fine coloured man who piloted these slaves some 20 miles to his house from Carolina County, was betrayed by one who started with the rest, (then) turned back and informed of the man who piloted them, and told where they went to stop over the first day. The poor man was tried and convicted and sentenced to the Maryland Penitentiary for ten years. They were preparing to have Benjamin arrested when his master secretly advised him to leave. His wife belonged to another plantation, and the old man, wisely concluding it would be more agreeable to have her along. She left without so much as asking leave, and with such an experienced guide as Harriet, they passed safely on.

Harriet has still one sister and her 3 children yet in slavery. She has tried hard this summer to get them all away together, but two of the children are separated some twelve miles from their mother, which has caused the difficulty — her sister refusing to leave without bringing all her children away with her.

Harriet's health has much improved, and I hope she will be spared many years yet. Since Harriet's parents were here, I passed on a poor broken-hearted coloured woman, near 70 years of age, the mother of 13 children. She left husband and children behind. Her husband's master lived some distance from her. For some offence, her master was about to sell her. She secreted herself in the woods two days and nights, nearly naked, and suffered dreadfully with the cold. She said she had good clothes at her master's, but could not in any way get them. We had to keep her a week before she was able to travel. My wife fitted her out with two suits of underclothes, good worsted frock, stockings, bonnet, and when fully rigged, she really seemed to almost forget her troubles. I furnished her with money to carry her to New York, and sent a pilot with her to Philadelphia.

I am fully aware that I cannot give the history of those particular cases without appearing to strangers, egotistical, but I can assure thee, it is only from necessity of the case that self figures so much in what I write to you. I know I have nothing to boast of. Sometimes I feel as though I had not fully done my duty. But of one thing I am certain, that I have never had cause to regret all I have ever done for those poor creatures. When I see how happy they are in the prospect of freedom, I cannot do less than partake with them in their joy. As a general thing, the poor creatures think themselves almost as safe when they get here as when they arrive in Canada, and it has proved to be so to an astonishing degree, [that] out of 2072 I have passed, I have never heard of but three that were taken back to bondage!

We are here, at present, living under one of the most tyrannical and corrupt governments on the face of the earth. The whole United States are ruled by about 300,000 slave-holders and their northern dough-faced allies who, for the sake of power and gold, will stoop to any mean, despotic act.

12th: I was aroused early this morning by the arrival of three fugitives, a man, wife, and son, 20 years of age. They had traveled three nights, and are now 60 miles from home. The man and wife have been owned by different persons, and lived 20 miles apart for more than 20 years. They will leave this morning on the Underground Railroad for Canada. The man and wife are quite intelligent, and well dressed. They met with kind friends to pilot them all the way here. It would have made the heart glad to have spent an hour with them this morning as I did. They were so cheerful and full of hope for the future. The parents were about 43 years of age, and think they will have no difficulty in maintaining themselves if they arrive safely in Canada.

I have remembrances to all those kind friends who have been instrumental in raising funds for the slaves, and retain a full share for thyself.

         Thine for the slave,
         — Thomas Garrett

18

Miscellaneous Letters

LETTER NO. 1
Division of History and Cultural Affairs
Dover, Delaware.
[Author's Comment: The Joseph Watson was the mayor of Philadelphia.]

Wilmington, 2nd mo. 20th, 1826

Respected friend, Joseph Watson,

I find by our papers that thou hast received a communication from the state of Mississippi respecting several colour'd persons, said to be kidnapped, one of which is stated to have lived in this place. There is a female of the name Charity Fisher that left this place the 6th day of last 10th month, expecting to return in a few days that has not since been heard of by her friends. Every circumstance except the first name would induce me to believe it was the same. I will furnish thee with what information I have on the subject, and should anything transpire to make it necessary to have more in-formation on the subject, I will cheerfully attend to it at anytime. Her mother's name is, at this time, Elizabeth Hirous, and [she] lives here. She says Charity was born near Downingstown, Penna; that she removed, when young, with, or by, her mother, to the neighborhood of Smyrna. After living there five years, she was sent to James Downing, near Downingstown, where she stayed till the time above stated. When she left here it may not be amiss to state that she had, while here, and left behind her, a male child about 9 months old, named Matthew, and that she never was married. She is supposed, at this time, to be about 24 years old, lusty make and light complexion for a decedent of Africa — looks a little on our side, sewing, or doing any work of that kind — thinks she has a small blemish on her left eye. Her mother says she has a daughter living in Cherry Way, Phila, with friends of the name of William and Mary James. Her name is Debbie Fisher. I think it [is] probable [that] she can give some more information on the subject. If anything more transpires on the subject, I shall be glad to hear from thee, as the mother is anxious to hear the fate of her daughter. I am respectfully, thy friend,

—Thomas Garrett Jr.

LETTER NO. 2

Swarthmore College Library
[Author's Comment: Elijah F. Penneypacker was a Station Master in Phoenixville, Pennsylvania, to whom Garrett often sent fugitives. Both Smedley and William Still give a sketch of Penneypacker in their books. Thomas' brother, Edward, mentioned in this letter, is his youngest brother, who inherited the Garrett Homestead in Upper Darby. *A History of Upper Darby* mentions that Edward was also involved with UGRR activities (See page 119 of that book). Samuel Rhoads, mentioned here, is Garrett's cousin (see letter to William Still, No. 10).]

Wilmington, 7 mo. 5th, 1846

Respected Friend, Elijah F. Penneypacker,

Thine of the 2nd, as well as a former letter, came duly to hand, and I at once answered the first letter, which it would appear thee has not receiv'd. I wrote thee, I think, that a few days after the husband left here, a woman with two children came to town and inform'd me that she was the woman that was left by her husband at John Hunn's, to be forwarded to him as soon as he should get a situation. I then told her I heard nothing of him since he left. Some two or three days after, I received a letter from my brother, Edward, requesting me to have the woman and the children forwarded to Samuel Rhoads, near Waddingtonville. She and the children arrived safe there [the] next evening, one of my sons being there when they arrived. That was some 2 or 3 weeks since. There appears to be some mystery in this business, as I recollect no other man having a wife and children at John Hunn's. If there is any other person, I will make of John Hunn, inquiry—or thee had perhaps better write thyself to him. Direct thy letter to John Hunn, near Middletown, Delaware.

Thine respectfully,
—Thos. Garrett

LETTER NO. 3

Historical Society of Delaware, Helen Garrett Papers

Wilmington 8 mo. 2nd, 1847

To Isaac Updike:

I have for some weeks had my mind drawn at times to thy situation, and to that of thy family. In my very soul I pity you all. Although I look upon the crime of kidnapping more cruel and wicked than I do that of highway robbing, I hope and believe that thy own conscience has punished thee sufficiently with the deprivation thou hast already suffer'd by being separated so long from a kind wife and family. And, believing as I do, that thou will be hereafter more careful to live an honest and respectable life than thou hast heretofore done, I have proposed to William S. Boulden, to get up a petition to the Governor of the state for thy pardon, and I have agreed to head the list of petitioners for thy release. If the petition should be successful (as I hope it may) I sincerely hope that thou will resist all temptation to take strong drink to excess, or do any other act that shall again bring reproach on thyself or family.

I am not so circumstanced at this time ... to do as much as I once could have done to assist thee should thee again get in [to] difficulty, but will at all times be glad to do all in my power to render thyself or family, assisting by advice, or any other way in power, believing as I do if thee sincerely repents, the Heavenly Father will forgive thee all thy past crimes. So ought all His followers do the same. Hoping thou will deserve the Sympathy and Kindness of thy fellow men, I subscribe myself thy Sincere friend.

— Thos. Garrett

LETTER NO. 4

Taken from the *Liberator,* October 14, 1853

LETTER FROM THOMAS GARRETT:

> We take the liberty of inserting the following letter from Thomas Garrett, of Delaware, though we are not sure it was meant for publication. This brave old man has done duty for several years on the frontiers of Slavery, and many a fugitive owes his freedom to his good offices. He has endured, as our readers will remember, the spoiling of his goods for conscience's sake. His entire property, we believe was taken from him and passed over to a slaveholder, to whose slaves he had given food and shelter. And his reply, when this miscreant said to him, as he pocketed the fruits' of a life's labor for a deed of charity, 'I hope, Mr. Garrett, you will take warning by this punishment, and never violate the laws again!'— his reply will pass into the number of brave sayings which the heart of humanity loves to treasure up. Turning to the Sheriff, who had conducted the sale, and satisfied the execution, he said, quietly, 'Friend, if thee should see a fugitive slave in want of help to-day, thee will please send him to me!'

Wilmington, 10th mo. 6th, 1853

Robert F. Wallout, Esteemed Friend,

Enclosed you will find three dollars, which please place to my credit for the *Liberator*. I have [subscribed to the] paper almost from its commencement, and of all the papers I read, none has advocated so fully and fearlessly the cause of the oppressed bonds-man, and none has caused so much alarm to the slave-holders of the South as the *Liberator*, and the name of no living man has caused such fearful forebodings for the future, as William Lloyd Garrison. I have frequently been brought in contact with them, not only at home in little Delaware, but in Maryland, Virginia and Carolina. I have ventured, while traveling in the cars and steamboats, frequently to refer to Garrison as one of the greatest philanthropists of the age. A man who had thought and reflected much on the evils and cruelty of Slavery, and one who dared to express what he thought, and act accordingly. And I have often, on such occasions, ventured to say, that I united fully with him, in general, in his views. I have several times caused the storm to rage violently for a time, but by keeping cool, the whirlwind would pass by and a calm would succeed. Whether it was my age — 64 years— plain Quaker garb, or 'cool impudence,' as some would call it, that protected me, I cannot tell. But certainly it is, I never received a scar or bruise on such occasions, except once, when two or three Southerners took hold of me to throw me off the cars [trains] in this city, when I entered to save a free colored woman from being carried to the South. I was then slightly bruised by the railing of the cars, but well in a few days.

Thine very respectfully,

— Thomas Garrett

LETTER NO. 5
Swarthmore College Library

Wilmington, 11th mo. 29th, 1856

My dear Friend, Joseph A. Dugdale,

Thine of yesterday was handed me just now by thy John. I will endeavor to attend the meeting on Spiritualism if I can leave home. We shall be glad to have thyself, wife, and your friend from Pittsburgh, on 4th day next [Wednesday]. We expect to have Frances E. Watkins on 3rd Day [Tuesday]. We have engaged the Odd Fellows Hall for her on that evening, on 5th Day [Friday], Horace Greeley is to lecture in the evening, and will stop at our house while in the city.

I have a letter this day from Oliver Johnson, informing me of the safe arrival of that wonderful woman, Harriet Tubman. She passed through here on First Day [Sunday] last, with 4 men and 1 woman, for which there is a reward of 2600 dollars, offered in the Baltimore *Sun*. She left this morning for Canada.

My wife is pretty smart, the rest, as well as usual. My slave list is now 2038. Still they go.

Love to thy wife and all the friends of suffering humanity the world over.

As ever thy friend,

— Thos Garrett

LETTER NO. 6
Cornell University Library
[Author's Comment: Edward M. Davis mentioned in this letter is the son-in-law of James and Lucretia Mott.]

Wilmington, 6th mo. 20th, 1858

Dear friends, James Mott and Edward M. Davis,

Your circular soliciting funds in aid of the Anti-slavery cause was duly received. I need not tell you that I feel poor, and yet at times find it very difficult to get money to meet our payments with credit. But the Anti-slavery cause has long been very near to my best life, and unless I am very much disappointed, will send you ten dollars in all, next month, to aid the cause. If you have not already done, please do not send one of the circulars to Edward Webb of our town. He has talents, and was a faithful laborer in the Anti-slavery vineyard, but [he] has been compelled to yield to the pressure of the times, and made an assignment, and I presume from what I hear [that he] will fall very short of being able to pay dues. To make the matter worse, he has a young wife about ready to be confin'd with her first child. With sincere regard, I remain,

> Your friend,
> —Thos. Garrett

Letter No. 7
Delaware State Archives

> Wilmington, 2 mo. 7th, 1860

Dear friends, Joseph, Ruth [Dugdale], Isaac and Dinah [Mendinhall]

As Benjamin Kent is going to your place today, I write to say that I have not yet been kidnapped by the Marylanders, and hope by this time my friends may breathe freer. I have had sundry letters from friends, some advising me to leave home for a few weeks, and one to go to England for a year or two, and take my wife along. I presume you have not been so much alarmed about me. It is true, the papers have made very free with my name, but I have given myself no trouble about what has been said, until yesterday. I wrote a statement of my position respecting aiding slaves, and sent it to the Peninsular *News* for insertion. I will enclose a scurrilous piece cut from the Pennsylvanian of the 30th of last month, by which you will see that they have placed me in good company, but the writer has stooped so low that it is not worthy of notice.

The meeting here on the men's side abandoned the case on music, so long pending, without disowning Elizabeth Grubb. My wife keeps smart this winter. The rest, all well.

> Much love to you,
> T and R Garrett

Letter No. 8
Swarthmore College Library

> Wilmington, 10th mo. 20th, 1862

Dear Children, J. & M. McCollin,

We have not heard from you since we left you this day week. This is a sweet bracing morning, and I hope it may prove strengthening to Margaret. I presume that Arnie is all right again by this time.

I was in Philadelphia on 6th Day [Friday] and dined with John and Mary. They were pretty well, Emlen also. We got home nicely from the Valley, dined and fed the horses at the [Mansion's?] House, called on the Dr. He said he could not go that afternoon to see you, but would go next morning.

Got home by 5 P.M. without any rain. The women all well pleased with their visit.

There is to be a meeting here next 6th Day Evening to take into consideration the establishing of a Boarding School for children of what are called, Hicksite Friends. [A] Committee from New York, Phila. and Baltimore, are to meet here to consider the subject.

The Annual Meeting of the Pennsylvania Society [of] Anti-slavery meet at West Chester on 7th day next 25th, at 10 o'clock. I expect that Rachel and I will be there.

Samuel J. May, Jr., 1798–1871.

We left Margaret's shawl with Dr. Price to take to you next day, Catherine not needing it. Elizabeth and Penny got their family home last night, and commenced House Keeping again, after a month's absence, Love to all.

Your Father,
—Thos. Garrett

LETTER NO. 9

Boston Public Library.

Wilmington, 11th mo. 24th, 1863

Esteem'd Friend, Samuel May Jr.,

I received a few days since, the printed circular thee was so kind as to send, inviting me to attend the 3rd Decade of the American Anti-slavery Society, with thy request that I give a brief statement, of the flight of Fugitive Slaves through this city. I have ever at our annual meeting (when called on to do so) given the number of slaves I have register'd as having aided to escape, even when it was very unpopular to do so — it now covering a space of 38 years — but have never done (except) only when called on to do so, as I did not wish to appear egotistical. What I have done was from principle; from a conviction that it was my duty to aid all of God's poor in their flight from their cruel Taskmasters, and I have been abundantly blessed in all that I have done.

Since the first of the year I have had it in my power to aid so few it is hardly worth stating, but I will cheerfully give the number register'd at that time, and each year since:

    1st mo. 1st, 1860, I had registered, 2246

    during that year I forwarded 33

    during 1861 "" 22

    during 1862 14

    during 1863, to 11 mo, 24th 7

    making 2322

The last two were females, one of which we have in our family, a kind hearted girl of 19 years, from near Fortress Monroe. She is very desirous to get some book learning, and has made considerable progress for the opportunity she has had.

I shall certainly attend the Decade Meeting if nothing occurs to prevent, as I have always been richly paid for any sacrifice I may have made to get there.

I rejoice to learn that our efficient laborer and friend, George Thompson, expects soon to be with us in this country. How I should rejoice to have him, Wendell Phillips, or Garrison, or all of them, to attend a meeting in this place. Little Delaware has acted so creditably in the election last week in electing a thorough Anti-slavery man in the person, N.P. Smithers, as Representative to Washington that I hope one, or all, will find time to come during the coming winter; My house shall be open freely, and Gladly to entertain them or any other friend of the oppressed.

I believe if a vote was fairly taken tomorrow, whether or not Slavery should be abolish'd within the coming year, the majority would vote for it. But unfortunately, *our* Legislature only sets once in two years, and when Elected, serve two terms. They will not meet for 12 months, and about two thirds of them, last session, were copperheads — as they are term'd — of the strongest kind. But I cannot but hope that either Congress or the President, or both, will, during the coming session, declare Universal Emancipation to all.

These views are intended for thyself, and such of thy friends as thee may think will feel interest in the Cause. But I prefer not having my name published further than to state, as I have done, the number of slaves that have passed through my hands. That cannot effect my credit any with [of] my friends. And should Judge Taney, the hardhearted and unjust Judge, see it, it might make him feel uncomfortable. For when I was taken before him for aiding a family of slaves in 1847,[1] and through his charge to the juries, and his influence, fined 5,400 dollars. I promised before all the Court House that I would double my diligence in aiding all in my power at whatever cost.

I will now close. When I sat down to write, I did not intend to write more than one side of a page.

Farewell, Remember me to Garrison and Phillips, and all those who labor'd years back, as it were, in thick clouds. A brighter day is near at hand. Much nearer than any of us could have hoped for 10 years since. But when the first gun was fired at Fort Sumpter, I believed the fate of the slave-holders was sealed, and that slavery would be abolished before the war was over.

18. Miscellaneous Letters

As ever, thy friend, and the friend of the oppressed, without regard to the colour or country.

— Thos. Garrett

LETTER NO. 10

[Author's Comment:

The following letter is to Sarah Bradford, Harriet Tubman's first biographer. It is in response to Mrs. Bradford's request for Garrett's opinion of Harriet Tubman.]

Wilmington, 6th mo. 1868

My Friend:

Thy favor of the 12th reached me yesterday, requesting such reminiscences as I could give respecting the remarkable labors of Harriet Tubman, in aiding her colored friends from bondage. May I begin by saying, living as I have in a slave State, and the laws being very severe where any proof could be made of anyone aiding slaves on their way to freedom, I have not felt at liberty to keep any written word of Harriet's or my own labors, except in numbering those whom I have aided. For that reason I cannot furnish so interesting an account of Harriet's labors as I otherwise could, and, now would be glad to do; for in truth, I never met with any person, of any color, who had more confidence in the voice of God, as spoken direct to her soul. She has frequently told me that she talked with God, and he talked with her every day of her life, and she has declared to me that she felt no more fear of being arrested by her former master, or any other person, when in his immediate neighborhood, than she did in the state of New York, or Canada, for she said she never ventured only where God sent her, and her faith in the Supreme Power truly was great.

I have been confined to my room with indisposition more than four weeks, and cannot write too much; but I feel so much interested in Harriet that I will try to give some of the most remarkable incidents that now present themselves to my mind. The date of the commencement of her labors, I cannot certainly give; but I think it must have been about 1845. From that time till 1860 I think she must have brought from the neighborhood where she has been held as a slave from 60 to 80 persons, from Maryland, some 80 miles from here. [Mrs. Bradford gives the following footnote to the above statement by Garrett:

> Friend Garrett probably refers here to those who passed through his hands: Harriet was obliged to come by many different routes on her journeys, and though she never counted those whom she brought away with her, it would seem by the computation of others, that there must have been somewhat over three hundred brought by her the Northern States, and Canada.]

No slave who placed himself under her care, was ever arrested that I have heard of; she mostly had her regular stopping places on her route; but in one instance, when she had several stout men with her, some 30 miles below here, she said that

God told her to stop, which she did; and then asked Him what she must do. He told her to leave the road, and turn to the left; she obeyed, and soon came to a small stream of tide water; there was no boat, no bridge; she again inquired of her Guide what she was to do. She was told to go through. It was cold, in the month of March, but having confidence in her Guide, she went in; the water came up to her armpits; the men refused to follow till they saw her safe on the opposite shore. They then followed, and, if I mistake not, she had soon to wade a second stream soon after, which she came to a cabin of colored people, who took them all in, put them to bed, and dried their clothes, ready to proceed next night on their journey. Harriet had ran out of money, and gave them some of her underclothing to pay for their kindness.

When she called on me two days after, she was so hoarse she could hardly speak, and was also suffering with violent toothache. The strange part of the story was found to be, that the masters of these men had put up, the previous day, at the railroad station where she left, an advertisement for them, offering a large reward for their apprehension; but they made a safe exit. She at one time brought as many as seven or eight, several of whom were women and children. She was well known here in Chester County and Philadelphia, and respected by all true abolitionists. I had been in the habit of furnishing her, and those who accompanied her, as she returned from her acts of mercy, with new shoes; and on one occasion, when I had not seen her for three months, she came into my store. I said, "Harriet I am glad to see thee! I suppose thee wants a pair of new shoes."

Her reply was "I want more than that."

I, in jest, said "I have always been liberal with thee, and wish to be, but I am not rich, and cannot afford to give thee much."

Her reply was, "God tells me you have money for me.":

I asked her "If God ever deceived her?"

"No!"

"How much does thee want?"

After studying a moment, she said; "About twenty-three dollars."

I then gave her twenty-four dollars and some odd cents, the net proceeds of five pounds sterling, received through Eliza Wigham of Scotland, for her.[2]

I had given some accounts of Harriet's labors in the Anti-Slavery Society of Edinburgh, of which Eliza Wigham was Secretary. On the reading of my letter, a gentleman said he would send four pounds if he knew of any ways to get it to her. Eliza Wigham offered to forward it to me for her, and that was the first money ever received by me for her. Some twelve months after, she called on me again, and said that God told her I have some money for her, but not so much as before. I had, a few days previous, received the net proceeds of one pound, ten shillings, from Europe, for her. To say the least, there was something remarkable in these facts, whether clairvoyance or the divine impression on her mind from the source of all power, I cannot tell, but certain it was she had a Guide within herself other than the written word, for she never had any education.

She brought away her aged parents in a singular manner. They started with an old horse, fitted out in primitive style with a *straw collar,* a pair of old Chaise wheels, with a board on the axle to sit on, another board, swung with ropes, fastened to the axle, to rest their feet on. She got her parents, who were both slaves belonging to different masters, on this rude vehicle to the railroad, put them in the cars, turned Jehu herself, and drove to town in a style that no human being ever did before or since; but she was happy at having herself other than the written word, for she never had any education, arrived safe. Next day, I furnished her with money to take them all to Canada. I afterward sold their horse, and sent them the balance of the proceeds. I believe that Harriet succeeded in freeing all her relatives but one sister and her three children.

             Thy friend,
             —Thomas Garrett

LETTER NO. 11
Boston Public Library

             Wilmington, Del. 4 mo. 2nd, 1869

Esteem'd Friend, Samuel May Jr.,

 Thine of the 28th of last month is before me, soliciting aid for our valued friend, George Thompson. I presume thee is aware that I lost all I had when about 60 years of age, by the mismanagement of my partners in the manufacture of Iron. At 60 years of age I commenced business again with a cash capital of 850 dollars, with an addition of a large amount of credit, not only with my friends, but also at (the) Bank where I had kept my Bank account for near 30 years. I was quite successful, and in sixteen years had made what I thought was sufficient for the interest to support me for the rest of my life. I then sold my interest in the store to one of my grandsons and a young man that had been in our store for many years, neither of which had any capital: I loan'd each of them 15,000 dollars at 6 per cent, which enabled them to take my interest, my youngest son, Eli, having one half the store. It proved a wise move to leave the store, a few months after my health failed, and for 2 years I could, with difficulty, get about. I paid different Physicians over 600 dollars. At last they owned they could not cure me. I was then for 5 months without any Physicians but took some medicine from a Doctor in New York for 3 months that seem'd to help me. It then lost its effect. Early last month, an old Physician, name of Wooley, called to consult me about some business of his own, and finding my situation, he thought he could, help, if not cure, me in three weeks. He had a good recommendation from John G. Whittier and from Dillyn Parrish of Phila. I told him to go to work, and in 24 days he left quite comfortable, and I now enjoy better health than I have for several years. He boarded with me while attending me, and charged me 150 dollars, which I paid freely, as he done me more good than all the other Physicians to whom I paid about 600 dollars.

 The claims on my benevolence for sometime past has been heavy for my circumstances. Last week I paid 20 dollars toward educating the freed men of this state, as our Legislation will do nothing for that class of people. I also have a brother, quite poor, a farmer. He had no horses sufficient to do his work, and in a few days since I paid 125 dollars for a Horse for him. I have also agreed to pay 80 dollars more (I have already paid 200) towards Friends Boarding School. Those payments have left me pretty bare, so that I cannot well do what I would wish to do for my valued friend, but I will enclose thee my check, payable to thy order, for twenty-five dollars, but small as it is, it may add somewhat to his comfort. I hope that sufficient may be raised in some way for his relief. If he could only be induced to give up the use of snuff, I think his health would be much better. Please acknowledge the receipt and oblige thy friend,

— Thos. Garrett

LETTER NO. 12
From the *Liberator*
Letter from Thomas Garrett.

Wilmington, Del. 4th mo. 5th, 1870

Aaron M. Powell, Esteemed Friend,

I received an invitation from thee and our kind friend, Mary Grew, to attend a meeting in New York, the 9th of this month, to commemorate the ratification of the Fifteenth Amendment. I certainly would be with you on that interesting occasion were it in my power to do so. Some five weeks since I received an injury, getting out of a carriage, in one knee, and have been confined to my room with it for the last four weeks, and cannot walk across my room without crutches, [and] therefore have no hope of being able to get to attend the meeting, which I fully intended to do, as it would give me great pleasure to meet my old friends who have so long [been] with me in the cause of the slave, and join with them in the last meeting of the American Anti-Slavery Society. I rejoice that I have lived to see this day, when the colored people of this favored land, by law, have equal privileges with the most favored. And I have faith to believe that ere long equal justice will be granted to the poor Indians, and the Chinese.

In the year 1818, I became a member of the Abolition Society of Pennsylvania, and labored therein till 1822, when I moved to Wilmington, Del. That year I was appointed, with William Chandler, by the Delaware Anti-Slavery Society, to investigate the case of two colored bound girls, they were sold as slaves to a trader in slaves, who took them out of the State and sold them. From that time I neglected no opportunity to aid all those oppressed people who called on me for aid, and I have cause to be thankful that I was placed in a situation where I could aid those abused and down-trodden people. No labor during a long life has given me so much real happiness as what I have done for the slave. And I now rejoice most heartily that African Slavery is forever ended in this country. But there is much yet for philanthropists to do for this people before they can fully enjoy the great boon granted them by the Fifteenth Amendment. In this city, on 7th Day last [Saturday], at an election for school directors, the colored people's vote was taken at seven of the nine wards. At two wards with Democratic inspectors, their votes were refused. This state of things cannot continue long. The friends of the slave may now profitably turn their attention to the Sixteenth Amendment, and the Woman Suffrage question,[3] for that, too, must soon be settled by granting equal suffrage to male and female alike.

Sincerely thy assured friend,
— Thomas Garrett

Appendix A:
Thomas Garrett Genealogy

Thomas Garrett's Parents

Garrett's father:
Thomas Garrett, born Oct. 29, 1748 — died Aug. 24, 1839.

Father's first wife:
Margaret Levis, born (?) — died Aug. 11, 1776. They were married November 18, 1773, at Springfield Meeting (PA).

Children of Garret's father and first wife:
Mary, born Aug. 1, 1774 — died July 9, 1775.
Samuel, born July 19, 1775 — died (?).

Mother (father's second wife):
Sarah Price, born Apr. 30, 1759 — died May 30, 1839. They were married April 15, 1779, at Darby Meeting (PA).

Children of Garrett's father and second wife:
Twins born, May 13, 1780, Phillip — died Feb. 14, 1851, Sarah — died (?)
Thomas, born Nov. 15, 1782 — died "young"
Charles, born Apr. 4, 1785 — died 1811
Margaret, born Oct 8, 1787 — died Apr. 7, 1860
Thomas, born Aug. 21, 1789 — died Jan. 25, 1871
Benjamin, born Oct. 17, 1791 — died Apr. 4, 1884
John Knowles, born Dec. 4, 1793 — died (?)

Isaac P., born Jan. 18, 1796 — died Jan. 24, 1869
Ann, born May 5, 1798 — died Feb. 17, 1892
Edward, born Dec. 17, 1800 — died Sept. 16, 1863

Thomas Garrett's Wives and Children

Thomas Garrett's First Wife:
Mary Sharpless, born Oct. 15, 1793, — died July 13, 1828. They were married Oct. 14, 1813, at Birmingham Meeting.

Children:
Elwood, born Dec. 19, 1815, Upper Darby — died May 25, 1910, Wilmington. Married Catherine K. Wollaston, Jun. 6, 1830.

Sarah, born Apr. 15, 1819, Upper Darby — died Sept. 3, 1853, Wilmington. Married Edward C. Hewes, Sept. 9, 1841.

Anna, born Feb. 2, 1822, Upper Darby — died Aug. 23, 1853, California. Married James Edwards, MD., Nov. 2, 1852.

Henry, born Nov. 22, 1824, Wilmington — died 1903, Wilmington. Married Catherine Ann Canby, May 7, 1846.

Margaret M., born, June 13, 1827, Wilmington — died Aug. 30, 1863. Married James G. McCollin, Aug. 17, 1848.

Thomas Garrett's Second Wife:
Rachel Mendinhall, born Dec. 25, 1792 — died Apr. 20, 1868, Wilmington. They were married Jan. 7, 1830, at Wilmington Meeting.

Children:
Eli, born, Dec. 2, 1830, Wilmington — died May 25, 1886, Wilmington. Married Frances Sellers, Apr. 26, 1855.

Grandchildren

Elwood's Children:
Charles Alfred, born 1840 — died 1891.
Howard, born 1842 — died (?).
Maurice, born 1842 — died 1928.
Elizabeth W., born 1845 — died 1872.
Warren, born 1848 — died 1926.
Emily, born 1850 — died (?).

Agnes, born 1852 — died (?).
Twins, born 1856 — Catherine W., — died (?), and Anna Elwood — died (?).

Sarah's Children:
Mary, born 1842 — died 1874.
Emlen, born 1845 — died 1907.
Charles, born 1847 — died (?).

Anna:
No children

Henry's Children:
Mary, born 1847 — died (?).
Charles Canby, born 1849 — died 1891.
Thomas, born 1851 — died 1923.
Twins, born, Dec. 3, 1854, Henry — died (?), William R. — died 1928.
Katie C., born 1858 — died 1944.
Arthur H.G., born 1863 — died 1912.
Margaret M., born 1865 — died 1893.

Margaret's Children:
Georgianna, born 1849 — died 1850.
George Malin, born 1852 — died 1853.
Margaret M., born 1854 — died 1855.
Anna G., born 1855 — died 1940.
Frances B., born 1860 — died (?).

Eli's Children:
Helen Sellers, born 1857 — died 1945.
Rachel Mendinhall, born 1860 — died 1910.
Ann Robinson, born 1865 — died 1937.
Francis Sellers, born 1869 — died (?).

Appendix B:
Letters from John Hunn
to The Blue Hen's Chicken

THESE LETTERS IMMEDIATELY follow the trial in 1848 and give an account of the events that led to the trial.

For The Blue Hen's Chicken. Near Cantwell's Bridge. 6th mo. 6th, 1848.

Friends Jeandell & Vincent As you have volunteered in your last paper to publish a statement of the case tried at the last session of the United States Court for Delaware District, at New Castle, in relation to fugitive slaves, I have thought proper to write out a brief statement as far as I am concerned, in order to let my fellow-citizens know by what laws we are to be governed, and the application of the United States law of 1793 in particular. On the 5th day of the 12th month, (called December,) 1845, a free old colored man, with his wife and six children, came to my house at half-past seven o'clock in the morning, asking food and shelter, as they had traveled all night through a snow storm, and their horse was nearly ready to fall. In consequence of the deep fall of snow, they concluded to tarry with me until the roads should be open, and recruit both them-selves and their horse. The poor creatures were nearly frozen, and were very hungry. They were made welcome, and came and went as they pleased on my premises. At 4 o'clock P.M., of the same day, Thomas Schee Merritt came to my house (having received information, that there were some strange colored people there,) and at half-past four o'clock, P.M. Robert A Cochran, Robert T. Cochran, Richard C. Hayes, and Wm Chesney (all residing in or near Middletown) came to my house in a sleigh. I went out to meet them, and Robert A. Cochran asked me if any strange blacks were at my house. I told him yes, and he said he guessed they were run-aways. I asked him why so? And he pulled out an advertisement for some, in which a reward was offered for their apprehension. I told him he could walk round and see them. They were not in the kitchen; so they proceeded to the granary, where my folks were getting off the corn. Here they got sight of the old free man, and he ran from them. They gave chase, and finally he came back to my house, with two large knives in his hands. These he gave to me at my request, and showed his pass to his pursuers. They pronounced it a forgery, and said he must go before a magistrate. I protested, but it was of no avail: they took him up, and he acknowledged that his two older boys (one fourteen and the other sixteen years old) belonged to Charles W. Glanding, of Beaver Dams, Queen Anne County, Md., and that his wife and the four younger children (the eldest six years old and the youngest at the breast) belonged to Catherine Turner, of the same neighborhood, but that his wife and four younger children had lived with him for six years past in a house by themselves: they said Turner had not contributed to their support in any way; and, having a desire that they should be free as he was, he had concluded to take them to another State. Well the whole matter is that they took the whole family from my house and lodged them in the New Castle jail — since which I have never seen any of them — and here is the offence for which I am sentenced to pay $2,500, for feeding and warming helpless children when they were perishing with cold and hunger.

In conclusion, I have to say that the "negro catchers" testified before the Court to the facts of the case, with the exception to Thomas Schee Merritt. The jury was taken from the State at large, contrary to custom, as I am informed, and only three, who adjudged my case, were from New Castle County. Such a jury was summoned that my Attorney (Wm H. Rogers) thought there was no choice in them. No doubt that the Marshall knew what he was doing, as well as the Judge (Taney), when he told the jury that "any person who undertook to find runaways for the reward offered was in fact the agent and attorney of the owner, and had the right to seize wherever he could find them; and that any right-minded man would bring out any stranger (black) who might be about his premises and have them inspected, and that what I done in this case," viz: gave two meals to a starving family, "was heartburning within the meaning of the law."

Yours, respectfully, Jno. Hunn

• • •

Letter from John Hunn to William Still,
which Still published in his book, *The Underground Railroad,* in 1872,
giving an account of the events that led to the trial in 1848.

On the morning of the 27th of 12th month [December, 1845], as I was washing my hands at the yard pump of my residence, near Middletown, New Castle County, Delaware, I looked down the land, and saw a covered wagon, slowly approaching my house. The sun had just risen, as was shining brightly (after a stormy night) on the snow which covered the ground to the depth of six inches. My house was situated three quarters of a mile from the road leading from Middletown to Odessa (then called Cantwell's Bridge). On a closer inspection I noticed several men walking beside the wagon. This seemed rather an early hour for visitors, and I could not account for the circumstances. When they reached the yard fence I met them, and a colored man handed me a letter addressed to Daniel Corbit, John Alston or John Hunn; I asked the man if he had presented the letter to either of the others; he said no, that he had not been able to see either of them. The letter was from my cousin, Ezekiel Jenkins, of Camden, Delaware, and stated that the travelers were fugitive slaves, under the direction of Samuel D. Burris (who handed me the note).

The party consisted of a man and his wife, and their six children, and four fine looking colored men, without counting the pilot, S.D. Burris, who was a free man from Kent County, Delaware. This was the first time that I ever saw Burris, and also the first time that I had ever been called upon to assist fugitives from the Hell of American Slavery. The wanderers were gladly welcomed, and made as comfortable as possible until breakfast was ready for them. One man, in trying to pull his boots off, found they were frozen to his feet; he went to the pump and filled them with water, thus he was able to get them off in a few minutes.

This increase of thirteen in the family was a little embarrassing, but after breakfast they all retired to the barn to sleep on the hay, except the woman and the four children, who remained in the house. They were all very weary, as they had traveled from Camden (twenty seven miles), through a snow-storm; the woman and four children in the wagon with the driver, the others walking all the way. Most of them were badly frost-bitten, before they arrived at my house. In Camden, they were sheltered in the houses of their colored friends. Although this was my first acquaintance with S.D. Burris, it was not my last, as he afterwards piloted them himself, or was instrumental in directing hundreds of fugitives to me for shelter.

About two o'clock of the day on which these fugitives arrived at my house, a neighbor drove up with his daughter in a sleigh, apparently on a friendly visit. I noticed his restlessness and frequent looking out of the window fronting the road, but did not know that he had come to "spy out the land."

The wagon and the persons walking with it had been observed from his house, and he had reported the fact in Middletown, Accordingly, in half an hour, another sleigh came up, containing a constable of Middletown, William Hardcastle, of Queen Anne's County, Maryland, and William Chestnut, of the same county neighborhood. I met them at the gate, and the constable handed me an advertisement, wherein one thousand dollars reward was offered for the recovery of three runaway slaves, therein described.

The constable asked me if they were in my house? I said they were not! He then asked me if he might search the house? I declined to allow him this privilege, unless he had a warrant for that purpose. While he stood thus conversing, the husband of the woman with the six children, came out of a house near the barn, and ran to the woods. The constable and his two companions immediately gave chase, with many halloos! After running more than a mile through the snow, the fugitive came toward the house; I went to meet him, and found him with his back against the barn-yard fence, with a butcher's knife in his hand. The man hunters soon came up, and the constable asked me to go get the knife from the fugitive. This I declined to do, unless the constable should first give me his pistol, with which he was threatening to shoot the man. He complied with my request, and the fugitive handed me the knife. Then he produced a pass, properly authenticated, and signed by a magistrate of Queen Ann's county, Maryland, certifying that this man was free and that his name was Samuel Hawkins.

    William Hardcastle now advanced and said that he knew the man to be free; but that he was accused of running away with his wife and children who were slaves. He also said that this man had two boys with him, who belonged to a neighbor of his, named Charles Wesley Glanding, and that the four other children and mother belonged to Catherine Turner, of Queen Ann's county, Maryland. Hardcastle further expressed his belief that this man knew where wife and children were at that time, and insisted that he should go before a magistrate in Middletown, and be examined in regard thereto. He also expressed doubts as to the genuineness of this pass, and wished the man to go to Middletown before my friend, William Streets, who was then in commission as a magistrate. It was now after dark of this short winter's day. Soon after our arrival at the office of William Streets, Hardcastle put his arm lovingly around the neck of the colored man, Samuel Hawkins, and drew him into another room. In a short time, Samuel came out, and told me that Hardcastle had agreed, that if he, Hawkins, would give up his two older boys, who belonged to Charles Wesley Glanding, then he might pursue his journey with his wife and four children. I asked him if he would believe Hardcastle would keep his promise?

    He replied: "Yes! I do not think master William would cheat me."

    I assured him that he would cheat him, and that the offer was made for the purpose of not only getting the two older boys (fourteen and sixteen years of age), but his wife and other children to the office, when all of them would be taken together to the jail, in New Castle. Samuel thought differently, and at his request, I wrote to my wife for the delivery of the family of Samuel Hawkins to the constable. They were soon forthcoming, and on their arrival at the office, a commitment was made out for the whole party. Samuel and his two older sons were handcuffed, amidst many tears and lamentations, and they all went off to jail, a distance of eighteen miles.

    William Streets committed the whole party as fugitives from Slavery, while the husband (Samuel), was a free man. This was done on account of the detestation of the wicked business, as much as on account of his friendship for me. On their arrival at the jail, about midnight, the sheriff was aroused, and the commitment shown to him; after reading it, he asked Samuel if he was a slave? He said no, and showed his pass (which had been pronounced genuine by the magistrate). The sheriff hereupon told them the commitment was not legal, and would not hold them lawfully. It was now first day [Sunday], and the man hunters were in a quandary. The constable finally agreed to go back and get another commitment, if the sheriff would take the party into the jail until his return. Accordingly they were taken into the jail. The sheriff's daughter had heard her father's conversation with the constable, accordingly she sent word on First Day morning, to my revered friend, Thomas Garrett, of Wilmington, five miles distant, in regard to the matter, inviting him to see the fugitives. Early on Second Day [Monday], Thomas went over with John Wales, attorney at law. The latter soon obtained a writ of habeas corpus from Judge Booth of New Castle, which was served upon the sheriff; who, therefore brought the whole party before Judge Booth, who discharged them at once, as being illegally detained by the sheriff. Thomas Garrett, with the consent of the judge, then hired a carriage to take the woman and four children over to Wilmington. Samuel and the two older boys walked, so they all escaped from the man hunters. They went from Wilmington to Byberry, and settled near the farm of Robert Purvis. Samuel Hawkins and his wife have since died, but their descendants still live in that neighborhood under the name of Hackett. Soon after the departure of the fugitives from New Castle jail, the constable arrived with new commitments from William Streets, and presented them in due form to the sheriff; who informed him that they had been liberated by order of Judge Booth! A few hours after, William Hardcastle arrived from Philadelphia, expecting to take Samuel Hawkins and his family to Queen Ann's county, Maryland. Judge of his disappointment at finding they were beyond his control-absolutely gone! They returned to Middletown in great anger, and threatened to prosecute William Streets for his participation in the affair.

After the departure of the Hawkins family from Middletown, I returned home to see what had become of S.D. Burris and his four men. I found them taking some solid refreshments preparatory to taking a long walk in the snow. They left about nine P.M. for Wilmington. I sent by S.D. Burris a letter to Thomas Garrett, detailing the arrest and commitment of S. Hawkins and family to New Castle jail. They all arrived safely in Wilmington before daylight next morning. Burris waited to hear the result of the expedition to New Castle; and actually had the pleasure of seeing S. Hawkins and family arrive in Wilmington.

Samuel Burris returned to my house early on Third Day morning (Tuesday), with a letter from Thomas Garrett, giving me a description of the whole transaction. My joy on this occasion was great! And I returned thanks to God for this wonderful escape of so many human beings from the charnel house of Slavery.

Of course, this circumstance excited the ire of many pro-slavery editors in Maryland. I had copies of several papers sent me, wherein I was described as a man unfit to live in a civilized community, and calling upon the inhabitants of Middletown to expel such a dangerous person from that neighborhood! They also told exactly where I lived, which enabled many a poor fugitive escaping from the house of bondage, to find a hearty welcome and a resting place on the road to liberty. Thanks to God! for his goodness to me in this respect.

The trial which ensued from the above, came off before Chief Justice Taney, at New Castle. My revered friend, Thomas Garrett, and myself, were convicted of harboring fugitive slaves; Judge Taney delivering the sentence. A detailed account of said trial, will fully appear in the memoirs of our deceased friend, Thomas Garrett.

Appendix C:
Letter from Thomas Garrett to The Blue Hen's Chicken

LETTER DATED JUNE 9, 1848, giving his address delivered after the trial, the events that led to the trial, and his personal views concerning slavery.

To Jeandell and Vincent: I herewith enclose an address delivered immediately after the close of the Superior Court of the State of Delaware, sitting at New Castle, Judges Taney and Hall on the bench, 5th month, 29th, 1848, after the close of my trials, for the penalties of aiding the escape of certain slaves from their owners, where the penalties and damages were awarded by the Jurors for seven slaves (a mother and six children) from one to sixteen years of age, to be $5,400, after a verdict had been rendered against J. Hunn for $2,500 in the same case. One Judge, Taney, had left the Court before it adjourned; Judge Hall I invited to stay and hear me, but he left when I was about to commence. If thou art of opinion that it is worthy of a place in the *Chicken,* thou art at liberty to publish it, and oblige Thomas Garrett.

I have a few words which I wish to address to the Court, Jury and prosecutors in the several suits that have been brought against me during the sittings of this Court, in order to determine the amount of penalty I must pay for doing what my feelings prompted me do as a lawful and meritorious act, a simple act of humanity and justice, as I believe, to eight of that oppressed race, the people of color, whom I found in the New Castle jail, in the 12th month, 1845. I will now endeavor to state the facts of these cases for your consideration and reflection after you return home to your families and friends: you will then have time to ponder on what has transpired here since the sitting of this Court, and I believe that your verdict will then be unanimous that the laws of the United States, as explained by our venerable Judge, when compared with the act committed by me are cruel and oppressive, and need remodeling.

Information was sent me that eight colored persons were in New Castle jail, charged with being runaway slaves, and that the individual believed several of them were entitled to their freedom, and requested to have their case investigated. I went to New Castle next morning and took Edith Pusey along, and had an interview with Samuel Hawkins, Emily (his wife) and some of the children, in a private room, in the presence of the sheriff, Jacob Caulk. Hawkins and wife admitted to us that two of their sons claimed by Glanding were slaves; but assured us, in the most positive manner, that themselves and four small children were entitled to freedom; that himself and wife had been keeping house, and living together as free persons previous to the birth of the eldest of the four children. Neither the Sheriff, or myself, had the slightest doubt of the truth of their statement. The Sheriff thought the mother so good a Christian that she would not lie even to free her own children. I then requested to see the commitment of the Magistrate, which was handed to me. I at once saw that they were defective; and had no doubt, if the individuals were taken before Judge Booth, (by legal process) but that he would discharge the parents and four children, if not the two older boys.

After I returned home, I called on Wales; stated the facts of the case; and requested him to accompany me to New Castle, in order to take the family above-named before Chief Justice Booth for examination. The *habeas corpus* was prepared, and they were all taken before Booth, about eleven o'clock, on Second Day morning (Monday).

The investigation lasted about one hour. The business was conducted by Attorney Wales in such a manner that the Judge was induced to discharge the whole family; and with his decision I was well pleased; but had little or no hope when they were taken before him that the two boys would be discharged. The statement made by Samuel and his wife, in the Judge's office, was the same in substance as they made in prison to the Sheriff, Edith Pusey, and myself; and that was, that the mother and four young children were free — the two elder slaves. I then put this question to Chief Justice Booth, as those people have been discharged, will there be any impropriety in my employing a hack to take them to Wilmington? My impression then was, and still remains the same, that his reply was '*O no.*' I then, in the Judge's office, and presence, asked the Sheriff to procure a carriage. He sent his son for one, and the owner came into the Judge's office, where we made the contract for him to take them to Wilmington. In about half an hour, they were all in the carriage, and started for Wilmington, and arrived at my store at noon, nothing secret, or covert, in the transaction whatever. And now I most solemnly swear that they were discharged by Judge Booth, and for sometime after they arrived in Wilmington, I had not the slightest, even a suspicion, of the mother and four children being slaves.

If my statement above is correct, which I presume will not be questioned by anyone acquainted with my character, your verdict of $2,500 for the penalty as rendered by you on 7th day last [Saturday] was not just, as the Judge in his charge to the Jury, on that occasion, distinctly stated: 'I must at least have cause to believe them to be slaves to entitle the plaintiff to a verdict.' With that *small clause,* as explained in my favor by the Judge, I was entitled to a verdict of acquittal. I do not pretend to assert that I was able, with the latitude allowed to the witness, to prove my innocence in this case clearly to the Jury. The Judge's charge was positively against me, if I knew they were slaves, or had good cause to suspect them of being such, even though examined by and discharged by the Judge. The first case tried during my absence, while I was sick at home, was different — I believed the two boys claimed by Glanding to be slaves; but the Judge having set them at liberty, I thought there would be no breach of law, or risk of penalty, in providing them a conveyance, with the rest of the family, to Wilmington: and had I believed every one of them to be slaves, I should have done the same thing, after they had been released by the Judge, with the feelings of humanity which the Almighty has implanted in my breast, and the interest I have felt for this oppressed people of color in our midst. I should have done violence to my convictions of duty, had I not made use of all the lawful means in my power to liberate those people, and assist them to become men and women, rather than leave them in the condition of chattels personal. I am called an Abolitionist, once a name of reproach, but one I have ever been proud to be considered worthy of being called. For the last twenty-five years I have been engaged in the cause of this despised and injured race, and consider their cause worth suffering for; but owing to the multiplicity of other engagements, I could not devote so much of my time and mind to their cause as I otherwise should have done.

The impositions and persecutions practiced on those unoffending and innocent brethren, are extreme beyond endurance. I am now placed in a situation in which I have not so much to claim my attention as formerly, and I now pledge myself, in the presence of this assembly, to use all lawful and honorable means to lessen the burdens of this oppressed people, and endeavor according to ability furnished to burst their chains asunder, and set them free — not relaxing my efforts on their behalf while blessed with health, and a slave remains to tread the soil of the state of my adoption — Delaware; and after mature reflection, I can assure this assembly it is my opinion at this time that the verdicts you have given the prosecutors against John Hunn and myself, within the past few days, will have a tendency to raise a spirit of inquiry throughout the length and breadth of the land, respecting this monster evil (slavery), in many minds that has not heretofore investigated the subject.

The reports of those trials will be published by editors from Maine to Texas and the Far West; and what must be the effect produced? It will no doubt add hundreds, perhaps thousands, to the present large and rapidly increasing army of abolitionists. The injury is great to us who are the immediate sufferers by your verdict, but I believe the verdicts you have given us within the last few days will have a powerful effect in bringing about the abolition of slavery in this country, this land of boasted freedom, where not only the slave is fettered at the south by his lordly master, but the white man at the north is bound as in chains to do the bidding of his southern masters. Your verdicts against us I hope will prove as leaven put into a batch of meal that will ere long leaven the whole lump.

I am *sorry* to have to admit this truth, that the slave states and slave interests have ruled this nation from the Declaration of Independence till the present time. They have kindly taken the North and West under their care and keeping, and have provided a large majority of our Presidents, Cabinet officers, Foreign Ministers and Judges of our Supreme Courts, from the slave states, they have made our laws to suit their *peculiar institutions*. It was slave holders that demanded the Admission of Texas into this union, with her mix'd breeds and degenerate race of inhabitants of all nations: they knocked at the Halls of Congress for admission into our glorious Union; the North blustered a while, but were soon whipped into the traces by their masters; they knew it would be contrary to law to admit them; they also know there was no use to contend about that, as the south always managed to have it their own way; they consented, and Texas was admitted in a day with the dash of a pen, with her mixed and motley crew of inhabitants as good and loyal subjects of these United States; when at the same time the most foreigners coming amongst us and adopting this country as his future home, must knock for years for admission as a citizen before they can be admitted. They must then swear to support the constitution, and pay a fee for admission.

Surely the slave power is omnipotent. No other power in this land could have produced the same result; and what has been the legitimate fruits of the admission of Texas into the Union? We have the admission of some of the strongest minds, even at the south (J.C. Calhoun of that number) that the admission of Texas was the cause of the Mexican War; where hundreds of millions of the peoples' money has been wasted, and thousands of valuable lives sacrificed by sword and climate, all for the slave interest. No intelligent man doubts this fact, that it was the slave interest, cruel, disgraceful and unrighteous war.

But all those things are producing their legitimate fruits. A few years since, a Senator that would speak his mind freely on the subject of slavery, in Congress, was in danger of being expelled; now it is the all engrossing subject. It enters more or less into every subject brought before either House at Washington. It is an institution that cannot bear investigation. This subject is now fairly before the people — this is what Abolitionists have been laboring for, to have the subject fairly canvassed by the people — then I fear not their verdict. Look at the nations around us. The cause of freedom is progressing with railroad speed. Their object is about to be accomplished. I have not correctly read the signs of the times if the days of slavery are not numbered in this country. The south will have to yield to the growing anti-slavery feeling of the north and west; or before ten years from this date there will be a dissolution of this Union. There is a point of forbearance beyond which the north, and rapidly growing west, will not submit.

I have done, and thank you for your attention.

Chapter Notes

Preface

1. James E. Newton. "Diamonds of Delaware and Maryland's Eastern Shore: Seven Black Men of Distinction." University of Delaware, Harmon R. Carey Afro-American Historical Society of Delaware.

Chapter 1

1. *Encyclopaedia Britannica*, 1972, Vol. 20, p.
2. William Breyfogle, *Make Free: The Story of the Underground Railroad* (Philadelphia: J.P. Lippincott), 1958.
3. Larry Gara, *Liberty Line: The Legend of the Underground Railroad* (Lexington, KY, Univ. of Kentucky Press, 1961), p. 52, 54–55.
4. Ibid, p. 52, 54–55.
5. *History of the Negro Race in America*, vol. II, p. 58–59.
6. R. C. Smedley, *History of the Underground Railroad in Chester and the Neighboring Counties of Pennsylvania* (Lancaster, PA, 1883), p. 34–35.
7. Wilbur H. Siebert, *The Underground Railroad: From Slavery to Freedom*, (New York, Arno Press, 1968 ed.), p. 45.
8. Ibid, p. 35.
9. Thomas E. Drake, *Quakers and Slavery in America* (New Haven: Yale University, 1950), p. 76.
10. Siebert, op. cit., p. 33.
11. Ibid, p. 118.
12. Ibid, p. 121.
13. Smedley, op. cit., p. 317.
14. William C. Kashatus, *Just Over the Line: Chester County and the Underground Railroad*, Chester Co. Historical Society (W. Chester, PA, Penn State University Press, 2002).
15. Gara, op. cit., p. 96.

Chapter 2

1. The subject's first full-length treatment was written by a black minister, William Mitchell. Entitled *The Underground Railroad: From Slavery to Freedom*, it was published in England.
2. Ebony Classics ed. (Chicago, Johnson Publications, 1970), p. v.
3. William Still, *The Underground Railroad* (Chicago, Johnson Publications, 1970). From the introduction by Benjamin Quarles, p. vi.
4. Aaron Powell was a pastor of a New York church and the editor of the *National Observer*, an anti-slavery newspaper.
5. R.C. Smedley, op. cit., p.113–114.
6. Ibid, pp. 77–78.
7. Ibid, pp. 83–84.
8. Wilbur H. Siebert, p. 11.
9. Benjamin Quarles, foreword to Siebert. Arno Press/NY Times.
10. Charles L. Blockson, *The Underground Railroad: First-person Narratives of Escapes to Freedom in the North* (NJ, Prentice Hall Press, 1987) p. 3.
11. Benjamin Quarles, foreword to Siebert.
12. Larry Gara, *Liberty Line: The Legend of the Underground Railroad* (Lexington, KY, Univ. of Kentucky Press, 1961), p. 174.
13. Ibid, p. 190.
14. Ibid, p. 196.
15. Ibid, p. 190.

Chapter 3

1. Richard R. Wood, *William Penn* (Philadelphia Yearly Meeting of the Religious Society of Friends), p. 17.
2. *A History of Upper Darby*, by a Committee of Concerned Citizens, Under the Directorship of John H. Tyson, (Clark Printing House, Philadelphia, 1972), p. 7.
3. Ibid, p. 108.
4. Ibid, p. 117.
5. Ibid, p. 97.
6. Ibid, p. 8.
7. Ibid, p. 121.
8. Ibid, p. 14.
9. Ibid, p. 18.
10. Henry Graham Ashmead, *History of Delaware County, Pennsylvania* (Facsimile Edition, Concord Township Historical Society, 1968), p. 541–551.
11. *A History of Upper Darby*, op. cit., p. 33–41.
12. Ibid, p. 32.

Chapter 4

1. Geoffrey Hubbard, *Quaker by Convincement* (New York, Penguin Books, 1985), p. 1.
2. George H. Gorman, *The Amazing Facts of Quaker Worship* (London, Friends Home Service Committee, 1973).
3. Hubbard, op. cit., p. 9, fn.
4. George H. Gorman, *The Amazing Facts of Quaker Worship* (London, Friends Home Service Committee, 1973), p. 6.
5. Ibid, p. 9.
6. Excerpted from *Friendly Anecdotes*, collected and arranged by Irvin and Ruth Poley (New York, Harper & Row, 2nd ed., 1950), p. 20.
7. Ibid, p. 47–48.
8. Ibid, p. 47–48.

Chapter 5

1. Thomas E. Drake, *Quakers and Slavery in America* (CT, Yale University Press, 1950), p. 5.
2. Ibid, p. 11.
3. Ibid, p. 15.
4. *A History of Upper Darby*, op. cit., p. 119.
5. William P. Tilden, "Memorial Address."
6. Thomas E. Drake, op. cit., p. 78.
7. L. Hughes and M. Meltzer, *Pictorial History of the Negro in America* (3rd revised ed., Crown Publishing Co., 1968), p. 30.
8. Excerpted from Bradford Chambers, *Chronicles of Black Protest* (Mentor Books, New American Library, 1963), p. 62–64.
9. H. Clay Reed, *Delaware: A History of the First State*, p. 904–905.
10. Thomas E. Drake, op. cit., p. 125.
11. *A History of Upper Darby*, op. cit., p. 119.

Chapter 6

1. M.V. Brewington, *Chesapeake Bay: A Pictorial Maritime History*, p. 43.
2. Personal letter from George Shumway, author of *Conestoga Wagon — 1750–1850*, (NY, PA, Shumway Publishing Co.).
3. Benjamin Ferris, *History of the Original Settlements on the Delaware*, p. 242.
4. Wilmington, Delaware, was the original terminus of the Canal. However, by 1824, when actual construction began, a "lower" terminus, Delaware City (then called Newbold's Landing), was decided.
5. We have no evidence that this was Garrett's business before his move to Wilmington. *A History of Upper Darby* reports that Garrett worked as a blacksmith, and that his family owned and operated a number of mills in that area.

Chapter 7

1. Benjamin Ferris, *History of the Original Settlements on the Delaware*, op. cit., p. 204.
2. Ibid, p. 203.
3. Ibid, p. 204.
4. A linear measure, equal to 5.50 yards or 16.5 ft.
5. Benjamin Ferris, op. cit., pp. 203–205.
6. Ibid, p. 299.
7. Thomas E. Drake, *Quakers and Slavery in America*, pp. 31–18.
8. Ibid, p. 32.
9. Ibid, pp. 38–39.
10. Ibid, p. 39.
11. Geoffrey Hubbard, *Quaker by Convincement*, pp. 55–56.
12. Thomas E. Drake, op. cit., p. 116.
13. Benjamin Ferris, op. cit., p. 248.
14. Ibid, pp. 247–248.
15. William P. Tilden, "Memorial Address," op. cit., pp. 3–4.
16. Sarah Bradford, *Harriet Tubman, the Moses of her People* (Gloucester, MA: Peter Smith, 1981), p. 44.
17. William P. Tilden, op. cit., p. 11.
18. Geoffrey Hubbard, op. cit., p. 234.
19. Bradford Chambers, *Chronicles of Black Protest*, p. 54.
20. Ibid, p. 55.
21. Thomas E. Drake, op. cit., pp. 130–131.

Chapter 8

1. Thomas Mendenhall, *History, Correspondence & Pedigrees of the Mendenhalls* (Ohio, 1912) p. 78.
2. For a more in-depth discussion of this and

the Progressive Meeting of Friends at Longwood, see William C. Kashatus, *Just Over the Line*, op. cit., pp. 63–64.
  3. Ibid, p. 64.
  4. John Tyson, *A History of Upper Darby*, op. cit., p. 119.
  5. Carlton Mabee, *Black Freedom: The Nonviolent Abolitionists from 1830 Through the Civil War* (NY, Macmillan Company, 1971), p. 41.
  6. Ibid, p. 44.
  7. Ibid, p. 42.
  8. Ibid, p. 59.

Chapter 9

  1. Larry Gara, *Liberty Line: The Legend of the Underground Railroad* (Lexington, KY: University of Kentucky Press), p. 15.
  2. Harriet Beecher Stowe, *The Key to Uncle Tom's Cabin* (New York: Arno Press/New York Times, 1960 ed.), p. 1.
  3. Ibid, pp. iii–iv.
  4. Ibid, p. 98.
  5. However, according to Wilbur H. Siebert, John Hunn, in a letter dated September 1, 1893, speaks of himself as being "superintendent of the UGRR from Wilmington down the Peninsula." Siebert, op. cit., p. 117.
  6. Smedley, op. cit., p. 239.
  7. Ibid, p. 239.
  8. Drake, *Quakers and Slavery in America*, p. 79.
  9. Siebert, op. cit., p. 254.
  10. Tilden, op. cit., p. 13.
  11. Court Records, acquired from the General Services Administration, National Archives And Records Service, Washington.
  12. Still, op. cit., p. 650.
  13. Drake, op. cit., p. 81.
  14. Still, op. cit., p. 654.
  15. Still, op. cit., p. 650.
  16. Siebert, op. cit., p. 110.
  17. Tilden, op. cit., p. 13.
  18. Http://usconstitution.com/TreatywithSpain.htm
  19. Albert P. Blaustein and Robert L. Zangrando, eds., *Civil Rights and the Black American: A Documentary History* (New York, Washington Square Press, 1969).
  20. (NWL-46-MCCOOK-2(4))—Courtesy of National Archives and Records Administration.
  21. Ibid.
  22. "Africans in America," WGBH, PBS Online.
  23. Benjamin Quarles, *Black Abolitionists* (New York: Da Capo Press, 1969) p. 212.
  24. See the comment to Letter to William Lloyd Garrison, no. 1.
  25. Ibid.
  26. Sarah Bradford, *Harriet Tubman, the Moses of her People*, op. cit., p. 112.
  27. Ibid, p. 206.
  28. Charles L. Blockson, *The Underground Railroad: First-Person Narratives of Escapes to Freedom in the North* (NJ, Prentice Hall, 1987), p. 238.
  29. Milton C. Sernett, *North Star Country: Upstate New York and the Crusade for African American Freedom* (NY: Syracuse University Press, 2002), pp. 136–145.
  30. Ibid, p. 140.
  31. Sarah Bradford, *Some Scenes in the Life of Harriet Tubman*, op. cit., p. 27.
  32. Priscilla Thompson, op. cit., p. 18.
  33. William C. Kashatus, op. cit., p. 63.
  34. See the comments about this incident in Chapter 10, and the comment to the Letters to Eliza Wigham and Mary Edmundson, No. 1.
  35. Kashatus, op. cit., p. 63.
  36. *The Columbia Electronic Encyclopedia* (New York, Columbia University Press, 2000).
  37. "Education on the Internet." TeachingHistoryOnline@keepAhead.com.
  38. Benjamin Quarles, op. cit., p. 235.
  39. Ibid.
  40. James M. McPherson, *Ordeal by Fire: The Civil War and Reconstruction* (New York: Alfred A. Knopf, 1982), p. 94.
  41. Edwin A. Miles, "Franklin Pierce Biography," Grolier Multimedia Encyclopedia, 2000.
  42. Ibid.
  43. James M. McPherson, op. cit., p. 95.
  44. Oswald Garrison Villard, *John Brown, 1800–1859: A Biography Fifty Years After* (Boston: Houghton Mifflin & Co., 1910), p. 396.
  45. Benjamin Quarles, op. cit., p. 238.
  46. Edward J. Renehan, Jr., *The Secret Six: The True Tale of the Men Who Conspired with John Brown* (New York: Crown Publishers, Inc., 1995), p. 137.
  47. Earl Conrad, *Harriet Tubman, A Biography*, op. cit., p. 124.
  48. Benjamin Quarles, op. cit., p. 240.
  49. Harry Hansen, *The Civil War* (New York: Bonanza Books, 1961), p. 10.

Chapter 10

  1. William P. Tilden, op. cit., p. 3.
  2. James A. McGowan, *Station Master on the Underground Railroad*, op. cit., pp. 25–26.
  3. From private collection of Philip Rhoads, Thomas Garrett's great-great-nephew. Letters are in the Quaker Collection at the Haverford Library in Pennsylvania.
  4. James A. McGowan, op. cit., p. 76.
  5. Ibid, Miscellaneous Letter No. 9, p. 151.
  6. Ibid, p. 79.
  7. Ibid, p. 168.
  8. Thomas E. Drake, in *Quakers and Slavery in America*, op. cit., p. 79.
  9. R.C. Smedley, op. cit., p. xiii.

10. William Still, op. cit., p. 405.
11. Parker Pillsbury, *Acts of the Anti-slavery Apostles* (New Haven, CT, 1883; reprint, Arno Press/N.Y. Times, 1969), p. 57, 58.
12. R. C. Smedley, op. cit., p. 241.
13. J. C. Furnas, *Goodbye to Uncle Tom* (NY, William Sloan Associates, 1956), p. 198.
14. Sarah Bradford, *Harriet Tubman, the Moses of Her People*, pp. 44–45.
15. Thomas E. Drake, *Quakers and Slavery in America*, p. 77.
16. J. C. Furnas, op. cit., p. 289.
17. Ibid, p. 333.
18. Thomas E. Drake, *Quakers and Slavery in America*, op. cit., p. 120.
19. Priscilla Thompson, op. cit., p. 23. Thompson reports that Holland also worked as an UGRR agent for 40 years, and that he at one time (in 1850) lived with Henry Garrett, Thomas's son.
20. Wilbur H. Siebert, op. cit., p. 111.
21. James M. McPherson, *Ordeal by Fire: The Civil War and Reconstruction* (NY, Alfred A. Knopf, 1982), p. 79.

Chapter 11

1. Benjamin Drew, *A North-Side View of Slavery*, p. 31.
2. Benjamin Quarles, *Black Abolitionists* (NY: Da Capo Paperback, 1969) p. 148.
3. John Hope Franklin and Loren Schweninger, *Runaway Slaves: Rebels on the Plantation*, (NY: Oxford University Press, 1999), pp. 212–213.
4. Ibid, p. 213.
5. James A. McGowan, op. cit., p. 66.
6. Ibid, p. 62.
7. William C. Kashatus, *Just Over the Line, Chester County and the Underground Railroad* (PA: Chester Co. Historical Society and Penn State University Press, 2002), pp. 19–20.
8. Vincent O. Leggett, "Chesapeake Underground: Charting a Course to Freedom," http://www.dnr. state.md.us/naturalresource/spring2000/chesapeake.html.
9. Ralph D. Gray, *The National Waterway: A History of the Chesapeake and Delaware Canal, 1769–1985*, 2nd ed. (Chicago: University of Illinois Press, 1989), p. 302.
10. "The Chesapeake & Delaware Canal," from the US Army Corps of Engineers official US Government information system. For further information: E-mail: webmaster@nap02.usace.army.mil.
11. James A. McGowan, op. cit., p. 121, 155.
12. James A. McGowan, op. cit., p. 143.

Chapter 12

1. James A. McGowan, *Station Master on the Underground Railroad: The Life and Letters of Thomas Garrett* (PA: Whimsie Press, 1977), p. 90.
2. James A. McGowan, op. cit., p. 125.
3. Ibid, p. 125.
4. Ibid, p. 168.
5. Sarah Bradford, *Some Scenes in the Life of Harriet Tubman* (Auburn: William J. Moses, Printer, 1869), p. 12.
6. Ibid, pp. 13–14.
7. Ibid, p. 56.
8. Ibid, pp. 20–22.
9. James A. McGowan, op. cit., p. 153.
10. Ibid, p. 154.
11. Sarah Bradford, *Harriet Tubman, the Moses of Her People* (MA: Peter Smith, reprinted by arrangement with Corinth Books, Inc., 1981), p. 57–61. This story raises the question whether this was Harriet Tubman's seventh rescue mission.
12. Ibid, p. 131.
13. Ibid, p. 168.
14. Sarah Bradford, *Some Scenes...*, op. cit., pp. 112–113.
15. See Letters to Eliza Wigham and Mary Edmundson, No. 5.
16. James A. McGowan, op. cit., p. 135.
17. Ibid, p. 155.
18. Sarah Bradford, *Harriet Tubman, the Moses of Her People* (MA: Peter Smith, reprinted by arrangement with Corinth Books, Inc., 1981) p. 137.
19. Sarah Bradford, *Some Scenes in the Life of Harriet Tubman*, op. cit., p. 81.
20. Ibid, p. 112.
21. Sarah Bradford, *Harriet Tubman, the Moses of Her People,* op. cit., pp. 81–82.
22. Ibid, p. 114.
23. James A. McGowan, op. cit. (Letter to Eliza Wigham, No. 4).
24. Ibid, p. 79.
25. William Wells Brown, p. 538.
26. Sarah Bradford, *Some Scenes in the Life of Harriet Tubman*, op. cit., pp. 76–77.
27. Ibid, p. 77.
28. Ibid, p. 78.
29. Ibid, p. 21.
30. Sarah Bradford, *Harriet Tubman ...*, op. cit., pp. 96–97.
31. Ibid, p. 75.
32. James A. McGowan, op. cit., p. 125.
33. William Still, *The Underground Railroad*, op. cit.
34. James A. McGowan, op. cit., p. 143.
35. In a letter to this author, Kate Larson states "Henry Predo" (actual spelling Predeaux) was actually "thirty-five years of age, about five feet and eight inches in height, chestnut color and wears whiskers and mustache." Not a giant, but he must have been an imposing physical and personal presence for Still to write that he was a

"giant." Unless, of course, Still got confused, when he meant Bill Kiah, one of the other slaves who ran away with this group.

36. William Still, op. cit., pp. 57, 58–59.
37. Kate Larson writes: Those people [were] Tubman's brothers, Robert, Ben and Henry (ne John Stewart, James Stewart, William Henry Stewart); John Chase and Peter Jackson, and Jane Kane (ne Catherine Kane who then married Ben Ross, ne James Stewart). There were two other men, George Ross (relationship unknown) and William Thompson, who arrived with Tubman, too, and they were from Delaware ... and a third also arrived a day later, Arthur Fowler, alias Ben Johnson. Anyway, George or William probably went on with Harriet and the others to Allen Agnew's.
38. James A. McGowan, op. cit., p. 141.
39. Kate Larson, letter to the author, December 13, 2002.
40. Earl Conrad, *Harriet Tubman* (NY: Paul S. Eriksson, Inc., 1974), p. 92.
41. James A. McGowan, op. cit., p. 140.
42. Ibid, p. 95.
43. Ibid, p. 140.
44. Ibid, pp. 95–96.
45. Ibid, p. 141, 142.
46. Earl Conrad, op. cit., p. 97.
47. Sarah Bradford, *Scenes in the Life of Harriet Tubman*, p. 48.
48. Earl Conrad, op. cit., p. 94.
49. Ibid, p. 92.
50. James A. McGowan, op. cit., p. 140.
51. William Still, op. cit., p. 58.
52. James A. McGowan, op. cit., pp. 411.

Chapter 13

1. James A. McGowan, op. cit., p. 121.
2. Ibid, p. 151.
3. Ibid, p. 157.
4. Ibid, p. 79.
5. In his letters to William Still, and to others, Garrett does mention that he kept some runaways in his house, and that he gave shoes and clothing to others.
6. In a letter to Harriet Tubman's biographer, Sarah Bradford, Garrett wrote "I have not felt at liberty to keep any written word of Harriet's or my own labors, except in numbering those whom I have aided." See Miscellaneous Letters, No. 10.
7. Richard A. Biondo, "Samuel Green: a Black Life in Antebellum Maryland" University of Maryland, 1988, unpublished manuscript, Master Thesis. (Quote taken from Barbara Jeanne Fields, *Slavery and Freedom in the Middle Ground* (New Haven, Yale University Press, 1972), p.16).
8. Charles L. Blockson, *Hippocrene Guide to the Underground Railroad* (NY, Hippocrene Books, 1994), p. 25.
9. Ibid, p. 27.
10. Ibid, p. 28.
11. Ibid, p.28.
12. Ibid, p. 29.
13. Peter T. Dalleo, "The Growth of Delaware's Antebellum Free African American Community" U.S. Courthouse, Wilmington, Delaware.
14. Ibid.
15. Blockson, op. cit., p. 96.
16. William Still, *The Underground Railroad* (Chicago: Johnson Pub., Inc., 1970), reprint of 1872 ed.
17. Ibid, pp. 44–46.
18. Ibid, pp. 47–48.
19. Ibid, pp. 85–86.
20. Ibid, p. 101.
21. Ibid, p. 60.
22. Ibid, pp. 64–65.
23. Ibid, p. 202.
24. Sarah Bradford, *Harriet Tubman, the Moses of Her People*, (Gloucester, Mass, 1981, Peter Smith, printer [reprint of the 1889 edition]), pp. 57–60.
25. See Letters to William Still and J. Miller McKim, Nos. 2, 3, 6, 7, 18, 19, 26.
26. Priscilla Thompson, "Harriet Tubman, Thomas Garrett and the Underground Railroad in Delaware" (a research paper, funded by a grant from the Delaware Humanities Forum, April, 10, 1985), pp. 25–26. Thompson located a "James" Fountain on 6th Street in Wilmington. Garrett, however, specifically refers to the Captain as "Alfred" Fountain (see Letter to William Still, No. 31). Thompson also found a Mary E. Lambdin living at 607 Orange Street and says she (Mary) was very likely the wife of Captain Lambdin.
27. William Still, op. cit., pp. 161–162. Still goes on to report further incidents of Captain Fountain's bravery.
28. James A. McGowan, op. cit., see Letters to William Still, Nos. 6, 9, 13, 14, 18.
29. Ibid, Letter No. 31.
30. Peter T. Dalleo, op. cit. (no page given).
31. James A. McGowan, op. cit., p. 92.
32. Ibid, p. 94.
33. Ibid, p. 97.
34. Ibid, p. 99.
35. Ibid, p. 92.
36. Ibid, pp. 106–107.
37. Ibid, p. 96.
38. Priscilla Thompson, op. cit., p. 23.
39. Ibid, p. 23.
40. Charles L. Blockson, *The Underground Railroad: First-person Narratives of Escapes to Freedom in the North* (NJ: Prentice Hall Press, 1987), p. 166.
41. James E. Newton, "Diamonds of Delaware and Maryland's Eastern Shore: Seven Black Men of Distinction" (University of Delaware, Harmon R. Carey Afro-American Historical Society of Delaware).
42. Charles L. Blockson, *Hippocrene Guide to the Underground Railroad* (New York: Hippocrene books, 1994), p. 21.

43. James E. Newton, op. cit. (No page number given).
44. James E. Newton, op. cit.
45. Ibid, op. cit. (paraphrased).
46. William C. Kashatus, op. cit., p. 58.
47. Benjamin Quarles, *Black Abolitionists* (New York: Da Capo Paperback, 1969), p. 109.
48. William C. Kashatus, op. cit., p. 92.
49. Ibid, p. 57.
50. Ibid, p. 57.
51. Frances C. Taylor, *The Trackless Trail: The Story of the Underground Railroad in Kennett Square, Chester County, Pennsylvania, and the Surrounding Community.* (Kennett Square, PA, published privately, 1976), p. 12–16.
52. Ibid, 24–26.
53. R. C. Smedley, op. cit., p. 259.
54. Ibid, p. 164.
55. Ibid, p. 266.
56. Ibid, pp. 269–270.
57. Ibid, p. 243.
58. Ibid, pp. 288–289, 297.
59. Ibid, p. 292.
60. Ibid, p. 308.
61. Charles L. Blockson, *Pennsylvania's Black History* (ed. Louise D. Stone, PA: Portfolio Associates, Inc., 1975), p. 22.
62. William C. Kashatus, op. cit., pp. 55–56.
63. Ibid, p. 56.

Chapter 14

1. On June 1, 1973, the author received a letter from Jack Snyder, then the secretary of Wilmington Monthly Meeting. It stated that the oak tree was "struck by lightning" almost ten years ago and had to be taken down.
2. Tilden's "Memorial Address, Commemorating the 100th Anniversary of the Birth of Thomas Garrett." (Quaker Collection of the Haverford Library in Pennsylvania.)

Chapter 15

1. Russell L. Adams, *Great Negroes, Past and Present* (Chicago: Afro-American Publishing Company, 1969), p. 31.
2. William Still, *The Underground Railroad*, op. cit., p. 167.
3. Russell L. Adams, op. cit., p. 31.

4. The *Standard* mentioned here refers to the *National Anti-Slavery Standard*, an anti-slavery newspaper. For further information on the case of Captain Lambdin, see Letters number 3 and 7 in this section, and Letter number 2 in Garrett's letters to Eliza Wigham.
5. L. Hughes and M. Meltzer, *Pictorial History of the Negro in American*, 3rd ed., revised (Crown Publishing Co., 1968), p. 147.

Chapter 16

1. Carlton Mabee, *Black Freedom*, p. 10.
2. William Still, op. cit., p. 679.
3. William Lorenz Katz, *Five Slave Narratives* (Arno Press/NY Times, 1969).
4. J.C. Furnas, *Goodbye to Uncle Tom* (NY: William Sloan Associates, 1956), p. 217.
5. William Still, op. cit., pp. 382, 391.

Chapter 17

1. L. Hughes and M. Meltzer, *Pictorial History of the Negro in America*, 3rd ed., revised (Crown Publishing Co., 1968), p. 141.
2. This is probably Edward M. Davis, son-in-law of Lucretia Mott.
3. William Walker (1824–1860) was an American military adventurer in Nicaragua.
4. "A Guide to Historic LaMott," a booklet by David Jenkins Morrison, prepared especially for persons attending the LaMott Historical Celebration, May 5, 1974, by the Cheltenham Township Library Historical Commission (acquired from LaMott Community Center Library).
5. Benjamin Quarles, p. 179.

Chapter 18

1. Garrett's appearance before Judge Taney was in 1848.
2. See Letter to Eliza Wigham, No.5.
3. Mary R. deVou, writing in *The Woman Suffrage Movement in Delaware,* says that Garrett was a Vice President at large from the first Delaware Conference to the National Suffrage Association in Convention assembled in Washington (see Schar, *History of Delaware*, p. 657).

Bibliography

Adams, Russell L. *Great Negroes, Past and Present.* Chicago: Afro-American Publishing Co., 1969.
"Africans in America." WGBH, Public Broadcasting System Online.
Ashmead, Henry Graham. *History of Delaware County, Pennsylvania.* Philadelphia: L.H. Everts & Co., 1884. Facsimile edition, as reprinted by Concord Township Historical Society, 1968.
Bartlett, Edward P., ed. *Friends in Wilmington, 1738–1938.* Wilmington, DE: Chas. L. Story & Co., 1938.
Bentley, Judith. *"Dear Friend": Thomas Garrett & William Still, Collaborators on the Underground Railroad.* New York: Cobblehill Books/Dutton, 1997.
Biondo, Richard A. "Samuel Green: A Black Life in Antebellum Maryland." Unpublished master's thesis. University of Maryland, 1988.
Blaustein, Albert P., and Robert L. Zangrando. *Civil Rights and the American Negro: A Documentary History.* New York: Washington Square Press, 1968.
Blockson, Charles L. *Hippocrene Guide to the Underground Railroad.* New York: Hippocrene Brooks, 1994.
_____. *Pennsylvania's Black History.* Edited by Louise D. Stone. Philadelphia: Portfolio Associates, Inc., 1975.
_____. *The Underground Railroad: First-Person Narratives of Escapes to Freedom in the North.* New York: Prentice-Hall Press, 1987.
Bradford, Sarah H. *Harriet Tubman, the Moses of Her People.* Gloucester, MA: Peter Smith, 1981.
_____. *Scenes in the Life of Harriet Tubman.* Auburn, NY: William J. Moses, Printer, 1869.
Brewington, M.V. *Chesapeake Bay: A Pictorial Maritime History.* Cambridge, MD: Cornell Maritime Press, 1953.
Chambers, Bradford, ed. *Chronicles of Negro Protest: A Background Book for Young People, Documenting the History of Black Power.* New York: Parents' Magazine Press, 1968.
Columbia Electronic Encyclopedia. ©1994, 2000, Columbia University Press. Licensed from Columbia University Press. ©2000–2003, Family Education Network.
Conrad, Earl. *Harriet Tubman, A Biography.* (New York: Paul S. Eriksson, Inc., ©1943, 1969, by Earl Conrad; 2nd pr. 1974).
Dalleo, Peter J. "The Growth of Delaware's Antebellum Free African Community." Wilmington, DE: United States Court House. June, 1997.

Drake, Thomas E. *Quakers and Slavery in America.* New Haven, CT: Yale University Press, 1950.

Drew, Benjamin. *A North-side View of Slavery. The Refugee; or, The Narratives of Fugitive Slaves in Canada Related by Themselves. With an Account of the History and Condition of the Colored Population of Upper Canada.* Boston: J.P. Hewett and Co.; New York: Sheldon, Lamport and Blakeman, 1856. Reprinted by Johnson Reprint Corp., New York, 1968.

"Education on the Internet." *Teaching History Online,* www.KeepAhead.com.

Ferris, Benjamin. *History of the Original Settlements on the Delaware.* Wilmington, DE: Wilson & Heald, 1846.

Franklin, John Hope, and Loren Schweninger. *Runaway Slaves: Rebels on the Plantation.* New York: Oxford University Press, 1999.

Furnas, J.C. *Goodbye to Uncle Tom.* New York: William Sloan Associates, 1956.

Gara, Larry. *Liberty Line: The Legend of the Underground Railroad.* Lexington, KY: University of Kentucky Press, 1961.

Gorman, George H. *The Amazing Facts of Quaker Worship.* London: Friends Home Service Committee, 1973.

Gray, Ralph D. *The National Waterway: A History of the Chesapeake and Delaware Canal, 1769–1965,* 2d ed. Urbana: University of Chicago Press, 1989.

Hansen, Harry. *The Civil War.* New York: Bonanza Books, 1961.

Historical Society of Delaware. *Delaware History.* Vol. X, No. 4. October 1963.

Hubbard, Geoffrey. *Quaker by Convincement.* Harmondsworth: Penguin Books, 1974.

Hughes, Langston, and Milton Meltzer. *Pictorial History of the Negro in America,* revised 3rd edition. New York: Crown Publishing Co., 1968.

Kashatus, William C. *Just Over the Line: Chester County and the Underground Railroad.* West Chester, PA: Chester County Historical Society and Penn State University Press, 2002.

Katz, William Loren. *Five Slave Narratives: A Compendium.* New York: Arno Press, 1968.

Leggett, Vincent O. *Chesapeake Underground: Charting a Course to Freedom.* http://www.dnr.state.md.us/naturalresource/spring2000/chesapeake.html.

Mabee, Carleton. *Black Freedom: The Nonviolent Abolitionists from 1830 through the Civil War.* New York: Macmillan Co., 1970.

McGowan, James A. *Station Master on the Underground Railroad: The Life and Letters of Thomas Garrett.* Moylan, PA: Whimsie Press, 1977.

McPherson, James M. *Ordeal by Fire: The Civil War and Reconstruction.* New York: Alfred A. Knopf, 1982.

Mendenhall, Thomas. *History, Correspondence & Pedigrees of the Mendenhalls.* Ohio, 1912.

Miles, Edwin A. *Franklin Pierce Biography.* Grolier Multimedia Encyclopedia, 2000.

Newton, James E. "Diamonds of Delaware and Maryland's Eastern Shore: Seven Black Men of Distinction." Dover, DE: University of Delaware, Harmon R. Carey Afro-American Society of Delaware.

Pillsbury, Parker. *Acts of the Anti-Slavery Apostles.* Concord, NH: Clague, Wegman, Schlicht, 1883; reprinted 1969, New York: Arno Press and the New York Times.

Poley, Irvin, and Ruth Poley, eds. *Friendly Anecdotes,* 2nd edition. New York: Harper & Row, 1950.

Quarles, Benjamin. *Black Abolitionists.* New York: Oxford University Press, 1969; reprinted 1991, New York: Da Capo Press.

Reed, H. Clay. *Delaware: A History of the First State.*

Renehan, Jr., Edward J. *The Secret Six: The True Tale of the Men Who Conspired with John Brown.* New York: Crown Publishers, Inc., 1995.

Siebert, Wilbur H. *The Underground Railroad from Slavery to Freedom.* New York: Macmillan Co., 1898; reprinted 1968, New York: Arno Press.

Sernett, Milton C. *North Star Country: Upstate New York and the Crusade for African-American Freedom.* Syracuse, NY: Syracuse University Press, 2002.

Smedley, Robert C. *History of the Underground Railroad in Chester and the Neighboring Counties of Pennsylvania.* Lancaster, PA, 1883.

Still, William. *The Underground Railroad.* 1872; reprinted by Johnson Publishing Company, Chicago, 1970.

Stowe, Harriet Beecher. *The Key to Uncle Tom's Cabin.* New York: Arno Press/NY Times, 1968.

Taylor, Frances Cloud. *The Trackless Trail: The Story of the Underground Railroad in Kennett Square, Chester County, Pennsylvania, and the Surrounding Community.* Kennett Square, PA: Published privately, 1976.

_____. *The Trackless Trail Leads On: An Explanation of the Conductors and Their Stations.* Kennett Square, PA: Published privately, 1995.

Thompson, Priscilla. "Harriet Tubman, Thomas Garrett and the Underground Railroad in Delaware." Research paper. Wilmington, DE: Delaware Historical Society, 1985.

Tilden, William P. "Memorial Address, Commemorating the 100th Anniversary of the Birth of Thomas Garrett." Pennsylvania, Haverford Library, Quaker Collection.

Tyson, John H., ed. *A History of Upper Darby, Delaware County, Pennsylvania, by a Committee of Interested Residents.* Philadelphia: Clark Printing House, 1972.

Villard, Oswald Garrison. *John Brown, 1800–1859: A Biography Fifty Years after Boston.* New York: Houghton Mifflin Co., 1910.

Wood, Richard. *William Penn: A Retrospective of Penn's Life and Work* (Philadelphia Yearly Meeting: Quaker Books, 1961)

Index

Acts of Anti-slavery Apostles 174
Adams, John Quincy 154
Adams, Samuel Hopkins 106
African American Churches 123–124; played most significant role in UGRR 127–128
African Methodist Union Church 8, 39
Agnew, Allen 15, 125, 158
Agnew, John 125
Agnew, Lydia 125
Agnew, Maria 15
Alston, John 203
American Anti-slavery Society 189
American Colonization Society 35
Amos, Thomas 127
Anthony, Susan B. 47, 74
Anti-slavery Bugle 174
The Anti-slavery Caused in America, and Its Martyrs 162
Applin (ship captain) 152
Appoquinimink Friends 118
Armstrong, Louis 5
Asner, Ed 7
August Quarterly 123; used as a starting point for escapes 124

Barnard, Eusebius 15, 125
Barnard, Sarah 127
Barnard, Sarah Marsh 15
Barnard, Simeon 15

Barnard, William 15
Bartlett, Edward P. 21
Bartlett, Joseph 59
Beecher, Henry Ward 75
Benezet, Anthony 90
Bentley, Judith 7, 82
Bethel Ame Church 127
Birmingham Friends Meeting 34
Blackbird, DE 118
Blacks on the Chesapeake 118–121
Blacks on the Chesapeake Foundation, Inc. 8
Blockson, Charles 7, 8, 20, 71–72, 117–118, 119, 123, 127
Blondo, Richard A. 117
Blow, Anthony (runaway who arrived by boat) 119
The Blue Hen's Chicken 53–55, 60, 62 64, 105, 134; Garrett's letters 65, 68–69, 94, 201–202, 207–210
Blunston, John 24
Booth, Chief Justice 58–59, 62, 205, 208
Boston Anti-slavery Society 175
Bradford, Sarah 43, 88, 99–101, 106, 120, 191; misgivings about Harriet Tubman's psychic ability 102; reports on Harriet's stories 106, 112
Bradley, Elsey 148
Brinkley, William (Negro UGRR agent) 118

Brodess, Edward 70, 99
Brodess, Eliza 114
Brooks, Preston: attacks Sumner 75
Brosius, Daniel 125
Brosius, Edwin 125
Brosius, Mahlon 125
Brosius, Mary 125
Brosius, Samuel 125
Brotherhood of Thieves 174
Brown, John 75–76, 160; attacks Harpers Ferry 78–79; dubs Harriet Tubman "General Tubman" 78; found guilty of treason and hanged 79
Brown, Thomas (UGRR worker in West Chester) 125
Brown, William Wells 105
Buchanan, James 68; becomes president 78; proposed Kansas be admitted as a slave state 78, 170–171
Burk, Henry 151
Burns, Anthony 92, 163; trial 163–164, 203, 205
Burris, Samuel D. 55, 57, 59–60, 109, 118
Butler, Senator Andrew 75

Calhoun, John C. 68, 210
Camden, DE 118
Canby, Catherine Ann 51
Captain "B" 120
Carmichael, Thomas 140
Carver, George Washington 5

221

Index

Caulk, Sheriff Jacob 57–59, 208
Chandler, William 115, 194
Chapman Maria 80
Charles, Benjamin 17
Chesapeake & Delaware Canal 38, 95–96, 118, 172, 213; construction of 96; as shortest route to freedom 120; use by runaways 96, 118
Chesapeake Bay 8, 118–119
Chesapeake Underground 95–96
Chesney, William 55–56, 201
Chester, William Murphy 145
Chester County, PA 15, 117, 124–128; anti-slavery communities in 94–95
Chestnut, William 203
Christian Quakers 32
Christiana, PA 127
Christiana Riot 19, 72
Civil Rights Movement 5
Civil War 2, 5
Clark, Winlock 152
Clay, Henry 66–67, 70
Coates, Lindley 19, 126
Cochran, Robert A. 201
Cochran, Robert T. 55–56, 201
Coffin, Levi 88–89, 162
Colonization 35
Colored schools (in Wilmington) supported by Friends 170
Comfort, William W. 163
Concord, DE 118
Conestoga ("Covered") Wagon 37
Confederate States of America 79
Conlin, James F., OSFS 7
Conrad, Earl 111–112
Cookman, Alfred 130
Corbit, Daniel 203
Cornell University Library 187
Cowgirl, Henry 118
Cox, Hannah 47, 125
Cox, John 47, 125
Craft, Ellen 71, 93, 155–156
Craft, William 71, 93, 155–156
Craig, Harry 122, 128, 140, 141
Cuffe, Paul 35

Darlington, Chandler 127
Darlington, Hannah 127
Davis, Clarissa (runaway female who dressed as a male) 119

Davis, Edward M. 166, 187–188
"Davy" (UGRR conductor) 126
Day, William Howard 130
Dear Friends, Thomas Garrett & William Still, Collaborators on the Underground Railroad 7, 82
Declaration of Sentiments 48
Delaney, Martin 78
Delaware Anti-slavery Society 115
Delaware City, DE 118
Delaware Division of Historical and Cultural Affairs 133
Delaware Gazette 37, 43
Delaware: A History of the First State 34
Delaware Humanities Forum 7
Delaware Republican 61
Delaware State Archives 188
Delaware *State Recorder* 107–111
Delaware Technical & Community College 133
Delleo, Peter J. 8, 118
Desmond, Cornelius, OSFS 7
Diamonds of Delaware and Maryland's Eastern Shore, Seven Black Men of Distinction 8
Dictionary of Quaker Biography 46–47
Dorchester County, Maryland 70
Douglass, Frederick 5, 8, 11, 47, 74, 162; meets with John Brown 78
Dover Division of History and Cultural Affairs 184
Dover Jail 107, 112; Garrett's account of escape 178–181
Drake, Thomas E. 14, 22, 31, 32, 54, 62–63, 65, 86, 90
Drew, Benjamin 93
Dugdale, Joseph 151, 187–188
Dugdale, Ruth 188

Edinburgh Ladies Emancipation Society 51, 76, 97, 151, 162–164
Edmundson, Mary (also Mary Wigham) 43, 94, 97, 102, 107, 111–112, 142
Elliot, Thomas 108
Eshelman, Dr. 15

Fearn, Joshua 25

Female Anti-slavery Society of Boston 155
Ferris, Benjamin 37–38, 40–43
Fields, Barbara Jean 117
Fifteenth Amendment ratified 80, 194
Fillmore, Millard 70, 170
Finney, Joe (UGRR worker) 118
Fisher, Charity 184
Fitzgerald, Ella 5
Flint, Isaac 15, 123, 128, 157
Ford, George 160–161
Fort Sumpter 79
Foster, the Rev. Daniel 164
Fountain, Capt. Alfred 120–121, 128, 140, 142, 144, 146; joins McClellan's Army 153; vessel burned by rebels 152
Fox, George 31
Franklin, Benjamin 35
Frederica, DE 118
Free Blacks: aboard ships on the Chesapeake 118; in Delaware 39; supported Garrett 94; in Wilmington 39
The Free Press 154
Freeman, Benjamin 125
Fremont 169–171
Friends in Wilmington 21
Fugitive Slave Law 70, 156, 174; first armed resistance 71–72; reaction to 70–72
Fugitive Slave Law (book) 164
Furnas, J.C. 87, 89
Fussell, Bartholomew 15, 117, 126–127
Fussell, Edwin 15
Fussell, William 15

Gandy, Moses 155
Gara, Larry 22–23, 53
Garat, Nathan 25
Garat, Samuel 25
Garat, William 25–26
Garnet, Henry Highland: advocates violence 50; family helped by Garrett 50; meets with John Brown 78
Garrett, Alfred Cope 163
Garrett, Anna 37, 74
Garrett, Edward 51, 149
Garrett, Eli 21, 48, 151; children of 199
Garrett, Elwood 34; children of 198–199; and daguerreotype 34–35, 44, 51

INDEX

Garrett, Helen Sellers 7
Garrett, Henry 18, 44, 49, 51, 123, 130; children of 199
Garrett, Margaret H. 28, 44, 50
Garrett, Rachel (Mendinhall) 46–48
Garrett, Sarah 36, 51, 74
Garrett, Thomas 1, 6, 12; antipathy to slavery 31; anti-slavery beliefs 1; attack of bilious 159; birthday 147; as a blacksmith 43; and blacks in Wilmington 2; boyhood years 27; and Colored Schools 170; commitment to helping the runaway slave 32, 82–83; compared to Franklin Pierce 164; compromise settlements in his court case 63; convicted of helping slaves escape 61; critical of Franklin Pierce 77; death 17; death of parents 51; defining moment of life 91; describes Harriet Tubman physically 98–99; disregard for Millard Fillmore 77; family violated by slavery 2; fine 63; on the fugitive slave bill 156–157; funeral 129–133; gravestone 132; and Harriet Tubman 2; handwriting 134–137; human reaction to helping the runaway slave 84; interviews Samuel Hawkins 58; and John Hunn receive summonses 61; joins the PA anti-slavery society 35; jury stacked against him 64; letter to Harriet Beecher Stowe 65; letter to Sarah Bradford 191; letter to *The Blue Hen's Chicken* 207–210; letter to William Lloyd Garrison 71; and Maryland reward for his arrest 86; mercantile iron and hardware business 181; moves to Wilmington 38; mystical experience 32–33, 82–84; personal description 82; religious teaching of 32; religious views 28; rescue of Tubman's parents 107, 192–193; speech at end of trial 64–65; supported Union war effort 2; trial of 1848 7; and Tubman's psychic ability 102
Garrett, Thomas (father) 25–26, 197
Garrett family 26–27
Garrett genealogy 197–199
Garrett House 25–26, 94, 133
Garrison 186–187
Garrison, William Lloyd 2, 18, 23, 47–48, 51, 62, 71, 74, 85, 88, 92, 102, 130, 155, 162, 177; attacks slave-holders 45; letters from Thomas Garrett 154–161; as a non-resister 154; profile of 154–155
Genius of Universal Emancipation 34, 45, 155
Georgetown, DE 118
Gibbons, Daniel 126
Gibran, Kahlil 9
Glanding, Charles Wesley 54–55, 57; sues Garrett 61, 202, 204
Glasgow, Samuel 127
Glasier, Zenor B. 60
Goodbye to Uncle Tom 87
Gorsuch, Edward 71–72
Grace M. E. Church 130
Grant, Ulysses S. 79
Greeley, Horace 102, 187
Grew, Mary 194
Grub, Elizabeth 188
Gurney, Joseph John 41–42

Hambleton, Alice 127
Hambleton, Charles 127
Hamilton, Joseph 122, 128; sentencing 151–152
Hardcastle, Robert 55–57, 59
Hardcastle, William 55–56, 203–204
Harper, Frances Ellen Watkins 80–81, 175, 178, 187
Harriet Tubman, Conductor on the Underground Railroad 6
Harriet Tubman Historical Society 133
Harriet Tubman, the Moses of Her People 43
Harriet Tubman, Thomas Garrett and the Underground Railroad in Delaware 7
Harriet Tubman–Thomas Garrett Memorial Plaque 131
Harris, William Henry 67
Hart, Rebecca 145
Haverford Library 6, 21–22, 163
Hawkins, Emeline 54–55
Hawkins, Samuel 54–56; death 60, 204–205, 208
Hayden, Lewis 163
Hayes, Esther 15
Hayes, Mordecai 15
Hays, Richard C. 55, 58–60, 201
Helper, Hinton Rowan 150
Hewes, Edward 51
Hicks, Elias 41–42, 90
Hicksite Friends 44, 189
Hidalgo, Miguel 66
Hirous, Elizabeth 184
Historical Society of Delaware 7, 21, 34, 82, 185
History of the Original Settlements on the Delaware 37
History of the Underground Railroad in Chester and the Neighboring Counties of Pennsylvania 125–126
History of Upper Darby 22, 25, 47
Holland, Patrick 90, 122–123, 128
Hosanna (African American Church) 127
Hubbard, Geoffrey 41–42, 44
Hughes, Daniel 108
Hunn 5, 15, 33, 52, 55, 57, 58–59, 60–61, 185, 203; account of participation in slave rescue 53; and ire from pro-slavery Marylanders 205; letter from Thomas Garrett 205; letter to *The Blue Hen's Chicken* 201–202; letter to William Still 202–205; sued by Elizabeth Turner 61

Impending Crisis of the South 150
Inward Light 28–29, 44, 100
Irish Catholics 90

Jackson (Negro UGRR worker in Kennett Square, PA) 125
Jackson, Gen. Andrew 66
Jackson, Frances 177
James, Dorothy Biddle 6–7
Jeandell & Vincent 201, 210
Jenkins, Ezekiel 55, 109, 118, 203
Jerry Rescue 72, 160
Johnson, Mary Ann 160, 187
Johnson, Oliver 103, 106, 111, 174, 176
Johnson, Severn 97, 122, 128, 144, 146

Journal of the Times 154
Just Over the Line 8, 16

Kansas and Nebraska bill 74–75
Kashatus, William C. 1–3, 8–9, 16, 73, 95, 125, 127
Katz, William Loren 19
Keith, George 32
Kelly, Abbe 50–51
Kennett Monthly Meeting 2, 73
Kennett Square, PA 8
Kent, Benjamin
Kent, Hannah 47, 127
Kent, Thomas 27
Kent County, Delaware 203
The Key to Uncle Tom's Cabin 53–54
Kimbor, Emmor 16
King Charles II 24
Kirkham, E. Kay 135
Knapp, Isaac 45

Lambdin, Captain 97, 120, 138–139, 140–141, 164, 167, 174
Larson, Kate Clifford 9, 214–215
Laurel, DE 118
Layton (Judge) 148
Lee, Col. Robert E.: becomes general of the Confederacy 79; surrenders 80
Leggett, Vincent 8, 95
Levis, Margaret 25, 197
Levis, Samuel 25
Lewes, DE 118
Lewis, Esther 13
Lewis, Evans 15
Lewis, Graceanna 13
Lewis, Mary Elizabeth 13
Lewis Sisters 127
The Liberator 45, 48, 81, 91, 115, 155, 159, 174, 186, 194
Liberty Line: The Legend of the Underground Railroad 22
Lincoln, Abraham 5, 102; runs for president 79, 159
Loe, Thomas 24
Loguen, Jermain 78
Louis, Joe 5
Louisiana Territory 65–66
L'Ouverture, Toussaint 5
Lovejoy, Elijah P. 50, 85
Lundy, Benjamin 34, 45, 48, 155

Mann, William 140
Marcus Hook 38, 140

Maris, Narris 16
Marsh, Gravner 126
May, Samuel J., Jr. 115–116, 174, 177, 189, 193
McGowan, James. A. 2
McKim, J. Miller 116, 121, 137, 140–142, 146, 147, 149–151, 166, 169, 175, 182
Mendinhall (also Mendenhall) 46–47
Mendinhall, Aaron 159
Mendinhall, Dinah 15, 47, 86, 95, 110, 126, 160
Mendinhall, Eli 6, 51
Mendinhall, Isaac 15, 47, 86, 95, 110, 151; disowned by Kennett Monthly Meeting 73
Mendinhall, Joseph 147
Mendinhall, Rachel (also Rachel Garrett) 7, 21, 198
Meredith, Isaac 15
Meredith, Thamazine P. 15, 125
Merritt, Thomas Schee 55, 201–202
Middletown, DE 58, 185
Milford, DE 118
Millsborough, DE 118
Minkin (Negro porter) 119–120
Missouri Compromise 66
Monroe, James 68
Moore, Charles 13
Moore, Davy 128
Mott, Lucretia 23, 44, 130, 174–176
Mott, James 44, 47, 173–174, 188
Mount Holly, NJ 149, 175
Munson, Comegys 122, 128, 143

National Anti-slavery Standard 216
National Philanthropist 154
National Standard 18, 159
New Castle, DE 118, 145
New Castle Jail 57
New England Magazine 65
New Yorker 106
Newton, James 8, 123–124, 133
Non-resisters 48–50
North Star Country: Upstate New York and the Crusade for African American Freedom 72

Observations on the Slavery of the Africans and Their Decedents 42

Odessa, DE 118
Orthodox Friends 44
Otwell, Thomas 108, 112–113, 142, 179–180
Owens, Jesse 5

Parker, Theodore 163
Parker, William 19
Parrish, Dillyn 193
Peart, Lewis 127
Penn, William 7, 24–25, 27
Pennell, Jane 25
Pennypacker, Elijah F. 15–16, 127, 137, 141, 185
Pennock, Isaac 125
Pennock, Mary 125
Pennock, Moses 125
Pennsylvania Anti-slavery Society 2, 17, 35, 60, 121, 137, 175
Pennsylvania Freeman 60, 174
Pennsylvania Meeting of Friends 47
Perry, Jesse (Negro involved in scheme to trap runaways) 148
Petry, Ann 6
Philadelphia Anti-slavery Affair 175
Philadelphia Yearly Meeting 42
Phillips, Wendell 18, 145, 160, 162, 190
Pierce, Franklin 73, 76
Pierce, Gideon 15
Pillsbury, Parker 86, 174, 177
Polk, James 67–69; death 70
Powell, Aaron 115, 130, 194
Predo, Henry 108
Price, Jane 160
Price, Sarah 25, 197
Princeton Theological Seminary 137
Pritchett, Phoebe 46
Progressive Friends 2, 7
Progressive Meeting of Friends 47, 73–74
Prosser, Gabriel 33
Pugh, Sarah 169
Purvis, Robert 60, 205
Pusey, Edith 208
Pushkin, Alexander 5

Quaker by Convincement 41
Quakers 1–2, 26–32, 35, 48–50, 73, 90
Quakers and Slavery in America 15, 22, 31, 62–63, 65, 90
Quarles, Benjamin 75
Queen Victoria 165, 177

INDEX

Reed, H. Clay 34
Religious Society of Friends 1, 7, 24, 28–29, 41, 44; *see also* Quakers
Ressler, Paul 9
Rhoads, Samuel 109, 181, 185
Ross, Benjamin (Harriet's father) 111, 114, 182
runaway slaves 12, 93–94
Rust, Clem 148

Sanborn, Franklin B. 102–103, 105–106
Schadd, Abraham 39, 124–125
Schadd, Mary Ann 124
Scofield, Sarah Ann 158
Seaford, DE 118
Sellers, Abigail 51
Seminole Indians 66
Seminole Wars 66
Sernett, Milton 72
Seward, William H. 102–103, 106
Shadrach Rescue 71
Sharpless, Mary 34, 44, 198
Shipley, William 40–41
Shipley Street 38, 42
Siebert 13–15, 20–22, 65, 213
Sixteenth Amendment 195
slave catchers 86
slave owners 52, 85–86
Slavery and Freedom in the Middle Ground 117
Smedley 13–14, 19–20, 54, 61, 63–64, 86, 125–128
Smith, John (black UGRR worker in West Chester) 125
Smith, Gerrit 102–103, 106, 160–161
Smyrna, DE 118
Snyder, Jack 216n
Speakman, Micajah 13, 126
Speakman, William 13, 126
Spencer, the Rev. Peter 8, 39, 123–124
spiritualism 101–102
Stanton, Elizabeth C. 174
Station Master on the Underground Railroad... 2–3
Still, William 2, 7, 17–18, 43, 51, 53, 56, 60, 73, 85, 105–106, 111–112, 116, 119, 121, 169; appointed chairman of acting committee 137; letters from Thomas Garrett 137–153; meets with John Brown 78
Stone, George 18
Stone, Lucy 157; lectures in Wilmington 158, 175
Stowe, Harriet Beecher 47, 53–54, 64–65, 73, 102, 150
Streets, Magistrate William 57–58, 60, 204–205
Sumner, Sen. Charles 75
Swantko, Margaret 9
Swathmore College Library 185, 187–188
Swathmore Library 6, 21

table rapping 101
Taney, Judge Roger B. 61–62, 190, 202, 205, 207
Tappan, Arthur 45, 50
Tappan, Lewis 50, 85
Taylor, Frances Cloud 8, 125
Taylor, T. Clarkson 130
Taylor, Zachary 68–69; death 70
Teleduction 7
Texas: annexation of 65, 67; becomes independent republic 67
This Land of Boasted Freedom 7
Thomas, Zebulon 13
Thomas Garrett Historical Marker 133
Thompson, Anthony 113–114
Thompson, George 155–158, 160–162, 190, 193
Thompson, Priscilla 7, 73, 90, 120, 123, 171, 214–215
Tilden, the Rev. William P. 21, 43, 54, 61, 63, 65, 82, 129–133
The Trackless Trail 8, 125
The Trackless Trail Leads On 8, 125
Trial of 1848 52–62
Truth, Sojourner 5, 47, 74, 172
Tubman, Harriet, 5–8, 15, 23, 36, 43, 70–72, 93, 96, 98–101, 103–114, 118, 120, 134, 152, 163–164, 166–168, 171, 175–176, 181, 183, 191–193; birth 137–138; and dreams and omens 103; meets with John Brown 78; and spiritual manifestations 175; trust in Thomas Garrett 103, 104; and the voice of God 99–100, 191
Turner, Catherine 202, 204
Turner, Elizabeth N. 54, 56, 61
Turner, Nat 33–34, 48
Turnpike Roads 37–38

Tyler, John 67

Uncle Tom's Cabin 47, 53–54, 73, 130, 150, 182
The Underground Railroad 17, 53, 134, 137
Underwood, Blair 7
U.S. Circuit Court at New Castle, Delaware 53
U.S. Circuit Court of District of Delaware 53
Updike, Isaac 88, 185
Upper Darby, PA 24–27, 32
Upper Oxford Township 127

Van Buren, Martin 67
Vickers, John 13

Wales, Attorney John 205
Wales, Senator John 58
Walker, David 44–45, 48
Walker, James (freed Negro who helped Thomas Garrett) 125
Walker, Jonathan 85, 121
Walker, Joseph G. 15, 126–127
Wallout, Robert F. 186
Walls, George 127
Walls, William 127
Washington, Booker T. 5
Washington, George 14
Watson, Joseph 184
Webb, Benjamin 15, 123, 128
Webb, Edward 127
Webb, Thomas 15
Webb, William 15, 123
West, Vincent 16
Whipple, Charles K. 174, 177
Whispers of Angels 7
Whitson, Thomas 126
Whittier, John Greenleaf 45, 47, 74, 193
Wigham, Eliza 36, 41, 44, 65, 88, 98, 102, 162, 192
Wigham, Mary (also Mary Edmundson) 36
Williams, Elizabeth J. 18
Williamson, Passmore 97
Willing, Thomas 40
Willingtown 40
Wilmer, George 122, 139–140
Wilmington & Kennett Turnpike Company 38
Wilmington Daily Commercial 18, 63, 134
Wilmington, Delaware 2, 7–8, 21, 24–27, 37–45
Wilmington Friends Meeting 133

Wilmington Monthly Meeting 7, 21, 41
Wilmington Turnpike Company 38
Wilmington's Underground Railroad 121–123
Wolfe, David R. 59
woman's suffrage 195
Woodall, Alwin 9
Woodall, Cheryll 9
Wyman, Lillie B. C. 65

www.ingramcontent.com/pod-product-compliance
Ingram Content Group UK Ltd.
Pitfield, Milton Keynes, MK11 3LW, UK
UKHW050702160426
5217IPUK00038B/1878